Behold a time before clocks and calendars

Once we told time by the phases of the Moon and the cycles of the Sun and the Earth. We watched for signs in the land and in the animals that told us when to sow and when to harvest, when to prepare for winter and when to open the doors to spring. Of necessity, we lived in harmony with nature.

For most of human history, the seasons of nature have been the essence of the sacred. Our bodies still respond to the cycles of the Earth, and to the shorter cycles of the Moon. We are born with a natural wisdom that we have forgotten how to tap, a wisdom bred into us in blood and bone.

The calendar of moons expressed the mysteries of the Earth's sacred cycles through mythology and through the tasks which belonged to each season of the year, and to each season of a person's life. The stories are old, but somewhere, deep within, we remember.

About the Author

Annette Hinshaw (Oklahoma) was a wife, mother, and a leader in the Tulsa, Oklahoma, Pagan community. As Coordinator of the Tulsa Grove of the Pagan Educational Network, she arranged public information meetings on Pagan topics. She also developed and distributed an annual calendar and resource guide for local and regional Pagans of all paths. As the Oklahoma Director of the Witches' Anti-Discrimination Lobby, Annette helped Pagans who experienced persecution for their religious beliefs. She volunteered her broad knowledge of Pagan paths and of the occult to local agencies including law enforcement and the public library.

Annette came to Pagan religions from a deep and broad background drawn from a lifetime of study in folklore, mythology, comparative religion, the history of ideas, the history of language, and an intertwining of symbol systems, psychology, and anthropology. She studied mythology and language, and received a National Defense Education Folklore Fellowship to attend graduate school in the early 1960s. She taught classes in English composition and literature, research methods, radio electronics, religion, computer operation and programming, and team-building, and was a featured public speaker on religion, astrology, the process of divination, and how to achieve personal spiritual growth.

Annette Hinshaw

Earth
Time
Moon
Time

Rediscovering the
Sacred Lunar Year

1999
Llewellyn Publications
St. Paul, Minnesota 55164-0383

First Edition
First Printing, 1999

Cover design by Anne Marie Garrison
Cover art by Susan Goss
Interior illustrations by Carrie Westfall
Book editing and design by Astrid Sandell

Library of Congress Cataloging-in-Publication Data
  Hinshaw, Annette, 1939–1999.
    Earthtime, moontime : rediscovering the sacred lunar year /
  Annette Hinshaw. -- 1st ed.
      p.   cm.
    Includes bibliographical references (p.   ).
    ISBN 1-56718-396-4
    1. Religious calendars--Neopaganism. 2. Moon--Religious
  aspects. I. Title. II. Title: Earthtime, moontime.
  BF1572.F37H56 1999
  133.5'32--dc21   99–30355
                                                        CIP

Llewellyn Publications
A Division of Llewellyn Worldwide, Ltd.
P.O. Box 64383, Dept. K396–4, St. Paul, MN 55164–0383
www.llewellyn.com

Printed in the United States of America

Dedication

For Lou (Journey Moon),
my husband,
who keeps my eyes on
new horizons.

For Myrna (Milk Moon),
my sister,
who nurtured every page
of this book,

and

For Betty (Father's Moon),
my mother,
who raised six daughters, one son,
as her life work.

Acknowledgments

Annette Hinshaw did not get to make the list of acknowledgments that she had intended. I have tried my best to include those who she loved and felt she owed thanks to. There were so many, I apologize for anyone I have left out and to those whose names have been misspelled. The names are not in any order—except for Mike Hinshaw, her son and sounding board; and Astrid Sandell, her editor.

*—Lou Hinshaw
the author's husband*

Thanks to Jody Cunningham; Marc Campbell; Karl Knittig; Don Keene; Walt Steiger; Ed Dougan; most of the Baha'i communities of Omaha (Nebraska), Tampa Bay (Florida), Springfield (Missouri), Hays (Kansas), and Tulsa (Oklahoma) areas; Jack Chalker; Glen Cook; Ingrid Lanier; Dr. Baxter; Dr. Brazil; Andrea Merrill (now Dugan); Marc Tripp; Celia Powles; Meli Turpen; the Tulsa Astrological Society; Gloria Dialectic; R. A. Garrett; several radio amateurs in Clearwater (Florida), Springfield, Tulsa, and Hays; Johnny Dicus, Lou Braun; Dr. Kaplan; Dr. Edwards; Dr. Knight; Jim Mcdonald and Jim Sherwood; C. Bax; Ted Coombes; the utility people at Jonesboro (Arkansas) and other places; Jake Gage; Jerry Martin, DeAnn Rhea, Jan Wolverton, Yvonne Grewe, Jan Tatman; Ruby Keller; Bendis of Arlington (Texas); Pat Henry; Cindy Sheets, Wren Walker, Jason Cupps; Tamarisk; Silver RavenWolf; and many more than I can possibly recall. Also, to Dale McMasters of Jonesboro, who reminded me that I had said Annette wanted such a list. Thanks to all of you.

Contents

In The Beginning

Once upon a time, there was no time, at least not as we think of time now. When our race was new, we did not have clocks and calendars. We told time by the phases of the Moon and the cycles of the Sun. The Earth, our Mother, moved through the seasons in an unending cycle of birth and life, death and rebirth. We watched for signs in the land and in the animals that told us when we could gather certain kinds of food, when to sow and when to harvest, when to prepare for winter and when to open the doors to spring. Of necessity, we lived close to and in harmony with the Mother.

Our minds and the technology of our culture have evolved a long way since the dawn days of our species, but our bodies still respond to these cycles of the Earth and to the shorter cycles of the Moon. We are born with a natural wisdom that we have forgotten how to tap, a wisdom bred into our blood and bone. Many of the illnesses, both of body and mind, in our society arise from our attempts to operate contrary to that innate wisdom and natural knowledge. Even now, in the twentieth century, we can benefit from attuning ourselves to the moods of the Mother and from trying to put our bodies and our minds into harmony with the cell-deep wisdom that our species codes into its DNA and into our collective deep consciousness, the wisdom that helped us to survive when so many other lifeforms did not.

The purpose of this book is to immerse the reader in a different way of looking at the world, a way based on harmony with the Mother and acceptance of all Her cycles, of the birth that begins growth, and of the death that is necessary for transformation and rebirth. For most of human history, these cycles have been the essence of the sacred. Now, at the end of the twentieth century, a return to the sacredness of the Earth and the life that thrives on it can still create the healing we need to repair the damage caused by our alienation from the Earth.

The bridge I offer to enable this return is a lunar calendar that is an artifact of an Earth-based, Pagan religion, probably the work of Celtic and Germanic peoples who settled in northern Europe and the British Isles. Trying to align ourselves with such a calendar can help us remember the natural wisdom that is our heritage. Lunar wisdom is of the body, of the non-rational (not, I specify, the irrational), in the realm of what we now speak of as the right brain. The right brain finds the wholeness in our world even as the left brain picks the world apart to analyze it. Tuning into a process such as this lunar calendar, which violates our belief that the world can be indexed into neat categories, begins a healing (making whole) process that can integrate our inner, lunar wisdom, with our outer, solar experience.

We learn humility and gain wholeness from acknowledging the validity of lunar knowledge, which, like moonlight on water, will not settle into clear and stable forms. When we understand that everyone sees something different in the moonlight, we can learn the humility necessary to respect the views of others whose worldviews seem to contradict ours. We can learn, along with Hamlet, that "there are more things in heaven and earth, . . . than are dreamt of . . . ."

Studying the lunar calendar in this book will give you a peephole into a different reality, the world of our ancestors, where keeping track of Earth energies was a vital and necessary skill for survival. This reality arose from a culture in which most people knew very little of the world beyond their village. They lived on the cumulated wisdom of peoples who had begun as nomadic herders and evolved into farmers. Their world was shaped by both the harsh physical realities of their lives and the wonder and mystery of their participation in the great sacred cycles of the Earth.

Their calendar of moons expressed the essence of this cycle through their mythology and through the tasks that belonged to each season of the year and to each season of a human's life. Its pivots were the Wheel of the Year, four solar and four lunar festivals, which intertwined the seasons and the mythology that expressed the mysteries of the Earth's sacred cycles. The solar feasts were the solstices and equinoxes, which had fixed dates determined by the changes in the Sun in the solar year. The four lunar festivals were based on the cycles of the Moon that followed each solar festival. Like the changeable Moon Herself, these lunar festivals were movable feasts.

Imagine a world without refrigerators or the transport to bring strawberries to us in winter. Imagine a world in which mistakes about when to put food aside, and how much, resulted in death and disease, a world where understanding the seasons—the "moods" of the Mother—was essential to survival.

The Calendar of Moons

Life arises from death. We find this in the renewal of the Earth when life "springs" again from the devastation of winter. Our life continues because we eat dead plants and animals. We bury our dead so that they may rot and release the substance of their bodies to new living things. The year begins with the Death Moon, the beginning and the end, which are the same, two sides of the same coin.

The deaths in nature that characterize the Death Moon are caused by the waning of the Sun, whom we name Father even as we call both Earth and Moon Mother. Now, in the midst of winter, animals hibernate, plants die back into dormancy, the world seems headed for an icy end. Each day, the light grows weaker, departs sooner, and warms us less. Into this frightening time comes the defining event of the Birth Moon, the winter solstice, the traditional festival called Yule or Midwinter. The sun stops (literal meaning of "solstice") in its apparent southward travel and begins its journey north again, strengthening with every day. The Mother has given birth to the Son (Sun), the Divine Child whose coming is celebrated throughout the world at this time of year.

After the trauma of birth, the Mother is exhausted, but, as milk comes into the breasts of new mothers soon after birth, so in the Milk Moon (also called the Nursing Moon) does the Earth reflect the first faint signs that the Mother's ability to nurture us will return as the Sun strengthens. Winter herbs and flowers poke their heads up and show green promise if we know where to look. The buds of trees begin to swell on warmer days. Birds make mating sounds. Spring lambs are born.

The traditional festival of Imbolc, the beginning of spring in the old calendar, comes in the Milk Moon. Imbolc is a festival of renewal and of purification for the coming revival of life. It is the day on which the Goddess, in Her phase as the aged Crone, visits the sacred well and comes away the Maiden.

The promise of new life heartens us, but we must still endure the bitter end of winter's diminished resources. We come to the Fasting Moon (also called the Weaning Moon). Here the final stores from the fall harvest must be stretched until new green plants are available in sufficient quantity to collect and cook. The Mother is weaning Her children, preparing them to adapt to the changes and chances of the world. Humans fast so that today's forbearance may assure that dwindling food stores and precious seed will last until planting time and the green renewal of spring.

The vernal equinox, called Ostara, is the defining event of the Seed Moon. The Earth is warming and many plants respond to the longer days. Seeds fallen to earth in the autumn now awaken. Farmers sow their fields. All life "springs" forth in joyous renewal. In the mythological cycle, this is the moon during which the seed is planted in the Mother so that, nine months later, She may give birth again to the Father/Sun at the winter solstice. The light half of the year begins, the days are longer than nights.

Every two or three years, an intercalary moon must be inserted into the calendar to bring the named moons back on track with the solar season. This intercalary moon is called the Courting Moon. The name indicates that it is a "between" time, a time for dalliance and fun, a holiday between the sowing of the fields and the journeys of late spring and early summer.

The Mating Moon celebrates the resurgence of life and hope for the future. In the life of the Earth our Mother, plants send forth their pollen, animals mate or bring forth young, and, in the words of the poet, "young men's fancies turn to thoughts

of love." As green plants and other fresh foods are reintro-
duced into winter diets of salt meat and stored grains, bodies
respond to better nutrition and look beyond bare survival to
the production of new lives. The Mother looks upon Her Son,
now grown to manhood, and loves Him, and in Him, all Her
creation. At the traditional feast of Beltane, the beginning of
summer, the Goddess in Her Maiden phase unites in love with
the God to bring forth the bounty of the new season. The
Maiden metamorphoses into the Mother.

Humans make plans to travel to fairs and other communities
to find wives and husbands, to make alliances, to enhance their
own ideas of the world by seeking the ideas of others. The
Journey Moon occurs near the summer solstice, a soft time of
the year. This moon has long days and an abundance of food
that makes for easy traveling. Young men venture with the
herds to summer pastures full of new grass, or explore the
world to find salt licks or sources of rare plants and other
materials. They prospect for new resources for their communities while they await the time for harvest.

The summer solstice, called Litha or Midsummer in the traditional calendar, normally falls in the Mother's Moon, the
time of the greatest abundance of life and food in the entire
year. The life-giving power of the Sun is at its greatest strength,
and the Father pours His energy into the Earth. This moon
expresses the Earth's bounty to Her children, a cornucopia of
giving that fulfills her aspect as Mother. The Mother's Moon is
closest in mood to the idyllic feeling we associate with childhood, when all our needs were provided by our mothers and
when we experienced unconditional love (motherlove).

The Father's Moon takes a somber turn, and we experience
the message of fatherlove, that life has boundaries and limits,
and that what we receive must be earned. The Sun still warms
the Earth, but, since the solstice, He has turned again toward
the south, and each day He shines less than he did the day

before. Those who are wise see the coming autumn. The Father, whose energies have ripened the grain, now offers Himself for the good of his children. In His persona as John Barleycorn, He gladly sacrifices His life that His body, the grain, may be transformed into the bread that will sustain life until the next year, when the cycle begins again.

The festival of Lammas, which celebrates both this sacrifice and the first harvest—grain—is normally in the Father's Moon. This festival is specifically a celebration of the life-affirming transformation that follows willing sacrifice. It is the essence of the mystery that the Father, who dies with the grain, will return again in the spring from that dead grain. "All that falls shall rise again." In the old calendar, Lammas is the beginning of autumn.

Those who are prudent now prepare for the coming winter while the weather holds. The Nesting Moon is a time for building the nest and preparing the homestead for harsh weather ahead. Now is a time of planning for the coming winter. Humans prepare means to store food, replaster walls with insulating mud, and rethatch roofs. They also assemble materials for work that can be done indoors during the winter, such as reeds for baskets, fibers for spinning and weaving, and plant materials for dying the fibers or finished cloth.

Chilly mornings herald the coming of winter. It is time for the Harvest Moon. The full moon of this month is one of the most brilliant of the year because the moon rises above the horizon just after sunset. Traditionally, its name comes from the extra hours of light by which the harvests of the season may be gathered. All strive to bring everything useful under shelter for the winter.

The feast of Mabon—both autumnal equinox and the second harvest, of fruit and wine—normally falls in this moon. The Father, as the Wine God, again sacrifices His life for His children in the fruit that nourishes and is the seed of new plants. The equinox is the start of the dark half of the year, when nights are longer than days. The Mother offers Her second harvest, another flourish of gifts, in the late-ripening foods, especially fruits and nuts, which put all their goodness into the future before succumbing to winter dormancy. The harvested seeds are food for next spring's sprouts and the fat roots are stored strength for the plants, which will reawaken from them when life renews itself again. Perennial herbs are harvested for the final time this year. Grapes and other fruits ripen. It is time to make wine and cider, which will warm winter bellies as humans wait out the cold beside their hearths.

Finally, we come to the Sorting Moon (also called the Culling Moon). Humans set aside bruised fruit to eat now so that better fruit, which will store longer, can be saved for later. They cull the herds down to a number that can be sustained by the fodder and shelter that are available for overwintering. The slaughter of animals is the third and final harvest. The God, in his persona as the Horned One, Lord of the Beasts, sacrifices Himself for the last time in the third harvest.

The feast of the dead, Samhain, normally occurs in the Sorting Moon and marks the beginning of winter in the old calendar. Its mood accords well with the Sorting Moon, as we look past the veil of life and consider the greater questions of why we are here and what we should do to fulfill the Mother's desires.

The Mythic Background

The year of moons in this calendar, and the seasonal celebrations that thread through the calendar, also express one of the great cycles of ancient myth, a cycle that we find vestiges of throughout the ancient world. It is a cycle connected to the worship of the Great Mother, and parts of it probably date back to Neolithic times. As with all mythological cycles, it expresses those great truths that cannot be reduced to rational thought. It speaks to the heart rather than the reason. It resonates with the place at which we are all connected in the Mother, the place Jung called the "collective unconsciousness."

In this book, I call this mythic cycle the "great story," and it is specifically the story of the Earth through the seasons. This cycle is the story of the Creator/Goddess/Mother who gives birth to the Divine Child, the God/Son. When the God/Son matures, the Mother takes Him as Her lover and conceives from Him a new Son, who will be born after His Father's death. The Goddess/Mother and the God/Father complete each other, and, in their joining, create new life and all the bounty of our world. Then, in a mystery that promises the eternity of life, the God/Father willingly sacrifices Himself to make room for the new Son, who represents the renewal of life, and who will, in turn, mature and sire his successor. The Son is born, dies, and comes again, and the Mother endures forever, cycling from the Maiden's youth, through the productive years of the Mother, into the old age and wisdom of the Crone. Together the God and Goddess, Father and Mother, represent the mystery of how things can change always, yet somehow remain the same.

The moons of this calendar are a weaving of stories, both of human experience through the year, as the Sun completes a turn, and of the story of the Earth, personified as the Mother, the Goddess who brings both life and death. The stories are old, but even our modern hearts resonate with their symbols and metaphors. Somewhere, deep within, we remember.

2

On Time and Timekeeping

You may not realize it, but you structure your whole life around time. Clocks and calendars mark when you do which activities. How much you accomplish within a given amount of time is fundamental to measuring your own worth. Without some way to mark time, you cannot even arrange your personal history so that it makes sense to you or to others. In fact, in most societies, the structure of time is the fundamental ordering mechanism of the culture. This process is usually below the level of our consciousness; even though we don't think about it, our conventions for marking time have a profound effect on how we believe the world works.

We tend to think of whatever time system we use as so "natural" that we regard it as a direct reflection of reality. My favorite story to illustrate this tendency happened in Nebraska in the late 1960s. When Daylight Savings Time was mandated in Nebraska, someone wrote a letter to the newspaper to complain that the extra hour of sunlight was likely to harm plants, interrupt animal reproductive cycles, and increase cancer in humans! We forget how arbitrary our clocks and calendars are.

In fact, humans have tried many different patterns for keeping track of time. The earliest Roman calendar ended after harvest and did not begin again until early spring. Who cared what day it was when the requirements of the agricultural year were done? Days have begun at sunrise and sunset, as well as at noon and midnight. Our seven-day "week" is based on four moon phases, but the ancient Egyptians divided their "month" into ten-day periods to distinguish waxing, full, and waning moons.

Prehistoric stone structures (megaliths, menhirs), which occur throughout the world, are evidence that timekeeping was important to early societies. Most of them were apparently built primarily so their societies would know when solar events such as the equinoxes and solstices were going to occur. The most famous such monument, Stonehenge, may also have been used as a giant computer to predict lunar eclipses. Even further back in the mists of time, archaeologists speculate that scratches on some of the earliest human artifacts we have found may be attempts to develop calendars by recording moon cycles.

Reconciling Sun and Moon

The fundamental problem early humans faced in developing a calendar is that our natural units of time—the day, the month, and the year—have no simple mathematical relationship to each other. The month, defined by a cycle that begins with the first sight of a new moon to first sight of the next new moon, is about 29.5 days. The year, defined by a revolution of the Earth around the Sun, is about 365.25 days. There are about 12.4 lunations in a solar year. These numbers have been widely known at least since the first millennium B.C.E., and they caused problems for our ancestors as far back as we have records for calendars. Ancient peoples did not handle fractions very well.

The earliest calendars were lunar, because a lunation (new moon to new moon) is a convenient and easy-to-understand time unit for everyday calendars. Humans struggled for centuries with the problem of keeping the seasonal, or solar, year more or less in synchrony with the passing phases of the Moon. Lunations, or "moons," were usually named for seasonal events. Without adjustment, a moon named for the blossoming plum tree would rotate through all the seasons of the solar year instead of staying in the season when plum trees flower.

Some early societies ignored this kind of discrepancy. In others, rulers would periodically declare intercalary (within the calendar) periods for "catch-up," or just restart the calendar at an equinox or solstice from the solar cycle. Our own Gregorian calendar has never had a clear relation to lunar cycles. The Julian calendar on which it was based had already discarded the simple solution of alternating months of twenty-nine and thirty days that keeps the months in line with lunations.

That alternating pattern was in the Egyptian calendar, which Julius Caesar used for a pattern. The problem was that twelve lunar months add up to only 354 days, and the solar year has 365. Caesar used thirty-day months, which brings the days to 360, added an additional day to five other months, and called for an intercalary "leap day" every four years. Pope Gregory's contribution to an accurate solar calendar was to remove leapdays from the ends of centuries that are not divisible by four hundred.

Our basically thirty-day "month" and our "week" are artifacts of the time when all time was told by the Moon. Just as an interesting sidenote, the reason February is so short was to salve Augustus Caesar's ego. It was short to begin with to allow for adding the leapday. Julius Caesar chose the month of July, which was named after him, as one of those that would have thirty-one days. Later, his nephew Augustus named August after himself and stole a day from February to make "his" month equal to his uncle's. That's also why July and August are the only sequential months in the calendar year that have thirty-one days. You can see how ancient events become fixed in a calendar long after the reason for them is forgotten.

Nowadays, we assume solar calendars are naturally superior to lunar calendars. They seem more "scientific," and, of course, we are used to that pattern. The adoption of our Gregorian calendar for international business reinforces our sense that "solar" and "calendar" are a natural pair. In fact, the Gregorian calendar is one of only two purely solar calendars in widespread use. Lunar calendars are still used throughout the world in traditional calendars that mark local or religious holidays. In many localities, the lunar calendar is the "real" calendar, and the Gregorian is just a convention for communicating with people in the outside world.

The ancients did work out a calendar, called "luni-solar," which adjusts solar and lunar cycles to each other. The calendar in this book has that pattern, as do most of the surviving traditional lunar calendars. The luni-solar calendar's standard year is twelve lunar months. Every two or three years, an extra, thirteenth month, is inserted into the calendar (intercalated) to bring it back on track with the solar seasons. Ancient methods for doing such intercalation were erratic at first, but they finally settled into a pattern now known as the Metonic Cycle.

Meton was an Athenian astronomer who flourished about 432 B.C.E. He determined that nineteen solar years and 235 lunations come out about even (within hours of each other by modern measurements). Calendars that follow the Metonic pattern have a nineteen-year repeating cycle in which twelve of the years have twelve months and, at intervals of two to three years, seven of the years have thirteen months. This model corresponds with the 235 (19 x 12 + 7) lunations in nineteen solar years. The nineteen-year cycle is also a close approximation of the 18.6-year Saros cycle, in which the relative positions in the complex dance among the Sun, Moon, and Earth repeat themselves. Eclipse patterns are related to this Metonic period, which is commonly used in modern astronomy, and for determining the date of the Christian Easter each year.

This nineteen-year soli-lunar pattern eventually spread throughout the ancient world in the calendars of early Egypt, Mesopotamia, Greece, and China. The present-day Jewish religious calendar probably derives from the original Mesopotamian calendar. The Chinese calendar is still in use in southeast Asia, as is a Muslim religious calendar in the Near East. The Chinese New Year, beginning on the second new moon after the winter solstice, is a media event every January or February.

Lunar Calendars and Other Methods for Marking Time Tend to Be Irregular

A lunar calendar looks disorderly to us. Can you imagine using a calendar that varied in how many months there were in the year? Even in a soli-lunar calendar with the right number of intercalary moons inserted at the right intervals, we don't get a regular date correspondence between our familiar solar calendar and the wandering lunar months. The months are stabilized in the proper season, but, over the nineteen-year cycle, each named moon starts and ends on a date that ranges over about sixty days on our present calendar. See Appendix B, which shows new moon dates for each named moon in the calendar presented in the book for the years from 1890 through 2019.

A child in our culture does not typically master our time system until he or she is about twelve years old. One reason is that our time system is not anchored in our experience of natural cycles. From a biological point of view, our clocks and calendars are entirely arbitrary. Do you look at the Sun to see what time it is? Do you know what phase the Moon is in? Do you know what the temperature is outside and how it reflects the season? Does your body respond to seasonal changes? Or do you set your reality by clocks and calendars that no longer relate directly to the natural cycles from which they were derived?

People in our culture have been functioning without direct reference to the positions of Sun, Moon, and stars for so long that they have lost track of how recent some of our methods for marking time are. For example, we think of an hour as a precise amount of time. Yet, for most of history, the length of an hour was one-twelfth of the time between sunrise and sunset. The use of twelve may derive from the basic twelve lunations of a solar year in each day, but the base-12 stem of the Babylonians, which gives us sixty minutes in a hour and 360 degrees in a circle (probably from the solar year), has been replaced almost universally by our present base-10 mathematics. In early times, night hours were longer than day hours from the autumnal equinox to the spring equinox, and vice versa for the "light" half of the year.

An accurate and reliable mechanical clock is a relatively recent invention, less than five hundred years old. Until such clocks were invented, the sundial was the most accurate timekeeping device available, and it didn't work after sunset or on cloudy days. Water clocks were developed by medieval monks who wanted to say prayers at the same time every night, but the clocks were expensive, cumbersome, and subject to freezing in the winter.

By modern standards, even the best early clocks did not keep accurate time over long periods. One of the great challenges of the age of exploration in the fifteenth and sixteenth centuries was how to measure longitude, which requires a clock that keeps accurate time for long periods and under the adverse conditions of a ship at sea.

Our most fundamental time periods, all of which seem obvious to us, have subtle differences in various parts of the world, and even within our own country. For example, in some parts of the South, the period I call "afternoon" is called "evening," and most of us are confused about whether to call 3:00 A.M. "morning" or "night." We think of a day as beginning at 12:00 o'clock midnight, but, historically, most cultures have started the day at sunrise or sunset. Christmas Eve is a relic of a time when days ran from sunset to sunset. Our year essentially begins at the winter solstice, but we call our tenth month October ("octo" = "eight") from a calendar where the year began on the spring equinox. The Jewish sacred calendar begins at approximately the autumnal equinox, apparently because that is the beginning of the agricultural year in Palestine. Many Pagans begin their religious year with Samhain, or Halloween.

Misunderstandings across cultures are often based in not recognizing differences in ideas we have about time and how we "use" it. Our time chauvinism, like other forms of chauvinism, is hard to correct because almost all our attitudes toward time occur below our level of conscious awareness. Exploring this fascinating topic is beyond the scope of this book, but, for those readers who are intrigued by the idea, the books by Edward T. Hall listed in "For Further Reading" are an excellent introduction to cultural preconceptions about time and time use, among others. His book *The Dance of Life* is specifically on cultural time systems and how they affect a society.

Why Bother with a Lunar Calendar?

Earthtime Moontime presents a traditional Pagan religious calendar that has been handed down through generations, probably from the pre-Christian era. The people who developed this calendar thought of time in a much different fashion than we do. We visualize time as a line, and we often feel burdened by the past and apprehensive about the future. We see the events in our lives as unique, and worry about making choices that will alter our lives irrevocably for better or worse. Humans in our society do not, in general, see the passage of time as a sacred event. Clocks and calendars regulate our secular life. We tend to see events that celebrate the passage of time, our holidays and anniversaries, as outside of time, extracurricular to the mundane realities of our daily lives.

In contrast, earlier societies apparently visualized time more nearly as a circle, where events repeated in unending cycles. The progress of the year through the seasons, with its recurring patterns of birth and growth, death and rebirth, and the implications of those patterns in the lives of humans, was the essence of ancient religious mysteries.

The keeping of a calendar such as the one in this book was a sacred task. The calendar advised humans when to prepare for the work of life, such as planting and harvesting, when to venerate the mysteries embodied in the passage of the seasons, and when to celebrate the sacred cycles of death and life renewal that we observe in the natural world. The holidays in this calendar were truly "holy" days that marked the turnings of the Wheel of the Year.

The easiest modern figure that we might relate to this ancient worldview may be the sine wave we use to depict the movement of electrical energy in alternating current mode. Mathematically, a sine wave is a circular function even though we usually graph it on a line. In a classic sine wave, energy moves in cycles, going in one direction for half the cycle, and in the opposite direction the other half. We can distinguish the directions, but we recognize that the energy is identical whether we describe its movement and direction at any particular moment in time as positive or negative.

In the same fashion, when we see the passage of time as sacred, we can distinguish polar opposites at different points in the passage, but we must also recognize the essential identity of the underlying life processes that move through all the points implied by a recurring cycle. In the worldview of this calendar, life and death are such polar opposites, and, like the sine wave, are descriptions of places in a recurring cycle rather than a mark for beginnings and endings.

That is, life and death are not different processes, but different points in the cycle. The differences between life and death, and a host of other apparent opposites, is illusory. The illusion arises because we look at only one point at a time. More than that, the union of these divine polarities describes the mystery we call God/dess, that entity that exists in the place where all things are connected and where even those things that seem most different are essentially the same. The divine polarities define the mystery of God/dess, which is both beyond our comprehension, and yet contained within our hearts.

Getting outside the preconceptions of our culture is very difficult, and nowhere is this difficulty so great as in how we deal with the passage of time. Yet this "getting outside" is one of the most valuable experiences we can seek. Only in such an "outside" can we recognize, the ideas that determine our most common actions and, if desirable, correct these ideas. Only from a different perspective can we reach toward removing some of the invisible limits with which we bind ourselves. Putting ourselves inside the skin of another culture can open up our personal possibilities. Exploring the calendar in this book is one method for doing that.

In addition, the worldview of this calendar is close to the natural cycles of the Earth. Exploring it can help us reconnect meaningfully to the physical world around us and to the deep cycles in our own bodies that evolved in resonance with such natural cycles. Scientific studies are only now beginning to discover the profound effects that changes in sunlight and weather conditions have on our daily lives and attitudes. In our urban surroundings, we feel sheltered from the real world of Nature by heating and air-conditioning, by artificial light and inorganic transportation devices. We like to think we can rise above our natures and ignore the realities of our biology. We are mistaken.

However advanced our minds and technologies may be, our bodies have not changed significantly since the Stone Age. Our only real hope for rising beyond the limits of our physical selves is to understand more clearly how natural cycles affect our bodies and how they influence how we feel and behave. The next step for our species, whether it be moving into space or just learning how to live more rationally with our Mother, the Earth, lies in learning where we can bend our potentials without breaking something essential. We must learn to work with our biology and not in spite of it. This book is a device for moving in that direction.

Making a Window into Our Inner Selves

In addition to expanding our understanding of the world in which we live, *Earthtime Moontime* also offers an avenue for exploring our inner landscapes through the ideas encoded in the lunar calendar. A year can be understood as a metaphor for the life of a human, and each moon in this calendar expresses energies that can be associated with specific human characteristics and experiences. One of the underlying ideas of this book is that we may feel the energies associated with such characteristics and experiences most clearly and strongly during the annual recurrences of the moons that reflect them. In turn, these experiences correlate to our changing physical and psychological environment as the seasons change.

I further suggest that the characteristic Earth energies associated with the moons may "imprint" us at birth. I believe that the influences associated with our birth moon are part of the template from which we develop our own peculiar characters and personalities. If this sounds similar to astrology, it is, and for the same reason. Astrology also reflects Earth energies at different seasons, but in a more direct, solar fashion.

I do not believe that your birth moon, or the positions of the planets in your natal horoscope, determine your life, or that their influences force you into certain attitudes and experiences. I do believe these facts about you reflect a portion of a whole spectrum of influences that cause you to tend in specific directions.

My experience indicates that such effects are subtle but easily detectable. Our lives have so many vectors that even a mild pressure, if consistent, can shape what we become as our personal choices interact with that pressure. Our lives are a continual intertwining of our freedom to choose with the consistencies in our physical and psychological landscapes that limit our choices.

The Purpose of this Book

This book is meant to open those choices for you. That this calendar incorporates ancient knowledge is not as important as the use you are able to make of it. We should not assume that old ways have an intrinsic virtue that is not present in modern ways, or vice versa. The ideas in this book must stand or fall on their relevance to us here and now. The ultimate test of any system is, "Does it work?"

The primary purpose of this book is to provide a bridge to the real and present wisdom this lunar calendar encodes. The names of the moons, simple but evocative, reflect the passage of a year, the life of a human being, the relationship between humans and our Mother the Earth and our Father the Sun. These names convey the sacredness of the basic processes of our lives, a sense we tend to lose in our complicated modern world.

The energies reflected in this calendar are mundane, a mirror of fundamental, everyday human experiences. They relate to birth, death, and mating, to planting and harvesting, to journeying and holding household. They reflect the nature of human love, comprised of an unconditional motherlove, by which we accept, or are accepted in, the community because we are alive. They also reveal a conditional fatherlove, by which we accept others, or are accepted by them for who we are and what we accomplish. As with all divine polarities, when we are whole, we need both, and we express both, in our lives.

These mundane energies of everyday life are the foundation and source for the "lofty" spiritual energies that we have extrapolated from them. Such energies as mind and matter, order and chaos, yang and yin define our personal wholeness and our experience of God/dess.

This calendar mirrors both simple and profound human experiences with an ebb and flow of power that speaks to our hearts and to our bellies, which speaks to what we were before we allowed our intellects and advanced technology to overrun the rhythms of the natural world and to alienate us from our roots.

I offer the ideas in this book as something to consider, to play with, for whatever use they may be to you. Please take what I offer in the spirit in which it is given, as a device for opening your personal possibilities, and not as a prescription for how your life must evolve or as a definition of who you are.

3

Definitions, Cosmology
and All That Jazz

The worldview of the society that developed the calendar in *Earthtime Moontime* was very different from ours. I touched on some of these ideas in the last two chapters. In this chapter, I cover them in greater depth.

The underlying ideas of how the world works in this ancient society are often almost diametrically opposed to ideas that we consider to be obvious truths about the nature of reality. Understanding the differences between our view and theirs is critical to understanding this calendar. The purpose of this chapter is to help you recognize and understand some of those differences, whether or not you accept these diverse views as a valid model of reality.

History

To the ancient society of this calendar, history was not a line, but an ascending spiral. The ascending part of this figure acknowledges that there are events, such as our own births, that seem to be unique and from which we measure other events. However, the unique events of our personal or cultural histories are less important than the eternal and sacred repetition of the patterns of life on Earth, which in turn reflect in the patterns of our own histories. The circular direction of the spiral describes the form of the primary sacred mystery: we, and all that lives, are born; we live and grow; we die; we are reborn into a new cycle. The more things change, the more they remain the same. Time and eternity are different ways of looking at the same process.

The Moon's cycles are the original model for this idea. In each lunar cycle, the Lady is born in an almost invisible sliver of new moon, She waxes to full, and then wanes and disappears into the dark of the moon. Mythologically, She is, in succession, Maiden, Mother, Crone—youth, maturity, old age. We accept the death and disappearance of the Moon, and we mourn the loss of Her light. Then She returns to us again in the ghostly crescent of another new moon.

The Sun, our Father, moves through a similar cycle. Each year, from the height of His power at the summer solstice, He declines into winter. As His warmth decreases, the Earth, our Mother, and the lives upon Her, dwindle and face death. Many lifeforms expire and die from the cold and lack of light. The Sun retreats ever further toward the south, and the days become short and dim.

In this dark time, just as primitive humans despair of being able to continue to find the sustenance needed for life, the Sun seems to stop in the sky (solstice) and change direction, returning toward us. Mythologically, the Divine Child is born to bring new vigor to life on Earth, a vigor lost when last year's Divine Child grew old and died. After the winter solstice, days again grow longer, the life-giving warmth of the Sun increases, and, in the fullness of time, spring comes and all life is renewed once more.

The mystery of this sacred drama plays throughout nature. The dying grain that gives up its seed to the reaper sustains the lives of the humans who harvest it. That same seed brings the grain to us again, in the next season, and every season. Mythologically, the Father, whose energies are embodied in the grain— which some ancient people personified as John Barleycorn— gives His life at the harvest to nourish us, His children, and then returns once more in spring for a new cycle of love and sacrifice.

Animals and humans grow old and die, but they beget new animals and humans to take their places. In the eternal repetition of these cycles, we can take comfort that when we die, we shall also return to live again. In the words of a Pagan song, "All that dies shall be reborn." Our deaths, and our births, are merely punctuations in the greater eternal dance of all life, a dance that includes stars and molecules, and encompasses all that lies between.

In our present Western society, we see history's objective as "progress," which is measured on a line. Many of us assume we are moving toward an end of history, such as the Last Judgment, Nuclear Winter, or, perhaps, the somewhat utopian New Age. In our personal lives, we are taught that our goal should be to transcend the desires of the material world in order to merit the reward of an ideal world beyond this one (Heaven), or to avoid eternal punishment (Hell) for our failure to become sufficiently "spiritual."

All these ideas are alien to the worldview of the ancient society that made this calendar. To them, the purpose of the journey is the journeying, for the process of living is sacred. The material and the spiritual are both part of that process, and are equally sacred. The physical world and our emotional and mental experiences are both sources of pleasure and pain, to be enjoyed or endured, as the events of our lives play through both joy and sorrow. For those whose lives repeat and renew eternally (the many-born), Heaven and Hell are chapters in people's lives, not final destinations. Heaven and Hell come to every human, in his or her own time, and by his or her own choices and actions.

Cosmology

Joseph Campbell says that God is a metaphor for all the things we don't understand. Since God is by this definition beyond our comprehension, It is very hard to talk about. However, I shall try to convey my understanding of how God, by Campbell's definition, works in the worldview of this calendar.

Beyond and within, surrounding and permeating all that exists, is God/dess, the Order, the Tao, the All, the Universe, the One Power, or whatever other term you may prefer for that which we call God. In *Earthtime Moontime,* I use the term "Tao" for this transcendent mystery, the God beyond all gods and goddesses. The word "Tao" means "the Way of Nature."

The Tao is the fundamental stuff of the universe, the laws by which the universe works, and all the manifestations of those laws, including the Earth and we who live on Her. The Tao is the matrix from which everything springs, and to which everything returns in everlasting sacred cycles, cycles reflected in our personal histories and in all Earth processes. The Tao is the place at which everything is connected, the Way in and through which all that is—from galaxies to lone hydrogen atoms—behaves and relates. It is the universal melody in which we, and all that lives, are individual notes. The Tao is the sacred dance of life.

We can only approach the nature of the Tao through metaphor and mythology. With that understanding, consider that, in the beginning, the Tao existed alone and unchanging. Because there was no change, time did not exist. Because there was nothing beyond the Tao, space could not be measured. Because It had no reference point outside Itself, It could not know Itself. In order to contemplate Its own reality, the Tao evolved into the Goddess, who gave birth to Her polar opposite, the God, and from the union and interplay of God and Goddess, change was introduced into the Way, and all that lives was created. God and Goddess are at once separate and the same, opposites and also complements, and together make a single whole, which is the Tao.

Gods and Goddesses Dwelt among Us

In truth, all local gods reflect the God, and all local goddesses reflect the Goddess, and each is a facet of the Tao. All gods partake of the same divine essence, and each member of a pantheon of gods and goddesses represents an aspect of deep reality. Even as the union of God and Goddess expresses the whole, so do the various gods and other paranatural beings in the lore of a specific culture express a complex picture of the Tao.

The people of this calendar had gods who were very nearly human. Humans prefer gods and goddesses to whom they can relate directly to the impersonal, intangible reality of the Tao. We see this even in Western monotheism, where people often relate more closely to humans such as Jesus or Mohammed or to various saints and prophets than to their transcendent God. Humans live in the world of time and space and almost always explore the transcendent, insofar as they are able, through concrete and tangible means, or at least what seems so to them.

To relate to the Tao, ancient peoples created local gods whom they could see and touch, as "access ports" to the unknowable. The immanence (indwelling) of Deity was more real to them than the transcendence (existence beyond) of Deity, although they acknowledged both, even as we do.

The people in the culture that developed this calendar experienced their gods and goddesses "up close and personal." The gods dwelt among them and interaction with Deity was a normal part of everyday experience, from prayers and invocations to literal meetings. There are many stories of gods visiting humans disguised as travelers. The understanding that gods might temporarily take up residence in the bodies of a shaman or priestess explains many wonder stories in folklore. We have archeological and historical evidence that the gods were believed to literally inhabit groves, springs, and sacred wells, as well as sacred images and other objects.

These people honored the gods, but did not "fear" them or grovel before them as we sometimes seem to do today. The gods were clearly human, and might visit those who honored them in human guise, to share wisdom, to give warnings, or even to seed mankind with the blood of the gods through sexual unions with human women. The gods valued the same things as humans: good food, good friends, the joys of love, courage, and honor.

People could talk to their gods as easily as to each other. They could complain of how the gods treated them as well as offer praise and gratitude. They revered their gods, but their reverence and honor were not precisely the worship we associate with present religious practice. Worship implies that the gods are far above us and that we are unworthy of their attention.

To the people of this ancient civilization, gods and goddesses were friends, influential powers to enlist and propitiate, or perhaps difficult personalities whom it is not politic to anger. Like humans, the gods enjoyed the world in which we live, and humans expected them to manipulate the natural forces under their command in a responsible way. If certain gods did not perform satisfactorily, people might transfer allegiance to other, more useful deities.

Life was hard for the people in the society that developed this calendar, but the world was not divided into what "should" be here and what should not. Humans of that culture belonged in the world in a way we do not, and so did their gods. The sacred seasonal cycles were the key to that sense of belonging, and the stories of gods and humans that go with these cycles, as expressed in this calendar, were the means these ancient people used to achieve their sense of integration with the Tao.

Divine Polarities

In Western society, we believe that everything is what it is, and nothing can be other than what it is. That is, "A" cannot simultaneously be both "A" and "not-A." All things can be defined as separate fragments, distinct from each other, and each thing is absolutely and always whatever it is that comprises its definition. Thus, day is different and distinct from night, male from female, sacred from mundane.

This model of the world is not universal. In Eastern thought, reality is modeled as a single whole that can most clearly be understood as a complementary duality. The symbol called the *tao chi* (the yin/yang symbol) exactly expresses this relationship. The name "tao chi" means "life energy of the Tao." The familiar nested black and white teardrops, each with a spot of the other color at its center, is a portrait of the Tao, an icon that represents the true nature of deep reality.

In the tao chi model, everything is all mixed together. We can distinguish, for example, male and female energies as concepts or even directions in the flow of energies in people we know.

(Remember the sine wave?) However, all males manifest female energies, and all females are mixtures that include male energies as well as female. Day and night are not discrete events, but processes that include the clines of dusk and dawn into greater darkness or light. Even at noon, caves and wells are dark. Even at midnight, there is light from the heavenly bodies. Every thing partakes of its opposite and shares qualities with its complement. Nothing is discrete, separate, unconnected to the whole.

The idea of what I call divine polarities (divine because they describe the nature of the Tao) sounds strange to us in Western society, but the experience of them is common. For example, in the tao chi model, beauty and ugliness are different aspects of the same thing. We are used to ascribing these qualities to different things, and tend to assume that what is beautiful is much different from something that is ugly. We also assume that we will be attracted by beauty and repelled by ugliness.

Yet all of us have met a person who has what we have been taught to believe is an ugly face or body but whose character is such that they are beautiful, and we are attracted to them. We have all met people who are good-looking but so self-involved that we experience them as ugly and are repelled. We know of objects so perfectly ugly that their very ugliness is a kind of beauty, and of others that are so perfect in their beauty that we are alienated by their flawlessness. It is commonplace that the most beautiful women have flaws that, rather than detracting from their beauty, add piquancy and special charm to their faces.

Corollaries to the Tao Chi Principle

Every quality includes its opposite, the mirror that reflects it perfectly but in reverse. A perfect example is the photographic positive/negative pair. This pair represents exactly the same image, except that one shows light where the other shows dark.

Throughout *Earthtime Moontime*, I use the words "positive" and "negative" in this sense, meaning *direction* rather than *value*.

In our society, we tend to map value on a vertical line. Everything is measured by rank above or below a certain point, and we tend to think that above is "superior," "better," more valuable, more nearly "right." We strive to "move up the ladder." We worry if our fortunes "decline." We evaluate ourselves and everyone we know by whether they are "one up" or "one down" from us.

The Cartesian X/Y number grid tells us exactly how to classify everything. What is to the left and down is "negative" and therefore "bad." What is to the right and up is "positive" and therefore "good." The further below the line you are, the "worse" you are. The further above the line, the "better" you are. In this way, we tend to mix up metaphorical positions in space with not only "value" but also "right" and "wrong," "good" and "bad."

When we map the divine polarities on the Cartesian grid, one side or other of the mirror is mapped below the horizontal zero, the line separating the "positive" and the "negative." As a result, our society tends to evaluate the "negative" side as "bad" or at least less desirable than the "positive." This subliminal mapping is the reason why "feminine" (yin, the dark, "negative" side of the tao chi) is often valued as less good, important, and valuable than the "masculine" (yang, the light, "positive" side of the tao chi). Other common polarities get the same treatment, so that light, day, rational, logic (left-brain), analysis, and the spiritual are all considered "superior" (our vertical line again) to dark, night, non-rational, intuition (right-brain), synthesis, and material.

Some of the racist ideas in our society spring from this unrecognized assumption that dark is "inferior" to light (note the spatial metaphor). Some of the sources for our renewal as a society are devalued, as when we assume that science takes a "higher" ground than art, or when we dismiss non-rational experiences as invalid. We invent the Devil because we cannot imagine God manifesting the "negative" aspects of existence. All of these ideas arise from the use of a vertical line as a map for value.

Directions are Different in a Circle

When we map our values onto a circle, we soon find that (a) no place on the circle is intrinsically "better" than any other by its position in space, and (b) all points on the circle are necessary for the circle to be whole and complete. We need dark to understand light. Without night to demark the passage of time, "day" would not exist as a concept. We need the balance of the non-rational to understand the truth underlying what we learn in rational processes, or our rationality becomes sterile. Intuition gives logic somewhere to look. Analysis will fragment the whole world if we do not bring the product of our thoughts to some kind of synthesis. Without the grounding of our bodies, our souls can never engage with reality, for matter and spirit are merely mirrors of each other, as we learn in Einsteinian physics, where matter and energy are different forms of the same thing.

In this book, "positive" and "negative" are directions, not a statement of value. When I talk about any polar duality, I assume that it may manifest in either "positive" or "negative" form, on either side of the mirror. I assume that both forms are resident in either manifestation, so that, for example, "industry" also includes "laziness," and "love" also includes "hate." I also assume that the polar extremes define the ends of a range of qualities that exist in an infinite cline from one to the other, as black fades gradually to gray and then lightens to white.

The three words *whole, heal,* and *holy* all originate from the same root word. In order to heal our Selves, we must consciously acknowledge both sides of the divine polarities within us, and find productive ways to express them both in our actions. What we attempt to deny will betray us. Jung characterized this process as integrating the "shadow self." The process of recognizing and accepting that our unacknowledged "bad" qualities mirror and mimic the "good" qualities, which we believe we wish to manifest is the basis of many metaphysical systems that claim to heal the Self.

Finding the wholeness within can free us of guilt and self-blame. When we operate from a position of such internal wholeness, we are fully responsible for our actions, but we have better control of what we do and of the results that come from our choices to act. As we learn to act from wholeness instead of our fragmented sense of Self, we achieve "health" and become its sister-word, "holy." For all that lives is sacred, and all that we do, as individuals and as a society, should be in celebration of that knowledge.

Lunar Knowledge

This book centers around a lunar calendar, and the wisdom encoded in that calendar is lunar knowledge, which is labyrinthine by nature. Roughly, lunar knowledge is right-brained, multi-layered, symbolic, and holistic. Solar knowledge, by contrast, is left-brained, single-tracked, verbal, and analytic. Lunar modes of thinking twist and turn in unexpected ways, and can confuse and disorient. Like seeing objects in the moonlight, forms shift and blur before our eyes. What we see is evocative rather than definitive, a sense of direction rather than a map.

Lunar knowledge opens onto new worlds and wild magic. Just when we think we've got a handle on a bit of truth, it squirms out of our grasp and we're off chasing a different moonbeam. Lunar knowledge arises, at least in part, from our intuition that all things are connected somewhere. It has a strong preference for finding the unity and sameness of things, just as solar knowledge focuses on the way things are separate and different.

Exploring lunar paths can be frustrating and frightening, for the territory is usually unfamiliar. Our society does not value the lunar side. Such exploration can also be exhilarating and full of self-discovery. The important thing to remember is that, without lunar knowledge, we have only half the story. The object of our journey through the labyrinth (into the underworld, or perhaps into our subconscious mind) is to return with insights that we could not have discovered in sunlight (the upperworld, the world of normal consciousness). As we alternate our seeking between solar and lunar modes, we gain the best from each. We can correct the errors that creep in when we try to navigate through life with only one way of looking at the world.

"Mother" and "Father" are Multiple Symbols

The interweaving of symbols in this ancient society's worldview can be mindboggling, but the metaphors work when we let them shift as images in the moonlight, and forgo the hard clarity of straight logic (solar mode). The multiple images and symbols are like the skins of an onion, the same in essence, even though we may discriminate among their specific meanings.

In this book, when I say "Mother," I usually mean the Goddess as she is embodied in Gaia, our Earth, but occasionally I mean to suggest other layers of meaning above or below that fairly specific definition. Just to keep you on your toes, and because the material I am working with is naturally multilayered, I also use the term "Mother energies" to signify the "yin" side of the divine polarities. The word "Mother" can also refer to the mature form of the tripartite Goddess, who manifests as Maiden, Mother, and Crone. These three forms are, among other meanings, metaphors for the processes of beginning, fulfillment, and death; and for youth, maturity, and old age. Naturally, "Mother" can also refer to the Goddess who unites with the God to comprise the whole of the Tao.

In the same fashion, I use "Father" most often to mean the Sun, which is an embodiment of the God as solar energy. He is the fundamental source of the energies by which we live, providing both solar energy and the weather cycles driven by such energy, giving us both sunlight and life-giving rain. However, the "Father" is also personified as the food that nourishes us. This personification is appropriate because the plants at the bottom of the food chain are literally made from the energy of sunlight (photosynthesis), and all other life is sustained, directly or indirectly, from plants.

In folklore, the Father is personified as John Barleycorn, the grain that makes our daily bread, and He is also the Horned One, who represents the animals that sacrifice themselves so that we may live. The Horned One is a relic of a time when the people of this society were nomadic hunter/gatherers who lived by following the wild herds. Again, the Father "provides" what His children need to sustain themselves.

While the archetypes of the God are less well-known than the avatars of the tri-partite Goddess, He also appears in forms that depict youth, maturity, and old age. The most common names for these three forms are Warrior, Hunter, and Sage. However, only the Hunter, or Provider, is clearly represented in the myth cycle of this calendar. Representing the harvest as the Father's self-sacrifice at the height of His vigor, so that His full strength returns to the world when He is reborn, is a central theme of this mythos. The Wise Old Man and the Young Fool, who are other permutations of the Father's triple archetypes, have come down to us more prominently in folk tales than in myth.

Beyond these specific identities for the God, which are well known in folklore and myth, we also find the Father/God of the great story, alternately Lover and Son to the Goddess, who sires His successor, who is essentially Himself returned to play out the same drama in a new year. I also use the term "Father energies" to signify the "yang" side of the divine polarities.

Time has Wheels within Wheels

In the ancient culture that made this calendar, the waxing year begins with the winter solstice and marks the growth of the Father's strength from this nadir to the time of His highest powers at the summer solstice. The waning year marks the decline of the Father's energies from midsummer to midwinter. The light half of the year is the period from the spring equinox to the fall equinox, when days are longer than nights. The dark half runs from fall to spring, when night has dominion over day.

The energies of the divine polarities "contend," forming everchanging "mixes" of the polar opposites. This contention is the engine of change in the universe. The people who celebrated the mythic cycle of the great story saw "Father" energies, which are associated with limits and bounds, striving to contain the unlimited potential of "Mother" energies. The Father grows in strength and His light overcomes the dark of winter. At the spring equinox, Father and Mother energies balance exactly. At Beltane (Mayday), which is the beginning of summer in the old calendar, the Father is strong enough to have His way with the Mother, and from their union of limits (the Father) and potential (the Mother) comes the bounty of summer.

As the light of the Father wanes after the summer solstice, so the dark power of the Mother increases, and the two are equal again at the fall equinox. (Remember, "dark" does not mean "evil.") The Father sacrifices Himself, a sacrifice expressed in the harvests of grains, fruits, and livestock, all of which come to maturity and die to provide us with food. These harvests will sustain the Father's children, both humans and animals, through the dark and cold of winter.

The Father cannot sustain His summer vigor forever, any more than a man sustains His virility indefinitely. Better that the Father die at his prime, by His own choice, and return in the vitality of youth, than fail from age, and, by that failure, grant death a permanent victory. The seed of plants and the animals that survive the winter are the means for the Father's return. When life is renewed again in the spring, John Barleycorn returns in the sprouting of a new crop, even as the Horned One, Lord of the Animals, who presides over spring births in the herds.

After delivering the bounty of summer, and in sorrow for the death of the Father, Her lover, the Mother rests. Just as humans need to rest after hard labor, so does the Earth rest as the year winds to its end. By Samhain (Halloween), the beginning of winter in the old calendar, the Goddess, in Her aspect as winter Crone and death-bringer, triumphs fully over the God. Yet the triumph of death implies the victory of rebirth.

Please note that the Goddess's twin roles as life-bringer and life-taker are equally sacred and necessary to the balance of the Tao. Indeed, in this mythic cycle, she is simultaneously the life-taking winter Crone and the life-giving Mother who brings forth the Divine Child at Yule, the winter solstice. The society of this calendar recognized death as an essential part of life, for in death we are renewed and can re-enter the Mother's womb, which is the Grail, the cornucopia, the endless cauldron of rebirth from which all life flows.

Unlike the Eastern concept where rebirth means a return to sorrow and suffering (to be bound on the wheel of life), the concept of rebirth in this calendar is underlaid with joy. The death-bringing winter Crone triumphs for the moment in the depths of winter, but the coming rebirth of the Father at winter solstice anticipates that, as time goes on, His strength will build again. The Crone Herself transforms into the Maiden at Imbolc (Candlemas). At the opposite pole of the year to Samhain, Beltane, the Mother triumphs in her role as life-bringer, as the bounty of summer returns.

A Word About "Energies"

I use the word "energies" in *Earthtime Moontime* to mean a field of force that directs thought and action, a tendency or potential at the center of human actions. For example, when I say that "nurturing" is an energy, I mean that a lot of emotions and actions in our lives relate to giving and receiving, or to not giving and receiving, what we and others in our lives need to thrive physically, emotionally, and spiritually.

As I use the term, "energies" always reflect the tao chi, and manifest as equal and complementary opposites, each with their own validity and appropriate domain. From a universal perspective, positive and negative energy forms always balance each other. When a portion of reality seems to manifest only one aspect of the dual forms, you can be sure that you are looking at a local, and temporary, phenomenon. Balanced humans also exhibit both positive and negative components of these energies in varying proportions.

In truth, both positive and negative polar energies are productive when they are used in their proper places. For example, I mentioned "nurturing" as an energy. Its negative form is "not nurturing." Every human needs both. When we are born, we need a lot of nurturing. For us to reach our potentials as adults, our parents must gradually cease to nurture us in certain situations so that we can learn to nurture ourselves and to live independently. We mature most easily as whole people when our parents know how to balance the mix of nurturing and not nurturing, and change that mix appropriately as we grow.

As the divine polarities interact, they renew and sustain each other. This continuous mingling of positive and negative forms provides the "motor" by which the universe runs. In the process of contending, these divine pairs generate all the richness and variety that are our delight and our heritage as members-in-process of the Tao. This variety, forever changing and growing, offers us an infinite number of paths to explore through all the lives of our souls' journeys.

The bipolar energies are fundamental to our experiences of the Mother. Her cycles of birth and death, growth and decline, renewal and stagnation, mark the tides of our lives. We journey through similar cycles in our physical lives, in our relationships, even in our jobs, through birth and growth, to maturation and through the transitions we call death or completion. Cycles dance through our lives in a dizzying array of patterns, as brief as a mayfly's life, as long as the time since the Earth formed from whirling dust.

Sometimes, out of the corner of our psychic eyes, we catch a glimpse of the fact that our lives are journeys. A passing image stimulates this experience, like the brilliant, sudden joy of a child, or the surprising sadness of a faded rose. Our unexpected connection with deep reality may come naturally in a time of transition in our lives, such as when we witness a birth or death. It may be our birthday or the beginning or end of a year. I mean for this book to be a tour guide to places where you may experience such epiphanies often. In the words of Ecclesiastes, "To every thing there is a season, and a time to every purpose under heaven: a time to be born, and a time to die; a time to plant, and time to pluck up that which is planted; a time to kill and a time to heal . . ." May *Earthtime Moontime* be a time for your healing, for your becoming whole, for your becoming holy.

4

A Guide to Using the Moon Chapters

Your mission in reading this book, should you choose to accept it, is to keep your models of reality from degenerating into any orderly, easily graspable pattern. Nature is intractably squiggly. If you want a true glimpse of how reality works, jump in with both feet and grab whatever comes to hand or mouth. The more surprising your catch is, the more likely it is that you are gazing at a genuine strand of truth.

I hope the chapters on the individual moons in *Earthtime Moontime* will be a "lunar" experience for you. Don't go into this book with expectations of coming out with organized little bundles of knowledge that you can file in tidy categories and then forget. Like the experience of great art, you may feel enlightened by your experience of this book, but you may have trouble putting what you learned into words. If your experience is especially successful, what you gain from reading this book will disturb your comfortable ideas and make you rethink some or all of the ways in which you conduct your life.

Please understand that the moon chapters probably contain more ideas than you're likely to want to use at any one time. They are meant to be dipped into for what attracts you now, and then revisited later to find new insights. My hope is that, in the words of Robert Frost's *Directive,* you'll find, by the time you finish reading the book, that "you're lost enough to find yourself . . ." My further hope is that what this book may do for you is also expressed in that same poem, "Drink and be whole again beyond confusion."

Follow, Follow, We're on Our Way down to the Labyrinth

My intent in this book is to explore, in an organized and understandable fashion, ideas and events that arise on the right-brained, slippery side of our experience. Our culture, which is predominantly left-brained and rational in its outlook, teaches us to take things apart and gather facts. When we want truth, and a holistic view, we have to turn to our right-brain, and the non-rational processes of intuition, symbols, and metaphors.

If *Earthtime Moontime* speaks to you in a useful fashion, your experience could be unsettling. We are, after all, exploring lunar knowledge, so we expect inconsistencies and overlapping information, shifts and things we can't quite grasp. In addition, our lunar, right-brain side functions primarily via our physical, animal energies, some of which we have been taught to feel ashamed of. Consider yourself warned: Some woods in this book may be dangerous, and the bears are not tame.

How the Moon Chapters are Structured

Each moon chapter begins with left-brained lists. (Sorry, I have to start with where I am.) I give a "mirror" and "stage" for each moon. These ideas are discussed more fully in a later chapter, called "Moon Mirrors." The section called "Range of Dates" tells how early and how late on our Gregorian calendar a particular moon may occur in the nineteen-year cycles, and whether any of the seasonal festivals associated with the Wheel of the Year normally fall within it. This information is all empiric. I collected it from analyzing the data in astrological ephemerides.

There is also a later chapter titled "The Seasonal Festivals" to give you an overview of the eight celebrations—Earth holy days—which are associated with this lunar calendar, in case you are not familiar with them. These festivals were widely celebrated, in various forms, throughout Europe during the Bronze Age and later times. We still retain many vestiges of these special days in present-day seasonal celebrations and folklore.

Modern Pagans celebrate all eight festivals as the Wheel of the Year, but there is really no evidence that any ancient society celebrated all eight within its culture. There is, however, ample evidence that each of the festivals was celebrated in various localities.

The section of each moon chapter called "Mood of the Mother" blends images from the state of the Earth at the season when a particular moon falls, and some ideas about how the season affected humans in the society that made this calendar. The ideas of how humans from that time felt and thought are, of course, filtered through my modern eyes. Another short section, titled "Images and Reflections" is a quasi-poetic expression of the same ideas.

"Related Energies" tries to identify the human experiences that are most closely related to each moon, and also identifies my correspondences with astrology and the tarot. "Primary Energies of the Moon" lists divine polarities that I associate with each moon and its season.

The section titled "Manifesting Moon Energies" is an attempt to show how the seasonal energies manifest in our personal lives, both in positive and negative forms. "Meeting . . . Moon Challenges" offers strategies for integrating such energies into our lives in a productive fashion.

"If You were Born in the . . . Moon" operates from the premise that the energies of your birth moon affect your life and your character by making the issues associated with that moon a significant factor in your success or failure in life. This section goes somewhat more intensely into the essential issues I associate with each particular moon and offers some ideas for dealing with uncomfortable or unsatisfactory aspects of those issues in your life or personality.

This section is fun to play with. Tables in appendix B will enable you to find what moon all your friends were born in, and you can see whether what I say about those born under a particular moon works or not. However, the energies of all the moons are present in all of us, for we all live in the world through the whole cycle of the seasons.

The energies of each moon affect us at different times in our lives and are relative to different aspects of our experience. For example, I was married in the Death Moon, and the central issue of my marriage has always been the essence of Death Moon energies: ending, letting go, and transformation. Perhaps it is coincidence, but seeing the energies of the Death Moon expressed in my marriage has helped me gain perspective and has helped me integrate some of the disruptions that tend to accompany Death Moon energies.

Moon energies can manifest in a wide variety of ways, over the entire spectrum of material and spiritual experience, and in both positive and negative forms of the divine polarities. These manifestations can also range from trivial to profound, and from almost absurdly literal to highly metaphorical. For example, I know a Milk Moon woman who had trouble weaning her babies, and a Courting Moon man whose favorite vacation place is Tahiti. A Nesting Moon man of my acquaintance focuses so hard on "feathering his nest" that he neglects his family, his body, and his spiritual development.

It is important to keep speculations on the influence of birth moon energies in perspective. The birth moon imprint is an interesting hypothesis, similar to astrological ideas and probably related. I find it useful, as I do astrology, but its usefulness is more in the ideas and connections that it evokes rather than because knowing someone's birth moon gives me a definition of that individual's personality.

For example, I began my own working with the birth moon idea by trying to understand how I personally might express the energies of the Harvest Moon under which I was born. The energies of the Harvest Moon center around harvesting—or, more specifically, gathering—and releasing. At first, I wasn't even prepared to classify "harvesting" as an "energy." When the connections hit me, they were flashes of light that illuminated some previously dark inner corners.

My personal history is full of times when I was reluctant to accept help or love or credit that I had earned, and other times when I pushed something to closure too early, or refused to accept that a situation was dead and couldn't be recovered. That is, I am uncomfortable about reaping my just harvests, and I tend to make mistakes about when to harvest.

In addition to helping me make peace with past mistakes, the insights I gained by thinking about Harvest Moon energies help me avoid the same kinds of mistakes in the future. When I hear myself being self-effacing, I remind myself to accept my just harvest. When I notice I am hell-bent on resolving something right now, I remind myself that the harvest may not be ripe yet. When I try to hang onto things or people that no longer work for me, I remind myself that whatever I haven't harvested by now may be too rotten to gather, and it may be time to move to another field.

As you explore the moons in this book, especially your birth moon, I suggest you let the ideas I offer soak in, sit in the back of your mind, and flower out in words and images that fit your personality and your life. The ideas in this book do not define what you are. They are meant for skimming, like cream, so you can use what rises to the top. That is, they are meant to speak to your inner self in such a way that your own inner wisdom can surface in your conscious mind in a useful way. I hope you have as much fun, and "harvest" as much insight from reading *Earthtime, Moontime,* as I have had in discovering these ideas for myself.

"Self-Discovery Journal: . . . Moon Issues," found in each moon chapter, asks questions designed to provoke useful insights and to help you identify specific places in your life or habits that you may wish to change. If journal work is not your preferred method for self-discovery, you may wish to skip this section. You can read over and respond to the questions without using a journal, but you will gain less from the exercise if you "do it in your head."

If you hate to write but would like to try using the journal section, consider taping your answers. A permanent record captures insights that may otherwise evaporate overnight. It also allows you to evaluate both your insights and your progress over time. This "Self-Discovery" section could also be fun to work with in a discussion group. Ideally, you would work through this section during the moon whose energies you are exploring.

When you work with this journaling section, ask yourself each question in turn. Answer as specifically and concretely as you can. Keep focused. Use the old formula of who, what, when, where, how, and why to keep you grounded and connected to specific facts or actions, past, present, or future.

For example, the Death Moon has to do with handling endings and change. When exploring those issues, try to think in terms of real endings and changes that are important to you. Don't overlook matters that might sound trivial to others, like the death of a pet, or how changing cars or clothing styles affected your life. If it was significant to you, it's worth looking at.

You may wish to work on the questions for each chapter over several days or weeks. Take your time. Think about how each question relates to your physical or psychological self, to your family and other relationships, to your job, and to any groups that are important in your life. To get you started, I have included notes in parentheses on some questions. Don't let my suggestions limit where you go.

If you're actually writing in a journal, you may wish to leave room so you can add to your answers later. You might also want to review your answers periodically, such as every year in the same moon, and add to your earlier insights.

The final section of each moon chapter, "A Healing Process," is the heart and culmination of *Earthtime Moontime*. All the other material I provide in this book is auxiliary to it. What I hope for you is that these chapters will open a constructive passage between your everyday, public persona and your inner self. Your inner self is root (the underworld) to the branches you display in the everyday upperworld. Both are essential to your health (wholeness)—physical and spiritual. The exercises listed under the heading of "A Healing Process" are meant to facilitate such integration.

The passage between outer and inner self is twisty, as befits the traditional journey into the labyrinth or into the underworld. The objective of our journey is to become more nearly whole. It is also to make the untapped resources of the non-rational parts of ourselves more reliably available in our daily lives. Like moonlight, our goal is effervescent. Like moonlight, it may be magical.

I suggest you approach the exercises in the moon chapters with prudence. If something feels uncomfortable, think about it before you jump in. Trust your intuition to decide whether it's the right thing for you to do at this time. All spiritual journeys begin and end with learning to trust your own wisdom.

Sage Advice?

On the other hand, don't be too cautious. This book is designed for right-brain use. Part of the right-brain experience is what used to be called a leap of faith, that resolute decision to dive into the mystery of the labyrinth that we hope will thrill us and chill us, and then lead us back to the light wiser and more nearly whole. Don't forget that part of the experience of the labyrinth is getting lost in the dark.

You may sometimes feel that I jumble trivial material matters with "high" spiritual concepts. It's not a mistake. I did it on purpose. I believe that all spiritual and material experiences intertwine. They connect, if they are different, on a Möbius strip, and no one can say where one ends and the other begins. Material and spiritual are not separate. Like birth and death, they are different modalities of the same experience.

The moon energies described in this book originate in the down-and-dirty realities of life. In my opinion, so do all the important things we feel and think, even the most noble and ethereal. If you don't let your psyche play in a little mud once in a while, you miss all the good stuff. Those of us who seem earthbound may not appear, to outer eyes, to fly the lofty spiritual heights. But to inner eyes, our spiritual experiences may be more profound for staying connected to material reality.

There are sermons in stones and those who only look to heaven never see them. Don't skip the mundane ideas in these chapters. Such ideas are more likely to result in immediately useful insights than those you find in esoteric metaphysics. If you fully integrate the material implications of the moon energies, the spiritual truths will follow naturally.

I suggest that, as you go through the moon chapters, you target a general objective, like healing or personal growth, or, perhaps, a more intimate knowledge of nature. Learn what you can from each moon, then let it rest for a while. Come back to it later for another go-around, to try to open another level of understanding, or to see and hear and feel from a previously invisible direction. Use the ideas in this book as a springboard for new layers of understanding, not as directions on how and where you ought to be.

If nothing in a particular chapter connects for you, try the next one. If you go through the whole book without sparking an insight, get another book. *Earthtime Moontime* contains nothing you can't find somewhere else, perhaps in some metaphor system that speaks more directly to your heart. On the other hand, if this book prompts your profound spiritual growth, remember it contains nothing you couldn't have found somewhere else. Whatever part of truth it speaks resonates in you. My words are a chance vessel. The credit is yours. Good journeying, pilgrim!

5

Death Moon

Mirror, Waxing Half of the Year: Journey Moon.
Stage: Cycle Change.
Range of Dates: The Death Moon may begin as early as October 27 or as late as November 26. It ends as early as November 25 and as late as December 25. Total range of dates over which the Death Moon may occur is from October 27 to December 25.

Samhain, which usually falls in the Sorting Moon, falls in the Death Moon in years with a Courting Moon. Yule, the winter solstice which normally occurs in the Birth Moon, falls in the Death Moon twice in the nineteen-year cycle, following a year when the Courting Moon starts in April. Traditionally, Yule in the Death Moon is considered an evil portent, perhaps because when Yule falls in the Death Moon, Ostara, the spring equinox which is ordinarily in the Seed Moon, falls in the Fasting Moon.

Mood of the Mother

The Sun has weakened every day for weeks. Now His wan light seems only a pale reflection of His summer splendor. On a cloudy day, even bright colors appear washed out. The Earth grows cold, and life retreats. Vegetation is sparse and most of what remains is brown and sere. Bright-feathered birds have flown to warmer climates. Only dun birds huddle in hidden nests. Some animals have also moved south. Others have died of hunger or fallen to hungry predators. Still others doze in full or quasi-hibernation to preserve their meager resources for sustaining life. Humans grow torpid and sit by the fire. All life conserves its energies against the deprivation of winter. Even dead bodies slow in their rotting. The Mother sleeps.

The land is quiet. The buzz of insects and the chitter of birds is gone. Dead leaves crackle as we walk on the ruin of summer's glory, and the wind sounds harsh and cold as it whips through empty branches. The sounds of the Death Moon are crisp, hard, sometimes almost explosive. The muffling provided by live vegetation is no longer available to disperse and mellow the sounds of movement.

The ripe abundance of smells that accompany other seasons is muted. As heat decreases, smell molecules grow sluggish and do not rise to our noses. We smell and taste less keenly. So, too, does our sense of touch diminish. Our hands grow numb from cold, or we insulate them in wrappings. In the first chill of winter, when our bodies have not yet adjusted to low temperatures, we huddle in on ourselves, shivering at temperatures that would seem mild in January. We feel remote, sense-deprived as though wrapped in a soft blanket, like snow that covers the ground, that protects next spring's seeds from the full harshness of the weather.

The Mother slumbers, and all Her rhythms slow. You may call Her mood weary after the abundant bearing of summer, or expectant as She rests that She may bear again in the coming year. The landscape reminds us that everything changes, that all cycles come to an end, renew, and begin again.

Images and Reflections

Dormant seeds, slumbering until spring. The snake, torpid and listless before it sheds the old skin that binds its new growth. The chrysalis of the butterfly, a seemingly lifeless bit of detritus that hangs on leafless branches. The reaper who scythes the dead grain as he harvests the means to sustain existence and the seed of new life. Dead vegetation, plowed under to fertilize new growth.

The melancholy of recognizing that "you can't go home again," that what is past cannot be remedied. The lethargy of a woman far gone in pregnancy, awaiting her time. The death of a person or a relationship. The mourning of Demeter for Persephone, of Venus for Adonis, of Valhalla for Balder.

Related Energies

Journey Moon: changes

Father's Moon: transformation

Harvest Moon: endings

Feasts

Yule: change in life state

Samhain: otherworld journeying

Lammas: transformation

Zodiacal signs
    Scorpio: transformation
    Sagittarius: enterprise
Planets
    Pluto: transformation, rebirth
    Jupiter: seeking knowledge
Tarot cards
    Death: transformation
    The Tower: major change and renewal
    Kings: releasing

Primary Energies of the Death Moon

Endings/New Starts

Death/Rebirth

Transformation/Stability

Change/Stagnation

Recognition/Ignorance of the mysteries of transition

Manifesting Death Moon Energies

On the most fundamental level, we are dying and being transformed every day. Every minute we live, three billion cells in our body die, and three billion other cells are born. Over a period of years, every cell in our body is replaced so that we are literally, physically, not the same person we were yesterday, last year, a decade ago. Yet, all these changes occur within an unchanging blueprint, the DNA program encoded in our cells at birth. This program sets the basic shapes and cycles of our bodies. It defines not only the parameters of our daily processes, but also the timing of life changes such as maturation and puberty. It determines how easily we reproduce, and, at least in part, how quickly we age in the journey to the inevitable transition we call death.

This tension between minute-by-minute changes and unchanging basic patterns is the essence of Death Moon energies. Our cells die by the millions, to be replaced by millions of other cells just like them. The particular changes in our lives, which are peculiar to us, have a basic commonality with the changes in the lives of all other humans. Life has many kinds of deaths, but also many kinds of births. The final death of our body is a birth into another form or stage of life.

Our lives are full of changes and periods of rest. Many of our experiences with transition are related to our bodies and to biological processes. Consider the miracle that transforms a helpless baby into a child that walks and talks. Think of the changes related to the onset of puberty and our first sexual experiences. We are transformed by the commitment of mating, by the begetting and bearing of children, by the weaning of children from the breast and from the home, by the loneliness of the empty nest, by the grief of losing family and friends, and by our final release from this turn of life.

We experience many other kinds of transitions also. We enter the work force or leave it. We change, or choose not to change, our jobs or our religions. We move from one house to another, from one place to another. Every relationship begins, evolves, and comes to a closure as if it had a life of its own. We fail or succeed at what seems most important to us, and we change how we judge a particular event to be a failure or a success.

We express the balanced energies of the Death Moon when we accept the necessary changes that occur in our lives with grace, and do not try to force changes before their time. As we forge a productive equilibrium between change and stability, we learn to recognize when some part of our lives, material or non-material, has ended, and we move on to what follows it with joy and anticipation.

In this state of balance, we are able to accept the natural rhythms of the Mother, both in the natural world, and in our minds and bodies. We do not disturb ourselves with undue grief for what passes, or with undue desire for what is not part of our current cycle. The balanced energies of the Death Moon show us the long view, the cycling pattern of birth, growth, and death that forms our lives and expresses the Tao.

The Death Moon takes us into the heart of the mysteries, with the profound message that death and birth are the same process. From death and decay come new life, which in turn will die and decay to provide impetus for the cycle of life beyond it.

The Death Moon teaches us to constructively confront both our own physical deaths and the other transitions of our lives. It teaches us to trust in the promise: all that dies shall be reborn.

Meeting Death Moon Challenges

Change is the one unchanging factor in our lives. Any attempt to hold our lives still is doomed to failure and pain. When we resist unavoidable change, we only exacerbate the unpleasant results. When we learn to submit to what will be, we can find, in that submission, the release of renewal and transformation. Each stage of every cycle has its own joys and its own sorrows, its own lessons and its own challenges.

When we focus on what we have lost as we pass through this life, we miss what is before our eyes, rather like longing for the joys of spring and missing the passion of summer. If we focus too strongly on the future, we may seek change before its time. We lose sight of lessons in our present, rather like longing so hard to be grown up that we miss our childhood.

To use Death Moon energies productively, we must learn to live in the present and to focus on what we have rather than on what we lack. Many life changes have natural rhythms. We cannot hurry the time it takes to make a baby, or forestall the coming of old age. We can disrupt some cycles by trying either to slow or hasten the pace, but such attempts succeed only locally and temporarily. No matter how we try to bend the fundamental cycles of our lives or of the world, unexpected displacements will erupt, other parts of the process will make temporary adjustments, and the natural periods of such changes will return, over time, to their preferred rhythms.

The only strategy that works for dealing with change and transformation is the advice of the Alcoholic's Prayer: Change what we can, accept what we cannot, and strive for the wisdom to know the difference. We must let go of what is dead or yet unborn in our lives, and focus on what is alive and here and now. We must replace mourning for what has passed with joy in today. We must learn to build our futures on present actions rather than ungrounded hopes.

Our inner selves already know how to do this. We can open a line to our hearts and listen to our own wisdom. We can get in tune with natural cycles and learn to appreciate the lessons for each turn of the wheel.

If You were Born in a Death Moon

The greatest strength of people born under a Death Moon is likely to be their ability to turn existential corners with panache and then to look eagerly forward to the changes they will find around that corner. People balanced in this moon's energies have a deep sense of the cycles that underlie such transitions and a reverence for the mysteries of dissolution and renewal. The greatest weakness of people born under the Death Moon is likely to be a tendency to make transitions in their lives unnecessarily difficult, either by holding onto what has already passed, or by drawing problem changes into their lives.

Everyone experiences change and transformation, death and renewal, throughout their lives. You who are born under the Death Moon are likely to have a certain fascination with death and with the mysteries associated with death and renewal. This fascination may manifest itself in mysticism or in an absorption with piercing veils to the otherworld. It can also show up as a determined materialism that attempts to deny that anything exists beyond the transition of death, literally a "whistling past the graveyard."

In addition to a concern with the greater issues, those born under the Death Moon may experience more major life changes than most people. People born under this moon naturally draw change into their lives so they can learn to deal with transitions and with the transformations that accompany them. If your conscious self does not seek suitable changes to meet your strong interest in this process, your unconscious self may see to it that you have opportunities to practice. Its selections are usually less comfortable than those changes that you consciously shape.

As you work with the energies of this birth moon, focus on developing effective strategies for handling change and transformation. Begin by learning to recognize, as early as possible, when change is inevitable. Try to minimize your discomforts during the transitions associated with such changes. Evaluate your performance after every important transition and think about how you can do better next time.

Another possibility is to actively seek small changes in your life, to stretch your skills for handling transitions without overwhelming your ability to cope. Your psychic muscles grow from exercise just like muscles in your body. With practice, you can improve your strength and endurance for dealing with the emotional turmoil of change.

If you have drawn many difficult transitions into your life, try to identify the change agents you have used and try to determine what you can do to avoid such agents or to minimize their influences in your future. For example, if you always fall in love with a particular kind of person who interacts disastrously with your personality, try first to make wiser choices. If you can't avoid a relationship whose prognosis is poor, try to end it more quickly than you did in the past. Any ending that you influence or control instead of having it forced on you will be easier to deal with.

The ways you "force" yourself into unpleasant transitions may include overspending your money or your personal time and energy resources so you "have no choices" when a crisis comes. You may also tend to "not have time" for the maintenance required for a car, a home, or a friendship, and then be unable to recover when you have a breakdown. You lose a job because you can't get to work, or you have a financial disaster when the porch roof collapses, or your friend won't give you the support you want to weather a rough spot.

You may not recognize how you draw uncomfortable transitions into your life, but often you can infer that you did from the results. Consider using as a rule of thumb that if you experience similar patterns over and over, you are somehow encouraging those patterns in your life. Don't worry about how you do it. Just change how you operate. Any change in your behavior will affect the entire system of your life and help break loose old patterns. As your strategies for dealing with transitions improve, your transitions should become easier.

☾ Self-Discovery Journal: Death Moon Issues

1. How, specifically, do you feel about change and transitions *(changes in body, home, family, friends; changes in community, country, the world; changes in how you see the world)*?

2. What specific transitions are occurring in your life right now? Think about trivial things as well as larger matters. Small changes often reflect more fundamental changes *(physical fitness, education, home or job; personal style in clothes, furnishings, or behavior; hobby or organizations; a job or lover you're in the process of gaining or leaving)*.

3. Which of the changes in your present life seem to you to be under your control? How, specifically, are you controlling such changes?

4. Which changes in your present life seem to be beyond your control? What specific actions can you take to gain more control or to ease the transitions for yourself?

5. What specific transitions have occurred in your life in the last year, the last five years? Do these changes suggest changes in your personal values and attitudes?

6. How, specifically, have you responded to past changes in yourself or in others? List specific events and how you felt about them, how they influenced your actions, what you learned (or did not learn) from them.

7. What was your last major life transition? What specific changes did it make in your life? *(Major life transitions include, but are not limited to, entering or leaving school, marriage or divorce, birth or loss of a child, moving to a new locale, starting or leaving a job, religious conversion, or deaths of close friends or family.)*

8. Chart all your major life transitions. How, specifically, could you have changed your attitudes and behavior to make those transitions more comfortable or constructive for you? Do your particular life transitions suggest a pattern that you may be able to change?

9. What kinds of transformation do you desire in your life, and how, specifically, do you mean to achieve them? *(Focus on inner changes and specific personal actions that may help you make the changes you desire. Transformations that depend on external forces are not in your control.)*

10. What specific transformations are occurring in your life that you are pushing or resisting? Why, specifically? *(Try to tune into your inner wisdom to determine whether your pushing of, or resistance to, these changes is appropriate.)*

11. How, specifically, do you feel about physical death? Of others? Of yourself? Does your attitude influence how you feel about other kinds of endings?

12. How, specifically, does your attitude toward your inevitable physical death influence your life? Is that influence beneficial or counterproductive?

A Healing Process for the Death Moon

Take a walk in a natural area such as woods or a park or even your own back yard. Notice the evidence for both death and renewal in the living things around you. Each season has its own signs of life and death, its own plant and animal life cycles.

Many species of birds mate in February, before the last cold of winter has left us. Spring brings us baby chicks and flowers that bloom for a few weeks and then withdraw their splendor until the following year. A spring landscape holds both the brown and yellow of dead vegetation and the promise of green growth.

Summer has ripening grain, and cool-weather plants that wilt and die back in the heat. Animals conceived in spring are born, and others begin to learn the skills they will need to survive independent of their parents. Some inexperienced young fall to predators.

Autumn offers us the harvest and the fruits that are a plant's hope for survival beyond the rigors of winter. The glory of autumn leaves is specifically caused by trees withdrawing into dormancy. In autumn, young animals strike out on their own, to find their successes or failures in continued life or death in the hard times ahead. Many herd animals mate now, at the peak of their physical condition, to produce early spring births.

In the deepest cold of winter, we can find precursors of new life. There are pregnant animals that will deliver in spring. When we have warm days in January or February, tree buds swell in anticipation of warmer weather. There are plants such as snowdrops, which flourish only in winter, and evergreens, carrying their color of life through the cold time. We are never left completely without the comfort of green life.

When we look, we can find both death and the promise of renewal in every corner. We may also observe that every change brings both gains and losses. Through the bodily changes of puberty, children gain the joys of sexual pleasure and of deep bonding to another. By that change, we also lose the unique ability of children to recover from injury. Never again will our body's cells be so able to renew and replenish themselves.

At menopause, a woman loses her ability to bear children and also loses the estrogen that protects her body from arteriosclerosis and heart disease. She gains freedom from many of her responsibilities, and the time to share her life's wisdom with those younger than she. Our bodies slow and deteriorate as we move into old age, but, in the comfort of realizing that we'll live over it, whatever "it" may be, we can leave behind much of the emotional turmoil that accompanies earlier stages of our lives.

As we learn to recognize and appreciate the cycles of life, we begin to synchronize into the deep rhythms of the Mother. We rediscover our connections to Her. We come home to the Mother when Brother Death, and the other transitions he symbolizes, become a natural part of our experience and, thereby, cease to be either a terror to be avoided or a release to be sought. Only when we fully accept our own deaths can we fully accept the joys of living. For life and death are merely turns on the wheel, alternate and unending patterns of light and shadow.

6

Birth Moon

Mirror, Waning Half of the Year: Mother's Moon.
Stage: Beginning.
Range of Dates: The Birth Moon may begin as early as November 25 and as late as December 25. It ends as early as December 25 and as late as January 24. The total range of dates over which the Birth Moon may occur is from November 25 to January 24.

The defining event of the Birth Moon is Yule or Midwinter, the winter solstice, which many cultures celebrate as the birth of the Sun or of the Divine Child.

Mood of the Mother

The energies of the Death Moon deepen, and the Sun continues to lose strength every day. Humans value evergreens and plants such as mistletoe and holly because they are green in this dark month, in seeming defiance of the withered remains that surround them. This time is fearsome, and even we "modern" humans surround ourselves with greenery, bright lights, and gaiety at this time of year, as a quasi-magical remedy to counter the apparent weakening of the Sun on which all life depends.

In the midst of this deepening of winter, hope lightens our hearts. The Father, who has been traveling to the south, further and further away from us, stops in His progress and returns. The old Sun, who has exhausted His lifeforce, is dead, and the Mother gives birth to a new Sun/Son who moves back toward us to brighten and revitalize our world with His young strength.

Like the first weak efforts of a newborn child, the changed motion of the Sun seems uncertain at first. His light is still pale and weak, but it strengthens every day. If we can endure the cold and the lack of greenery and the slow rhythms of the Mother for a while longer, winter will end, and spring will come again. The Mother speaks to our most primitive selves, and whispers to us, "Through cycles and changes, birth and death are one. All beginnings are also endings."

Images and Reflections

The sudden eruption of a sprouting seed. A newborn of any species. The sound of a frozen brook when it begins to run free. The first scent of baking bread. A raincloud after a drought. The sun after flooding. The rainbow, sign that the storm has passed.

The joy of beginning a new job, a new home, a new friendship. The euphoria of a mother who has successfully delivered a healthy child. "Unto us a child is born. Unto us a son is given." Pandora's hope, Prometheus' gift, Idunn's apples.

Related Energies

Death Moon: transitions

Seed Moon: beginnings

Mother's Moon: unconditional love, trust in the universe

Feast of Yule: birth

Zodiacal signs
   Sagittarius: enterprise
   Capricorn: productivity

Planets
   Jupiter: seeking new experiences
   Saturn: parenting

Tarot cards
   The Fool: venturing forth, opening to all possibilities
   Wheel of Fortune: new stages in life
   Aces: beginnings

Primary Energies of the Birth Moon

Beginnings/Completions

Birth/Stasis

Hope/Despair

Creation/Destruction

Manifesting Birth Moon Energies

The primitive within us, legacy of our animal selves, lives more in the eternal Now than we "civilized" moderns may recognize. We have come so far in learning to override our deep animal instincts that we sometimes forget that beneath our modern cerebral cortex lies the primitive brain we inherited from the first animals that walked on land. On an atavistic level, in the reaches of our reptile brains, the weakening of the Sun before the solstice is terrifying. Whatever our minds may know, our bodies cringe in fear that, this time, the light that nourishes all life may be extinguished, and, with it, our own lives.

If we are in tune with our inner selves, the turning of the Sun can be an extraordinary joy, a promise to our innermost selves that we will not cease to be when we pass over in the transition we call death. If we are not in tune with the whole cycle, and fear our own deaths in the apparent dying of the Sun, we may feel like retreating into a cave at this time of year. The glitter and abundance of holiday parties, evergreen trees ablaze with lights, even our tendency to stoke up on high-calorie foods, are symbolic expressions of our rage against the dying of the light and of our personal fears of being cast forever into outer darkness.

On a literal, material level, the Birth Moon celebrates the sacredness of making babies and of creating all other forms in the material world. It is also a celebration of the many ways we have of making, from planting flowers and digging ditches to composing symphonies. Those who risk resources (the trauma of birth) or risk the pressures of society (fear of failure) to make something new celebrate the energies of the Birth Moon. In order to take such risks, we have to trust that we have or can find what we need to carry through. We must also be willing, for some creations, to destroy what lies in the way, as we might raze an old building to make room to build a new one.

The obvious spiritual energy of the Birth Moon is hope. The Greek legend of Pandora is a precise metaphor for the energies of this moon. Pandora opened a forbidden box and released all the ills that plague humankind. All that remained in the box to defend us against their onslaught was Hope. As in this cautionary tale, we do not gain our happiness by denying unpleasant realities. However, in our hope for growth and rebirth, we can find the courage to begin anew, again and again, even as the Sun dies and returns to us each year.

The balanced energies of the Birth Moon teach us to accept the risks of making new starts, to destroy only what we must in order to create, and to act from hope for our futures. Sometimes, trusting the Tao to provide the resources we need to do what we desire is the most difficult part of such tasks. We may feel unequal to the challenges that face us. Sometimes we decline to act, hoping to preserve our resources for beginning some other day. Sometimes we act and fall on our faces.

None of these choices violate the essential message of the Birth Moon, which is that we must continue to strive, no matter how discouraged we may feel. What does violate this moon's message is repeatedly choosing to avoid bringing new things into the world, or choosing to destroy without replenishing. We are set on our life path with access to all the resources we need for our life's work. Jesus' advice, "Seek, and ye shall find. Knock, and it shall be opened unto you," is in the spirit of this moon. We are assured by the Birth Moon that we may begin an infinity of times, and that something productive comes from every trial, if only the knowledge of how to do it better next time.

The other important lesson of the Birth Moon is that we are responsible for what we elect to bring into, or not bring into, the world. We cannot choose to be disengaged. We make things, useful or not, whether we choose to shape what we produce or choose to stand aside and let our making grow as it will without providing our directed input. The joy of creating lies in actively shaping what we make in life. If we must try several times to get it right, that's fine. The process provides its own rewards. The sorrow of regret lies in missed opportunities which we failed to grasp, either from lack of courage or simple neglect.

Meeting Birth Moon Challenges

Birth Moon challenges cluster around beginnings. On a deep level, these challenges mostly relate to a failure of the hope that is symbolized by the miracle of birth. We may have trouble acting because we fail to hope, or we may act unwisely on hope that is not founded in fact and experience. Our despair may be expressed by giving up control of our lives to someone else, or by our inability to relate to other people without having full control of the relationship. We may destroy what we are afraid to create. Whichever is the case, the root cause is a fundamental insecurity about our ability to act effectively, and about our worthiness to succeed.

When we despair, we feel overwhelmed by the forces ranged against us, and we distrust our ability to overcome the obstacles that face us. We may even fall into a habit of despair, where we can't see beyond our belief that we have too little control and too few choices. The only way out of that corner is to resolutely quit looking at the huge pile of things we can't do, and to diligently search for the thread, however small, of what we can do. Action, even unwise or ineffective action, is an antidote to despair. With any action, our chances of succeeding, or at least of not failing so miserably, improve.

Those who operate on false hopes despair in a different style. In effect, they consider themselves of such little value that they have to inflate their self-worth or the assets available to them lest they reveal their inner poverty. When we deceive ourselves or others about the resources available to us, we set ourselves up for failure. Perhaps we feel that our need for help or for resources proves we are not worthy to succeed, or perhaps we just want to fail and get it over with. Fortunately, failure is an event, not a job description. We can fail over and over and still retain the capacity to succeed.

Like the hyperactive child who needs stimulants to slow down, false hopers need more hope, not less. Genuine hope is empowering. No one can promise us success just because we try, but if we wait to get into the race until conditions are perfect, we'll probably never run.

The alternative to hoping and trying is giving up and dying. While we sit on the sidelines and tell ourselves we can't make it, someone who's less able than we are is winning the race. None of us are that good at this business of life. Some people just don't let it get them down. To hope, we must develop an inner security, a trust that we can make it through. No one is born with that knowledge, and we all have lots of evidence that making it through is by no means guaranteed.

In fact, we have only one avenue to security: our personal decision that we will live over it, whatever "it" may be, from a failed love affair to a tornado that sucks up our house. Such a determination is a policy decision. We decide that, whatever happens, we'll find a way to survive it, somehow, some way.

The surprise is, when we refuse to despair, when we put ourselves in the hands of the Tao and try to muddle through as best we can, we always do find a way around our "overwhelming" obstacles. As we get past such difficult places, we also build the sense of self-worth that helps us to try the next time.

Trying doesn't assure that the way we find around a problem will be pleasant. It doesn't save us from having to stretch our resources to squeak through. It doesn't even promise we'll make it through whole. But once we internalize a decision to keep going, no matter what, we can draw from that decision for the strength to try again, and again. In that decision is an endless supply of the hope we need to start anew.

If You were Born in the Birth Moon

The special strength of people born under the Birth Moon is their creative potential. They are often energetic "idea people" who spend their lives inventing concepts and making new things happen. People balanced in the energies of this moon follow through on their projects and take responsibility for any misjudgments along the way. They have the courage to take risks, the wisdom to know when to stand down, and the persistence to try again when they fail.

The special weakness of people born under this moon tends to be diminished hope. That is, they do not so much despair as they do not develop the confidence to take risks. When they are unwilling to risk much, they have few failures, but their successes tend to be meager. They may wonder why the zest of life has passed them by.

When people born under the Birth Moon get "stuck," they tend, metaphorically speaking, to have trouble getting pregnant. They have difficulty delivering their creations, or have problems in owning up to what they produce. Common permutations of these "stuck" places include starting dozens of projects, but not finishing them, or being afraid to reach out and create unless success is guaranteed. Difficulty with this moon's energies also shows up in people who never quite seem to live up to their potentials, and in people who seem to spend all their abilities in destroying what others create.

The balance of energies for those born under this moon lies between their urges to create and their willingness to risk failure, between accepting the consequences of what they create and their skipping out on responsibilities. As one born under this moon, you may feel a sense of diminished achievement where you have not taken the risks necessary to manifest your full abilities. You may feel a sense of emptiness where you have left a string of unfinished projects, or have abandoned what you created because it did not turn out as you wished. You may be bitter where you have destroyed and not replenished, especially if your motivation was a fear that you lacked the ability to replace what you destroyed.

Many problems of people born under the Birth Moon stem from fear of failure. There is no simple formula for getting over that fear, and it doesn't ever go away by itself. The people you see succeed are just as afraid as you are; they just refuse to let the fear keep them from trying. Ignoring fear is a learned skill, like riding a bicycle. After you learn how to do it, it gets easier. Do it long enough, and you may forget you're afraid.

If risking is your particular challenge, work on starting small things and completing them successfully. Use small successes to develop trust in your own abilities. If you are willing to begin projects, but tend to leave your creations incomplete or to abandon them, finish something you've started or go back and reclaim something you have forsaken. Even if what you complete is not everything you envisioned, the energy of finishing it will help you to be more effective on your next undertaking. We have to learn to accept the imperfections of our creations as part of normal human experience. When we focus on what we achieve instead of how we fall short, we consolidate skills that lead to later success.

Indeed, learning to accept failure is probably the single most important skill required for success. An expert in any area of knowledge is one who has made more mistakes than most other people and then learned to recover from them. Those who never make errors can become competent users, but they never become experts, certainly never the creators who try the edges and make the breakthroughs.

As one born under the Birth Moon, you may need to focus on how to develop appropriate hope for success and how to sustain your will to try. Appropriate hope is based on real experience. You stretch the limits of your resources carefully, so the worst that can happen is that you may stumble and scrape your knee. Next time you stretch a little further. You don't have to risk falling on your face. Each time you dare to act, the distance you are able to stretch becomes greater, and what you can achieve comes closer to your inner visions.

All you need to try is to trust yourself. Trusting yourself is based on experience, and also in your willingness to accept that you intend to survive if things go wrong, that you can recover if you just keep going. I've a heard a lot of magic formulas for developing that kind of self-confidence, but they only work if you practice. Doing is the only road to building hope.

☾ Self-Discovery Journal: Birth Moon Issues

1. How, specifically, do you feel about beginnings *(beginnings in life processes and stages, physical fitness, job, family, friends; beginnings you see around you in your job, community, country, world)*? What kinds of beginnings make you feel afraid or excited? Why *(be specific)*?

2. What, specifically, have you begun today, this week, this year, to achieve your desires? *(No beginning is too trivial to mention. Little beginnings build the self-trust on which big beginnings are built.)*

3. What actions are you willing to take to achieve what you desire *(for your body, physical environment, relationships, job, community)*? Which of these actions can you take now? *(Don't set up too ambitious a program. Small achievements build confidence for acting. Small failures can increase inertia.)* What specific resources do you need? How can you get them?

4. What kinds of projects are you unwilling to begin? What parts of your life are you unwilling to change *(regarding your body, environment, relationships, job, the world you inhabit)*? Is

your unwillingness caused by comfort with what you have or fear of failure? Do your answers point to any specific course of action you can take?

5. How, specifically, do you define failure and success? *(List concrete evidences, not vague feelings.)* How, specifically, do you know if you have failed or succeeded? What specific inferences do you make about success or failure *(self-worth, the value of other people)*?

6. Do you need to change what you tell yourself about failure and success? What, specifically, should you say to yourself about failure and success in your self-talk? *(Write a script, use it whenever you catch yourself putting yourself down.)*

7. What new things, specifically, have you manifested in the world in the last year *(physically, in your life processes, for your family, job; new ideas, new ways of doing things, new areas of knowledge explored)*? Did you complete the project? Are you satisfied with your creation? What, specifically, did you learn from it?

8. What single thing do you most wish to give birth to *(a project, friendship, new personal wholeness, marriage, better relationship in your family or job)*? What specific action can you take immediately to make it happen? What specific actions and resources do you need to carry it through?

9. What specific processes are you afraid to begin *(self-assessment, loving someone, accepting someone for what they are, a new job, a fitness program, reaching for something you want)*? Why, specifically? If your fear is inappropriate, what, specifically, can you do to counter it?

10. Where, specifically, do you operate on false hopes *(waiting to act until your "ship comes in," buying things you don't have money for, putting up with a destructive relationship rather than be alone)*? How do you know your hopes are false? What

specific strategies can you use to improve your ability to make accurate assessments of your resources?

11. How, specifically, can you learn to use the empowerment of hope and belief in your own worth to improve your life? *(Don't be too ambitious at first. Enduring transformations begin with small, persistent actions. Choose one small, specific action and follow through until you prove your hope for success. Every action ripples through your life. Set yourself up for success.)*

A Healing Process for the Birth Moon

When we interact with the Mother in even the most peripheral way, we cannot fail to observe the extraordinary persistence of life. We spray our lawns and dig up every dandelion, and bright yellow heads still festoon the lawns next year. The bush we cut to the ground and painted with herbicide until it was black nonetheless hopefully sends out new leaves as soon as we turn our backs on it. One look at weeds pushing their way through tiny cracks in the sidewalk is enough to belie every science fiction story that shows a city, supposedly abandoned for hundreds of years, with intact streets and naked walls.

Humans and animals are as hard to kill. The media relates stories of pets that travelled a thousand miles to reunite with their families. Television broadcasts several "docudramas" every year about humans who managed unbelievable feats of endurance, who survived against unbelievable odds, beyond all expectations. Consider your own attachment to living.

Go for a nature walk, at any time of the year, or just take a close look at your front lawn or the trees that line your block. The evidence of life's persistence and diversity are countless. A square foot of lawn may have a dozen or more species of plants in various stages of growth or hibernation. In spring and summer, tiny pink, white, and yellow flowers hide within the forest of leaves. Poke around a little, and you may see several kinds of insects, flies buzzing around the flowers, pillbugs rolling into a ball as you turn your attention to them, grasshoppers leaping a foot off the ground when you disturb them. If the weather is wet, perhaps you'll even catch an earthworm disappearing into the soil.

The tracks of life appear everywhere. Can you find a spider's web, with a neatly wrapped bundle of eggs, or a paralyzed fly that is the spider's larder? Tree bark may show damage from insects or birds. A hollow place at the fork of the bole that collects water may be powdering from rot caused by microbes, or perhaps it hosts a rank of shelf fungi that live on rotting wood. Leaves reveal ragged holes from the ravages of hungry caterpillars, or the bumpy galls of insect eggs. You may even find the evidence of larger animals, as the nest of a bird or squirrel, or the acrid smell of a tomcat's territorial marker.

Notice how bravely all that lives persists in trying to live. Even death is food for some forms of life. The fundamental law of the Tao is, "all that lives has a right to live, if it can." In every nook and cranny of our lives we see evidence that all that lives keeps trying. Can we do less?

Find a natural place where you feel close to the Mother. In that place, draw an imaginary circle, a momentary safe place, around your body. Reach out to the Mother and feel Her life, and Her support of your life. Renew your determination to live while you can.

7

Milk (Nursing) Moon

Mirror, Waning Half of the Year: Father's Moon.
Stage: Growth.
Range of Dates: The Milk Moon may begin as early as December 25 and as late as January 24. It ends as early as January 24 and as late as February 22. Total range of dates over which the Milk Moon may occur is from December 25 to February 22.

The Feast of Imbolc normally occurs during this moon. Imbolc is the beginning of spring in the old calendar. The equivalent feast on the Christian calendar is Candlemas (February 2).

Mood of the Mother

As milk flows fitfully at first from a new mother's breasts, so the Earth shows the first signs of the coming renewal of spring. The Mother will nurture us. The cold may be bitter today, but a blanket of snow insulates the waiting seeds from its full force. Winter flowers, such as snowdrop and crocus, greet us like a promise in the mostly barren landscape. The first birds begin to return from their winter homes, and some species sound their mating calls, a herald of warmer weather. Spring-bearing animals begin to deliver their babies, and life, which seemed to have retreated during the winter, begins to stir once more.

The light of the Father is visibly strengthening now, and sometimes a few warm days catch us unaware, a false spring that makes us long for the real thing. If a warm spell persists more than a day or so, trees begin to bud and the soil takes on a damp, loamy smell that is not quite the fertile smell of spring, but hints of balmier days to come. Some grasses send up a few new blades, testing the promise of days of longer sunlight. Occasionally we hear the lazy buzz of a fly, awake too early to survive, but a reminder that his wiser brothers will return to plague us when summer comes. The light seems more substantial, and our spirits unfold in the sunshine.

The Mother, still drowsy from the labor of birth, reaches out to Her children. Her nurturing flow begins, and our hearts gladden. Life will continue. We shall experience Her full bounty again in the fullness of time.

Images and Reflections

Seedlings sprouting under the protection of last year's withered vegetation. A bird feeding its young or luring a predator away from its nest. Any young mammal at its mother's breast. An animal defending its offspring. A cat teaching her kittens to hunt. A bird pushing its babies out of the nest.

The hearth of a happy home. Children playing under a smiling parent's watching eye. Madonna and child. A group hug. The joy of fellowship. Isis nursing Horus.

Related Energies

Father's Moon: fatherlove

Mother's Moon: motherlove

Feast of Imbolc: promise of renewal

Zodiacal signs
> Capricorn: material productivity
> Aquarius: love of humanity

Planets
> Capricorn: responsibility
> Uranus: interconnectedness of all things

Tarot cards
> The Empress: bounty of the Mother
> Strength: lifeforce
> Threes: creative flow, preparing to manifest in the world

Primary Energies of the Milk Moon

Recognition of Self/Others

Nurturing/Not nurturing

Generosity/Selfishness

Independence/Dependence

Manifesting Milk Moon Energies

In a natural environment, a mother's milk is the child's first food, the primary requisite for its survival. After the trauma of birth, the safety of the mother's arms and the siren call of the milk smell of her breasts will ever after symbolize safety and nurture. That nurture, and all the other kinds of nurture we require in our lives, is necessary for us to prosper.

The energies of the Milk Moon revolve around two issues. We must find what we need to continue, not just what we need to survive, but what we need to thrive. We must also discover how to pass on the nurturing we received to a new generation, and, by extension, to all humanity. This moon deals with both giving and receiving, and with the appropriate balances between them as we travel through our lives.

We manifest Milk Moon energies when we seek whatever we need to grow and develop, and also when we provide an appropriately loving and caring environment to those around us, especially to our children. In the process of maturation, we seek experiences that develop the skills and knowledge we require to be independent in the world. When we reach independence, we have our turn at providing the components of nurture—material needs, love, and education—for those we choose to nurture, to insure their future successes as independent persons. Throughout our lives, we provide such support not only to our children, but to ourselves, to the other members of our families, to our friends and coworkers, and, through our taxes and in our personal expressions of charity, to those in our society who are in need.

To be able to appropriately nurture others, we must operate from personal wholeness. That is, we must first assure our own well-being, so we may have the resources we need to care for others. Without such resources, we cannot fulfill our obligations to provide those in our care with an environment where they can thrive, whether they be our children, our family and friends, or our employees. That environment has to be a suitable blend of giving and not giving, so that those for whom we care can develop a healthy and appropriate independence. Thriving is more than survival; it presupposes growth as well.

The balanced energies of the Milk Moon include both generosity and the wisdom to know when to be selfish; both support and the strength to refuse inappropriate support; both commitment to others and the recognition that, to be of value to others, we must first realize our own potentials. The backwards, inside-out theory of reality says that if we are not at least a little selfish, we aren't likely to be much good to others, that giving too much is as bad as giving too little. The answer lies in how we balance the demands of self and others.

A significant overtone in Milk Moon energies is love of humanity, where, in return for the nourishment we have received from the Tao, we reach beyond our immediate families and acquaintances to provide love and support to people we don't know and who do not offer us personal advantages. Our impulses to help a stranger change a flat tire, to give old clothes to a local charity, or to pay a tithe to our church or community chest, all express this moon's deep recognition of the interconnectedness of our species, and of our mutual interdependence. The Milk Moon teaches us that we are all valuable and sacred to the Tao, no matter what we do. The Mother loves us for what we are, rather than who we are.

Meeting Milk Moon Challenges

Most Milk Moon challenges center on the interrelationships between our own needs and the needs of others. Our first and most important task in working with Milk Moon energies is to recognize that both our own desires and the desires of others are valid, and that they are connected rather than separate. In the words of John Donne, "No man is an island, entire of itself; every man is a piece of the continent, a part of the main . . . ."

We have to begin with nurturing ourselves, and with learning to distinguish between what we must have to thrive and what is merely our desire. As a starving person has no energy for spiritual matters, so we cannot nurture others until we are whole enough to build resources beyond our own requirements for physical and emotional survival. When we fail to distinguish between our own needs and what we merely desire, we also fail to make valid judgments as to what resources we have available to help others.

If you tend to neglect self-nurture, practice being selfish. Remind yourself again and again that you are as worthy of time and resources as others are. We all have a right to ask for what we want, and the right to receive all of it we can manage to get. The catch is that everyone else has exactly the same right, so we must either learn to balance among needs for ourselves and others, or spend our lives fighting for that right. Eventually we have to manage both appropriate selfishness and appropriate giving. But the first step is to accept our own right to what is available.

If you tend to the self-indulgent side, you may have to remind yourself that we're all in this together. No individual human can survive for an extended period without the help of others. How many of us are fit to grow our own food, make our own clothes, and build our own shelters? Without the cooperation and help of thousands of other humans, we'd spend all our energy in keeping alive, and our life would be diminished below our capacity for pleasure or thought.

On a broader scale, our sense of wholeness and identity arises from our relationships with those around us, and, by extension, the whole human community. Humans are gregarious. Children who are neglected fail to thrive; sometimes they die of having no attention. Few adults are able to survive isolation, and none do it well. They become peculiar and inhuman and lose the ability to connect both to others and to their own inner worth.

As in many human experiences, we have an endless, chicken-or-the-egg situation. We are able to love because we are loved;

we are unlikely to receive love unless we offer it. Our advantage is served by learning to be effective givers, if only so we can reliably receive what we need from others when we need it. Surprisingly, extending ourselves to serve humanity is probably our most effective motivator for reaching our personal potentials, as we are most useful to others when we have most to offer, and we are genetically inclined to give and receive help from our own kind.

The knottiest issues associated with Milk Moon energies revolve around the changing mix of giving and not giving to nurture growth from dependence to independence. The most obvious place this pertains is with children, but the same pattern occurs in many other places. Any adult who encourages inappropriate dependence from another adult, or demands inappropriate support, displays this imbalance. Such relationships can develop between marriage partners, friends, or co-workers. Disentangling from such affiliations requires discipline, and, sometimes, a hardened heart.

My personal moral aesthetic says that I must do anything I can to help anyone who needs and can use my help. This rule is surprisingly limited. If someone has a need that I lack the resources to fulfill, I am off the hook. If someone wants something I do have resources for, I have the right to decide whether my giving it to them is an appropriate use of those resources. That is, will my giving benefit them enough to justify my spending my resources to fulfill their desire?

This second parameter, determining whether the one who asks deserves my help, is trickier than the first, but it works pretty well in practice. For example, if I have $100 I can spare, but I feel that if I give it to my son, he will waste it, I keep my money. I have not only the right, but the responsibility to make that judgment. I find that these two criteria are a useful guideline to help me balance between my own needs and what others want from me. Anyone can ask us for anything they want. No one, not even our own children, has a call on us that we may not choose to refuse for cause.

Ultimately, all that lives is one continuum, and the choices we make to fulfill our own desires must be tempered by the needs of others, who are really just more remote parts of ourselves. However, each of us has our own string of notes in the universal song, and our task is to harmonize with other notes rather than to sing all or part of the song that is another's life.

If You were Born in the Milk Moon

The great strength of people born under the Milk Moon is likely to lie in their ability to love and nurture everyone they meet. People balanced in these energies manage to be non-judgmental and nurturing, but also to lovingly help others recognize where they need to make improvements. The greatest weakness of people born under this moon is likely to be their difficulty in setting boundaries, in knowing when to refuse some of the souls that reach to them for love and to choose to nurture themselves instead.

The central focus of those born under the Milk Moon—nurturing others—is, in my opinion, one of the most difficult spiritual paths. Those born under this moon tend to be farsighted, with a clear perspective of how all of us are interconnected, yet also myopic about how the good of the whole depends on each of us taking care of business at home, within our own selves. Their greatest gift is loving; their greatest challenge is loving wisely.

A typical person born under this moon may focus so strongly on parenting that his or her children grow up believing they are the center of the universe, and then discover, to their great pain, that the world does not agree. Others may be humanitarians who feel such strong obligations to help the community that they neglect their immediate families or other personal responsibilities. Still another Milk Moon behavior defines a personal sphere, a group that is an extension of the emotional self and beyond which requests for help need not be honored. The sphere may include family and, perhaps, a small circle of friends. This strategy is one way to protect the Self from the unending emotional neediness in our world. The superior ability to love, which often characterizes people born under this moon, attracts all who want more love, and few of us are immune to that attraction.

The particular spiritual task for you who are born in the Milk Moon is to explore the definition between Self and others. The vagueness of this separation in your perceptions is the likely cause of any inappropriate balances you may have between your personal needs and the needs of others. You know instinctively that the right way to increase personal emotional resources is to give love and support to others, and to receive love and support in return. You may tend to make mistakes on how much return you are likely to get for particular transactions. You may go through life disappointed, usually giving more than you receive, or, perhaps, rationing what you give so tightly that you seldom develop strong enough relationships to get a good return on your emotional investment.

In order to correct any imbalances you may display in how you spend your emotional resources, learn to keep a strict emotional accounting, not only of what you give, but of how effectively you give. Consider the possibility that giving is not always the kindest and best thing you can do. Sometimes generosity hurts more than it helps if it fails to support the independence of others. If you have been hurt so many times that you now have trouble giving, work with making sure that what you give is used well. There is nothing ungenerous about wanting the best outcome for any investment.

As you work on a clearer definition of where your Self ends and where the selves of Others begin, you will come to your birthright of understanding the mystery of how we are each an individual and yet all connected, part of one whole. On the first level, you may recognize the commonality among us all. On the second level, you may recognize that the miracle of such commonality is that it is an infinitely rich pattern woven of unique and responsible individuals, each with his or her own place in the circle, each with his or her own contribution to the whole, which is the Tao.

☾ *Self-Discovery Journal: Milk Moon Issues*

1. How, specifically, do you nurture yourself *(your body, your mind, your spirit; through hobbies, group activities, intellectual, mechanical, artistic, or religious pursuits)*? Are the means you use sufficient to renew your physical and spiritual energies? How, specifically, do you know the answer to that question? Do your answers to these questions suggest any specific actions?

2. What specific nurture do you receive from others *(from parents, children, spouse or lover, other family, friends, co-workers; for your material, emotional, spiritual support)*? Do you ask for such nurture? Do you need it? Do you want it? If not, why do you continue to accept it?

3. Do you take responsibility for clearly communicating your needs and desires to others? Is what you ask for what you really want? How do you handle not receiving what you ask for? Can you identify the difference between what you want and what you need?

4. How, specifically, do you give nurture to others? *(List specific individuals, parents, children, spouse or lover, other family, friends, co-workers; and specific activities such as material support, love, education.)* How do you know that what you give is what they need and want?

5. Why do you choose to give nurture to specific individuals in a particular way? Is your mode of nurture effective? Can you think of other effective modes for giving nurture to others?

6. Can you distinguish between what others want and what they need? How, specifically, do you know the difference?

7. What specific actions can you take to nurture more effectively those whom you choose to give to?

8. What, specifically, do you consider your responsibilities in meeting the needs of others *(family, friends, community)*?

9. Do you ever offer to give what you cannot afford to give *(money, emotional energy, time)*? If so, why, specifically? What actions can you take to avoid overdrawing your resources?

10. Do you ever give what you know will not be useful to the person you give it to *(for example, support to a person who's overly dependent, money when the problem is something else, advice they won't listen to or can't benefit from)*? If so, why, specifically? What standards can you develop to evaluate the cost/benefit ratio of your gifts?

11. Do you ever take care of someone who needs to take care of him/herself? If so, why, specifically, do you permit this entanglement? What specific actions can you take to make whatever changes you desire?

12. Do you ever depend on others for what you are able to provide for yourself? If so, is it your desire or theirs for you to be dependent? What specific actions can you take to make whatever changes you desire?

A Healing Process for the Milk Moon

Begin by considering what happens in Nature when insufficient or inappropriate nurture occurs. Whether the soil is impoverished or over-fertilized, the result is the same—yellow, dying plants that do not provide for the portion of the food chain that depends on them. Without rain we have drought, and with too much, we have flooding. When we kill off the predators that winnow old and sick animals, deer and rabbits become pests that destroy their habitat. The Mother balances needs among all Her children, and allows the consequences of imbalance to run unchecked, for the greater good.

Now journey inside yourself. Go back in your own history and find times when you received appropriate love and support. Remember the beneficial influence such experiences had on you. Notice what characterized these positive experiences. What you were given was without obligation, for your own sake. It respected your individuality and your right to make choices. It was what you needed, neither more nor less. It allowed you room to grow without leaving you hanging out in space. It brought you to a greater independence and a greater ability to return similar love and support to yourself and to others.

Practice the form of appropriate nurture, which includes learning when not to give and how to give so that the independent nature of the one you give to is not damaged. Loving begets loving. Loving heals both the giver and the gifted.

8

Fasting (Weaning) Moon

Mirror, Waning Half of the Year: Nesting Moon.
Stage: Testing (Challenge).
Range of Dates: The Fasting Moon may begin as early as January 24 or as late as February 22. It ends as early as February 23 and as late as March 24. Total range of dates over which the Fasting Moon may occur is from January 24 to March 24.

In years that have a Courting Moon, the Feast of Imbolc usually falls in the Fasting Moon. Ostara, the spring equinox, occurs in the Fasting Moon twice during the nineteen-year cycle, in the same years when Yule, the winter solstice, falls in the Death Moon.

Mood of the Mother

As a loving mother weans her child to prepare it for maturity and greater independence, so does the Mother withhold Her bounty yet a while longer that we may learn forbearance and the skills of making resources last. Such skills are necessary to assure that we will use the coming abundance prudently, but learning the skills is uncomfortable, pulling us out of our material selves to the larger issues of the good of the community.

Keats' remark, "If winter comes, can spring be far behind?", rings hollow in this moon. We are at the bitter end of winter weather, tired of cold weather and of storage food, weary of staying indoors. There is little forage available, and some of the animals that have survived are gaunt or diseased as the dying winter collects its final toll. Many individual animals have already succumbed to sparse food, exposure, and hungry predators.

The growing strength of the Sun is still too weak for sustained warmth. The light has a brittle quality, as though it might break if we depend on it. The hints that spring is near, in birdsong and swollen treebuds, tantalize us like fruit beyond our reach. The wind that brings us occasional scents that hint of new life is still sharp and bitter.

The time remaining until spring fulfills its promise seems to stretch ahead as far as the winter stretches behind us. Our bodies, starving for the vitamins in fresh food, feel heavy and out of balance. Vitamin deficiencies manifest in swollen gums and bad skin. The smells of smoke and human bodies too long without a bath add their pall. The community needs a focus to distract people from the discomforts of their lives. We begin to question the meaning of life, the value of continuing to struggle. More people die in February than in any other month, though it is the shortest of all months in our calendar.

If we imagine how humans lived before refrigeration, we can glimpse the challenge of this moon. Food stores are dwindling to dregs, and the nourishment of what remains has diminished since it was harvested. Humans eat withered and decomposing food. Some kinds of spoilage produce mind-altering chemicals in the body. For some, the world becomes very strange. Only the strongest discipline preserves the sacrosanct seed grain, which is the hope of summer's harvest.

The Mother's bounty seems remote. Humans fast to stretch available stores, to cleanse their bodies from the effects of inactivity and unwholesome food, and to foster visions that they may understand the meaning in their deprivations. Many cultures preserve this race memory in observations such as the Christian Lent, the Muslim Ramadan, and the Baha'i Fast. The Earth yearns for full spring.

Images and Reflections

A bear, gaunt and testy after a winter's hibernation. A desert ecology, driven by the scarcity of water. The cactus with its water-miserly spines. The penguin's weeks-long fast as it holds its brooding eggs away from the life-sucking chill of the ice. Mouth-breeding fishes, which do not eat from the time eggs are produced until the young are hatched.

A community chest campaign. A concert or other benefit for victims of flood or famine. Aesop's fable of the grasshopper and the ant. A shaman fasting for a vision quest. A Hindu holy man with a begging bowl. A whirling dervish, reaching for an altered state. Drumming circles and trance dances. Odhinn hanging on Yggdrasil to gain the runes to teach to the folk.

Related Energies

Nesting Moon: wise use of resources

Father's Moon: sacrifice

Sorting Moon: choices

Feast of Imbolc: purification

Zodiacal signs
>Aquarius: concern for community, visions
>Pisces: spiritual seeking

Planets
>Uranus: breaking patterns, future vision,
>>greatest good for the greatest number
>
>Neptune: altered states

Tarot cards
>The Hierophant: spiritual seeking
>Knights: focusing

Primary Energies of the Fasting Moon

Forbearance/Indulgence

Wise/Unwise use of resources

Spiritual seeking/Contentment

Concern/Unconcern for community
>resources and future

Recognition/Lack of recognition of the
>limits and capacities of the physical self

Manifesting Fasting Moon Energies

Weaning a child is an excellent symbol for Fasting Moon energies. The child feels deprived, hurt by this separation that is its first challenge on the road to independence. Weaning is a blend of several issues. The most immediate concern is that the mother cannot indefinitely provide all the nurture required by a growing child. In addition to this limitation, she must also consider preparing to nurse other children who may be born later. In a longer view, a child's first task in gaining independence is to learn to feed itself. That task may be the child's first introduction to the lesson that every loss includes a gain, that every limitation opens new possibilities.

All our lives, we must make choices in using our resources to provide for our needs over time. Even in the midst of our society's abundance, we make unpleasant choices to achieve our long-range desires. We diet to improve our bodies' health, we accept the pain associated with exercise to gain strength and fitness, and we put aside money that we might spend for immediate pleasure to provide for special projects or our old age.

The fable of the grasshopper and the ant contains all the parameters that define Fasting Moon material issues. The ant spends her energies in providing for the future of the community. The grasshopper centers on present, personal gratification. The Fasting Moon is concerned with both present and future needs, for both individuals and the group. Its balanced energies address finding the best compromise among all four concerns.

Fasting Moon energies tend to revolve specifically around the issues of limiting resources to assure future needs. On a personal level, we may be asked to deprive ourselves, to consume less than we desire, for the greater good. The balanced energies of this moon are expressed both by prudent planning, which avoids having to be deprived, and by our willingly enduring hardship and suffering when they cannot be avoided. Without the flexibility to meet shortfalls in our resources, both for our personal lives and for our communities, we cannot survive, individually or as a society.

Recycling exemplifies many Fasting Moon issues, including wise use of resources, planning for the future, and involving the community to accomplish these goals for the benefit of society at large. Indeed, personal recycling is often hard to justify. For example, the money from selling our personal aluminum cans is seldom great enough to compensate for the effort and the costs of storing used cans. The biggest payoff in recycling aluminum is on a community level, in reduced waste management requirements, in avoided costs of mining and refining bauxite, and in reduced prices to consumers of aluminum products. Individuals derive their "profit" from this process both from the cash they get for the cans and from knowing they have benefited their community.

The experience of physical fasting brings us to another focus of the Fasting Moon, spiritual seeking, which is connected to physical fasting in two ways. First, depriving the body of food for any length of time produces altered states of consciousness. Such states are a traditional means to visions and spiritual illumination. Indeed, fasting is a time-honored method for gaining otherworld knowledge, and has been used since prehistoric times by shamans and seekers. Religious fasts are associated with spiritual growth, and with refocusing our attention toward long-term, spiritual needs, rather than toward immediate, material desires.

Second, the experiences of being deprived of food, and the suffering that is associated with it, naturally led humans, who are meaning-seeking animals, to probe the great questions: Why do we suffer? What is the purpose of life in a world that does not meet all our needs? Entwined with these questions is still another Fasting Moon concern, personal sacrifice for the good of others, as when parents go hungry to feed their children, or the community responds to the needs of disaster victims with gifts of money, food, and other necessities.

The Fasting Moon expresses both the material reality of human pain and the sublime ability of humans to reach beyond their suffering into courage, self-sacrifice, and spiritual vision. Here we find both the degradation of human greed, which hoards rather than shares resources, and also the exultation of the mystic's high spiritual vision. How we meet the challenges of Fasting Moon energies is one of the basic determinants of what we become as human beings.

Meeting Fasting Moon Challenges

The threads that run through Fasting Moon challenges are the human suffering that results from being deprived of material, emotional, or spiritual sustenance, and our strategies for handling or preventing that suffering. The main thrusts of this moon's lessons are to prevent deprivation by prudent planning and to learn to recognize whatever benefits we can derive from the suffering we cannot avoid.

On a direct, material level, the Fasting Moon echoes the old New England proverb, "Use it up, wear it out, make it do, or do without." We are advised to make sure that we have used all we have to its fullest extent before we ask for more. Some of us feel deprived in the midst of abundance because we have not learned to distinguish between our needs and our desires. That distinction is critical to making wise choices on the use of our resources. We must understand the baseline of what we need to survive in order to judge how far we are from crisis.

On a larger perspective, the Fasting Moon also advises us to keep track of the fact that our choices today affect the resources we will have available tomorrow, both for ourselves and for those around us. Our decisions for using what we have must balance the desirability of immediate consumption against the likelihood that our present indulgence might leave us short of necessities later. The resources we need to consider for such evaluations include not only our material resources of money and goods, but also our time and our personal energy.

In the Fasting Moon, we confront the limits to what is possible at a given time and place. Our task is to learn how to work within those limits. Even with the wisest planning and the widest ranging forethought, we cannot prevent all painful events.

Our first line of defense against suffering is to control how we respond to pain. We can wallow in our pain, or accept it. We can concentrate on how much we hurt, or think about something else. We can suffer silently, or try to entangle others around us in our pain.

Pain, either physical or emotional, intensifies when we give it our attention, and dissipates when we are able to move our attention elsewhere. One of our most powerful distractions from present anguish is to look for some desirable future outcome from our suffering. Sometimes that's easy to see, as our understanding that we can't lose weight without being hungry. Sometimes we have to reach deep to find the lessons in our suffering, but such lessons are always there. Painful incidents often teach us our most significant life lessons. The most important components of who and what we are usually derive from how we have handled our tough times.

Note that I do not suggest a strategy of avoiding the painful consequences of our actions. The time for that avoidance is in the planning stages, before we do something that makes us suffer. However, once we've committed to an action that causes us discomfort or pain, we cannot afford to add the suffering of regret for having made a wrong choice. We need to learn to take responsibility for what we do without taking on guilt for what went wrong.

Sometimes we need to consciously refuse the feelings of guilt and self-blame that we may have trained ourselves to feel. We also need to avoid unloading those feelings onto others who disappoint us. Guilt and blame are excess baggage, which not only fail to help us recover from an error, but actually impede learning what our painful episodes have to teach. Refusing to feel these emotions, or to heap them on others, requires practice, but the result is well worth the trouble. Without the extra freight of guilt and blame, we move lighter and more joyfully, and move more readily from such sorrows as come our way.

A major category of Fasting Moon challenges is connected to self-sacrifice and to the unlovely quality of self-righteousness. When people deprive themselves, they sometimes believe that the fact of sacrifice should give them control over those for whom they make the sacrifice. Balanced sacrifice is an act for its own sake, entered into freely and without the intent of trying to manipulate others.

Unfortunately, many of us have trouble managing that balance. We decide to make a sacrifice, and then decide that if we have to suffer, so should everyone else. This feeling is the source of puritanical moral and legal codes applied without considering variations in people and circumstances. It also begets the loud suffering of martyrs who make unnecessary and unwanted sacrifices to control others. Still another permutation of this feeling is demonstrated by the person who treats us with the amused contempt of one who knows the right way to do things and feels superior to us because of that knowledge.

Self-sacrifice is a really difficult issue, because a minor nuance in how we handle it can change a specific act from noble to controlling, from useful to harmful. Nothing is so likely to generate unnecessary and harmful guilt as this matter, whether it is a sacrifice we feel we should have made, or a sacrifice someone else made on our behalf.

When we choose to deprive ourselves for cause, or to accept the sacrifice of another, we need to consider the cost/benefit ratio for the interaction. Is this act likely to benefit self or others? Is the estimated benefit worth the cost? If the benefit is for others, do they want that benefit? Does the act have any hidden agendas to demonstrate moral superiority or to obligate others to us? If the benefit is for self, does it include an overtone of self-punishment? If another sacrifices for our gain, did we ask for the sacrifice? Did we want it? Is there a hidden cost for the sacrifice that we are unwilling to pay?

The essence of making wise choices in managing our resources is having a clear picture of the reasons, the costs, and the benefits, to ourselves or to others, of sacrifices we may consider or ask of others. We humans have no finer quality than our willingness to sacrifice ourselves for our fellows. Sacrifices performed to genuinely assist others or to benefit ourselves, without the taint of punishment or control, release enormous amounts of energy for growth and transformation. In the words of certain metaphysicians, they give good karma.

If You were Born in the Fasting Moon

People born under the Fasting Moon have a complex set of strengths, and the innate passion to exercise those strengths effectively in the world. Some are excellent resource managers, with a natural efficiency that may seem awesome to those less gifted. Others have an especially intense appreciation for the joys of being alive. Some are visionary, filled with lofty spiritual aspirations. Still others connect to the Mother so readily that earth-centered, grounded spirituality is as natural to them as breathing. They feel the pulse of life flowing through their bodies. The major weakness of those born under this moon is that they have trouble putting all these parts together at once.

People born under a Fasting Moon tend to lean toward being either grasshoppers or ants. Those who are predominantly ants are dynamite at getting the most out of their resources. Generous or miserly, they always know what things cost in time and money, and they have a keen aptitude for formulating the most efficient way to proceed in any job. Their generous actions are chosen to produce a requisite amount of pleasure or other value for themselves or others, and their miserly tendencies are to avoid the waste of precious resources like time, money, and energy.

If you tend toward an ant mentality, you may display a "forest and trees" syndrome, where you are so focused on getting the job done and on anticipating future needs that you neglect the pleasures of everyday living. Don't forget to leave yourself room to exercise such pleasures. If you have to, program time to "smell the roses" into your very efficient planning. Otherwise, whenever you slow down, you may feel an underlying emptiness, a sense that, while you seem to have everything important under control, some link between your planning and the purpose for the planning has been left out.

Those born under the Fasting Moon who tend toward being grasshoppers also have a "forest and trees" problem, but in a different direction. They may spend so much time "grokking" the forest that they tend to forget that we need to maintain forests by planting new trees and pruning old ones. People with this personality type have an acute appreciation for spiritual and human values. They are perhaps a little nearsighted about the practical underpinnings necessary to implement those values. They tend to be very relaxed, until they see others being hurt, at which time they may transform from fuzzy puppy to rampaging grizzly bear.

If you tend toward being a grasshopper, whom James Joyce wittily styled a "grace-hoper," you may need to work on lengthening your perspective to give more consideration for your long-term needs. Your joy in the present is a significant strength, but if you neglect your future, you may have fewer and fewer days where you are free enough from daily cares to stop and enjoy the laughter of children or the splendor of a sunset.

People born under the Fasting Moon are usually deeply interested in spiritual and ethical values. This is a natural outgrowth of your focus on how to make choices for the best use of resources. Notice that this focus is shared by both ant and grasshopper types; their difference is in direction rather than essence.

The pitfall in this interest can be your conviction that the personal values you have discovered are "right." You may not feel that your high standards make you personally superior, but you may be prone to a certain smugness, to a belief that the values you espouse are the best available—for anyone. You can fall prey to the righteousness dragon, the one who spends his life in solitude because no one comes up to his expectations.

Righteousness is a significant challenge for you who are born under this moon, especially as your devotion to your convictions is probably not self-serving. Indeed, your focus in the energies of this moon means you are likely to have an above-average understanding of how to choose values. As a result, your personal standards may really be more workable, and better thought out, than the standards of others in your life.

However, being "right" is a cold comfort. If you catch yourself trying to justify yourself or your actions solely on that basis, you may wish to consider whether having better standards, or knowing the "right" way to do things, is sufficient reward to make up for the barriers these qualities may place between you and others. Sometimes, being "right" isn't worth anything, if that's all you have. You need not give up your personal standards to learn to be more discreet about how you share them with others.

People born under the Fasting Moon not only have to guard against righteousness in their judgments of others; they also have to watch that they do not judge themselves too stringently. If you tend to drive yourself to achieve your objectives, to the neglect of either good sense or your self-nurture, one reason may be that you are trying to live up to unworkably high ideals. Perhaps you need to allow yourself some lapses from perfection. Perhaps your ideals are higher than they need be. Perhaps you need to lower them enough to give yourself room to live.

The finest leaders express the balanced energies of the Fasting Moon, and leadership is the natural birthright of those born under it who have balanced its difficult energies. You have passion and vision. You have an inherent aptitude for developing good plans that are founded both on an understanding of costs and on values that meet both individual and community needs. You have the stamina to carry your plans to fulfillment. When you apply your native enthusiasm to achieving without being judgmental, either of yourself or others, you are hard to beat.

Self-Discovery Journal: Fasting Moon Issues

1. How, specifically, do you feel about being deprived *(of food, material necessities, your desires, love and friendship, access to education or job resources, opportunities for advancement or self-improvement)*?

2. What, specifically, do you do when you are deprived? Of what you desire? Of what you need for survival? Do you know the difference? How, specifically, does knowing or not knowing the difference between desire and need affect how you handle deprivation?

3. List the deprivations that are hardest for you to bear *(material, emotional, mental; short-term, long-term)*. Why, specifically, are they a problem to you? How, specifically, can you decrease the likelihood that you will experience deprivations, or decrease their severity if they do happen?

4. What, specifically, have you sacrificed for the benefit of someone else *(material resources, time, personal energy; for family, friends, coworkers, strangers in need)*? In the last week, month, year?

5. Do you believe each of your sacrifices was beneficial enough to the recipient to justify its cost to you? If not, did you expect that before you made the sacrifice? Do your answers suggest specific actions in the future?

6. What specific obligations do you believe you have toward preserving community resources? *(List specific examples, such as contributing to charity, paying taxes, supporting environmental or civil rights causes, supporting parks, recreation, art, schools.)* Why, specifically, these obligations? What specific actions can you take to fulfill these obligations?

7. What resources, specifically, do you use wisely *(money, material things, relationships, personal energies)*? How, specifically, do you know you use them wisely? *(List specific examples.)*

8. What resources, specifically, do you use unwisely *(money, material things, relationships, personal energies)*? What specific consequences in your life cause you to make that judgment? *(List specific examples.)*

9. What specific actions can you take to improve your use of resources? What can happen if you don't take those actions? Worst case? Greatest benefit if you change your behavior?

10. Do you recognize the specific choices you make that have led to tough places in your life? *(List specific examples.)* What have you done or can you do differently in the future with the knowledge you gained from those experiences?

11. What specific actions define the line between sharing spiritual knowledge and trying to force others to accept your ideas? That is, if you believe you're right, how far should you go to assure that your vision can influence the lives of others?

12. Are there some people you feel you have a special right to influence *(children, spouse, other family, friends, co-workers, employees, fellow members of your religion)*? Where should you draw the line between influencing their values and demanding they agree with you?

13. Do you believe being right makes you superior to others who do not recognize the same truths you do? Can you define any action that is universally right for every situation, or universally wrong? Give specific examples, if any. How do you know they are universally applicable?

14. A wise man once said that most of us fail to live by what we say we believe, only a few of us live by what we think we believe, but all of us act on what we do believe. Using this idea, what specific beliefs can you extrapolate from the actions of people you know? From your own actions?

15. Does your list of what your actions say about your beliefs surprise you? What changes, if any, does this new knowledge suggest?

A Healing Process for the Fasting Moon

We spend much of our lives trying to fulfill our desires. Consider the cleansing, the "stripping for action" that accompanies our choices to do without something. Most of us have not had to live with the fear of going hungry or of having insufficient resources to sustain our lives. When we deprive ourselves, such as going on a reducing diet, we tend to focus on the pain of our loss rather than on the profit we may gain by our actions. This exercise is to help you recognize the profound truth that all experiences have their aspects of loss and of gain. Our challenge is often to recognize which is which.

If you are in good health, undertake a brief fast. Abstain from eating food for long enough to work past your first feelings of being hungry. You can accomplish this in as short a time as a half day, but a full day is a better period. Do drink water and, if you desire, fruit juice. Avoid coffee, tea, and most carbonated beverages. Caffeine makes it harder to fast.

Another fasting pattern you might try is to abstain from all food and drink between sunrise and sunset for several days. You rise before the sun to eat breakfast and have supper after the sun sets. This fasting model can be more difficult, as not using liquids is both harder to remember and physically more demanding than going without food. This is the pattern used in the Muslim Ramadan and the Baha'i Fast.

If traditional fasting sounds too strenuous to you, consider giving up one special food or drink that you use often, such as coffee or chocolate, for an extended period, perhaps several weeks. If you are a smoker, giving up your favorite vice for several hours or days will have a similar effect.

You can also give up activities that you normally enjoy for a specified time. Some possibilities include sexual activity, listening to music, or pursuing your favorite hobby. Stay away from the video store, or do without television and radio for a week. Try silence for a day, where you unplug the phones and don't turn on the stereo, the radio, or the television. The greater part an activity plays in your life, the more dramatic will be the effect of not doing it.

Whatever you choose to give up, be wise in your choice. Deprive yourself of something that you will miss, but whose lack will not endanger your health, of either body or mind. You don't get medals for doing a three-day fast instead of a one-day, for example. Your aim is new knowledge, not proving your "won't" power.

While you are fasting, notice how your body and your perceptions change, both while you are not taking the substance you have given up and when you return to your standard practices. Some common results from fasting from food, for example, are a noticeable increase in the sharpness of the senses, especially smell. Your body may feel light, and your mind may feel detached. Even a brief fast can have a side-effect of causing an unusual clarity of mind and a more sensitive perception of your body. You could also experience disorientation or a fuzzy mind. When you return to food, you may note that your senses of smell and taste are heightened, and that even ordinary food may taste exquisite.

Your primary purpose is a keener perception of how your body and mind respond to deprivation, and how the substances you put into them, or don't put into them, affect the way they behave. Do you focus on what you are missing, and neglect other things you should be doing? Do you feel empowered because you recognize that you control what you use? Do you find clarity and better operation result when you reduce the load on your body from too frequent eating or from overeating?

Explore how being hungry and thirsty feels. Consider the difference between hunger and thirst voluntarily undertaken and hunger and thirst as a fact of life. Consider what is abundant in your life, material or spiritual, and what you feel deprived of. Consider how you might help others who lack your abundance. Consider whether you really need what you feel deprived of.

If you happen to be one of those people who live on coffee or diet drinks and one small daily meal to control your weight, you may need to try the obverse of this exercise. Try eating a healthy breakfast, like a bowl of oatmeal and a glass of juice. Have a light lunch and a moderate supper. Pay attention to your body and listen to what it says about the temporary changes you have made. Do the body's messages suggest a different mode of operation?

All of living is a balance among too little, enough, and too much. When you learn how to zero in on "enough," many of the problems you may have in using your body or your mind, expending your energies or your material resources, may correct themselves.

9

Seed Moon

Mirror, Waning Half of the Year: Harvest Moon.
Stage: Maturation.
Range of Dates: The Seed Moon may begin as early as February 23 and as late as March 24. It ends as early as March 24 and as late as April 22. Total range of dates over which the Seed Moon may occur is from February 23 to April 22.

Ostara, the spring equinox, falls in the Seed Moon seventeen years of the nineteen-year cycle.

Mood of the Mother

The Mother lies ready for the seed. The black earth, warmed by the strengthening Sun, sprouts seedlings as early spring plants reach for their turn at life. Buds appear, swell, and explode into leaves and flowers. Daffodils and dandelions greet us like captured sunlight. Animals who spent long winter nights drowsing in their nests perk up and actively investigate the greening world.

This is a chancy time of year. Tiny seedlings rush to stake out growing room before more careful plants dare even a cautious leaf above ground. These plants risk dying in the erratic frosts of early spring. Plants that await clearly warmer weather risk losing their places in the sun or the competition for necessary soil nutrients to the now stronger, hardier plants that hazarded an early start. Once committed to their strategies of sprouting early or late, the infant plants thrive or die, according to the fortunes of the weather.

So, too, the farmer who sows in spring must choose his time carefully. If he plants too early, some or all of his seedlings may perish in a late frost, and the harvest will be diminished. If he waits too long, some crops may be unripe when the first killing frost of autumn strikes.

Despite the anxiety of choosing when to act, human hearts are lightened by the bursting joy of life returning and the beginning of the light half of the year at the equinox. Bodies, starved for the vitamins of fresh green plants, sing as they turn from the remains of winter stores to fresh food. Eyes and ears are delighted by sudden flowers and returning birds. The scents of new flowers catch humans unaware. They remember, once again, after the long nights of winter, that life can be good.

Images and Reflections

The sudden appearance of daffodils on a grey day. The scent of lilacs after winter. The first robin on the lawn. The Sun shining through a raincloud. The first thunder, the first smell, of warm spring rain. A new foal struggling to keep its legs under it. Baby chicks and brand-new bunnies. Eggs and other seeds.

The first snip of scissors in new fabric. A baby's first word. The first stroke of paint on a bare canvas. A child proud in brand-new Easter clothes. Resurrection. The Holy Grail. Persephone's return from the underworld. The Cauldron of Cerridwen, the womb of the Mother, from which all life is born, again.

Related Energies

Harvest Moon: committing to action

Birth Moon: beginnings

Mating Moon: fertility

Feasts
  Ostara: renewal of life
  Beltane: fertility

Zodiacal signs
  Pisces: faith
  Aries: risk-taking

Planets
  Neptune: the web of all life
  Mars: initiating

Tarot cards
  The Magician: the one who acts—left brain
  The High Priestess: the gateway to knowing—
    right brain (Together, the High Priestess and Magician cards represent the whole-brained balance needed to create)
  Pages: risking

Primary Energies of the Seed Moon

Beginning/Procrastinating

Commitment to action/Inaction

Faith/Fear

Renewal/Exhaustion

Manifesting Seed Moon Energies

Choosing to begin something is an act of courage. The potential for failure looms over every beginning. Once we commit to action, retreat may not be possible. If what we begin does not work out, we may look like fools, lose all we have, or just fall on our faces and have to get up again. Sometimes we are afraid that we won't recover if we fail. The Seed Moon promises us that, if our courage does not fail, we can find the resources to begin again and again, until we succeed.

Sometimes the issue is deciding not to act when others pressure us to commit our resources. Perhaps the outcome we anticipate seems less valuable to us than the resources we expect to expend in reaching it. Perhaps we believe that beginning now, or beginning at all, will lead to failure. Perhaps we think that our action may injure another. Choosing not to act can also be courageous, and making such a choice can make us vulnerable to ridicule, contempt, or rejection.

At the moment of decision to act, or not to act, we are alone. No one shares our choice to turn a corner from which there may be no returning. When we choose rightly and succeed, we earn any glory that accrues. When we choose wrongly, or fail, we are responsible for the consequences of our action. When we fail, all we can do is pick ourselves up and go on. An important value to our actions lies in learning what we can from both our mistakes and our successes.

The balanced energies of the Seed Moon teach us to have the courage to act or not to act, as is suitable to a particular occasion. It offers us faith that, if we should fail, we can recover and begin again, and it offers us an appropriate fear of failure to help us choose our actions wisely.

Most of all, the Seed Moon gives us the joy of renewal, the heart-singing jubilation of life returning, which is the peculiar happiness of spring. By acting, we affirm our aliveness. By choosing to participate in life, we expand our reality and the poignancy of living. By making our response to life, "Yes," we obtain the means to bring our individual and separate qualities to their full-voiced potential in the universal song.

Meeting Seed Moon Challenges

The challenges of the Seed Moon arise primarily in choosing to begin necessary tasks or in completing the tasks we have begun. We can meet these challenges by developing better strategies for keeping track of what we're doing, and by learning to consciously control our decision processes. That is, most of what we do is done without conscious thought. The reasons why we act, and when we choose to act, are often obscure to us, and we may feel controlled by "outside" forces. When we become more self-aware, we can more effectively change our behavior in the directions we prefer.

We are all victims of our unconscious choices. Anytime you wonder why you did something, you acted from such choices. Learning to catch our unconscious decision patterns "in the act," patterns which determine a lot of what happens in our lives, is not an easy task.

Uncovering our true motivations for such actions is even harder, especially when those actions are motivated by reasons we prefer not to acknowledge. When you set out to discover your personal hidden agendas, decide now to accept those underlying motivations, however self-serving they may sound. When you control your choices to act more consciously, you can make corrections if you want to. If you refuse to accept the reality and validity of how you feel, your actions will continue to have outcomes you don't want and can't figure out how to correct.

The only way to determine where our real motivations lie is by watching how things turn out. We have to separate the reasons we give, to others or to ourselves, from what we actually accomplish. For example, no matter how many justifications you may have for not painting the garage, you cannot escape the fact that you have not begun the project. We can ignore the mind-boggling implications of whether events that we had no direct control over, like an accident we didn't cause or an unexpected visitor, were somehow drawn into our lives to give us an excuse not to paint the garage. Those are speculations. We have one hard fact: we have not begun painting.

When you focus on that hard fact and ask your inner self why, an answer may float to the surface of your mind. The true answer may be subtle, perhaps a feeling you perceive only "out of the corner of the mind's eye." It takes practice to tease these nebulous feelings into full conscious thoughts, but it's worth the effort. In our paint-the-garage example, you might discover that you resent giving time to painting that you would rather spend, say, building a model railroad. The resentment isn't effective; all the time you're putting off painting the garage, you're probably not working on the railroad either. Worse yet, the resentment that keeps you from starting stretches the time over which you are engaged with the task, without increasing the wall area covered by new paint.

Once you discover reasons for your procrastination, you can explore other solutions, including, of course, to just do the job and get it over with. You can put off the painting until later or hire someone else to do it. You can get friends and family to help, to reduce the time spent, or just make the job more fun. You may even decide that you can wait another season to do the painting, or install siding that doesn't need painting every couple of years. Bringing our reluctance to do something to consciousness often resolves it.

The process sounds strange, but it works, and it gets easier with practice. When we let our real feelings surface without judging ourselves, those feelings help us make better decisions. Sometimes the new information doesn't make doing the project more palatable, but at least we don't waste energy in guilty procrastination. When we bring our true motivations to our conscious mind, we gain a better understanding of how we operate and where our true personal priorities lie. Let your inner self tell you why you procrastinate, and then apply your own values and wisdom to discover what to do about it.

Learning to take direct and conscious responsibility for our decisions to act, or not to act, sounds like taking on a heavy load, but it is actually very freeing. Instead of being the victims of our own unconscious choices or of the opinions of others, we become actors/magicians who are in control of what we do and we begin to shape our world to our desire.

If You were Born in the Seed Moon

The greatest strengths of people born under the Seed Moon are their kaleidoscopic intuitions about the consequences of actions and their courage to act when they are confident about the rightness of what they do. Their greatest weaknesses tend to be procrastination and fear of failure. Both sides derive from their strong intuitive awareness of the many possible outcomes of an action, and from their desire to gather all possible data and considerations before they act.

People born under the Seed Moon often struggle with beginnings, mostly with getting started, but also with an impatience that has them beginning too often or too soon. Fear of undesirable consequences is usually at the root of either approach. You may procrastinate to put off the bad results you fear, or you may rush in headlong, hoping the momentum of your precipitous action will carry you past the danger points. Some people born under this moon begin so many projects and keep so busy that they never have the time or energy to consider whether they are succeeding or failing. Such people also have trouble bringing individual projects to completion.

Fear of failure is not a trivial concern. Human brains seem to be wired to learn more readily from mistakes than from successes. Your strong desire to avoid mistakes is one of the tools the Tao gives you to learn wisdom. Used appropriately, that fear can guide you to right action and growth. Used without balance, when you focus too strongly on the possibility that what you begin may not prosper, you can fall into procrastination so deep it becomes paralysis.

You should not run roughshod over your hesitancy or assume that you put things off because you are lazy. People born under the Seed Moon are often strongly intuitive, a faculty that can give them access to significantly more data than most people operate from. Your intuition may recognize pitfalls and opportunities for mistakes that your conscious mind overlooks. The best strategy for dealing with procrastination is to bring the reasons for it to consciousness as much as possible, as we discussed earlier. Recognizing the need to satisfy the inner self's concern about failing can speed up the process of committing yourself to action. Once satisfied, your innate courage may move you strongly forward. A talent for making new starts is a special strength of the Seed Moon.

If you recognize that your hesitancy is often based on real information that happens to be hard for your conscious mind to access or to accept, you can relax and trust your own wisdom. To overcome that hesitancy, work toward balancing your trust in yourself, that your reasons for not acting may be valid, with the needs of people around you. Try to balance your special interest in initiating things with the resources you have available to complete what you begin. Try to balance your desire to start more projects than you have time to do with your need for renewal and the excitement of beginnings. Sow your seeds with an eye to the harvest.

☽ Self-Discovery Journal:
Seed Moon Issues

1. What kinds of projects, specifically, do you have difficulty beginning? List specific examples *(personal, job-related, requested by family or friends, "good" causes)*.

2. Why, specifically, are such projects difficult for you *(money, time, personal energy, mixed feelings, external pressure, others' opinions of you)*?

3. What kinds of projects are you so eager to start you may even tend to "jump the gun." List specific examples *(personal, family-related, job-related, religious or other group-related)*.

4. What specific things do these two lists tell you about yourself *(personal values, social consciousness, vulnerability to outside opinions or pressures)*?

5. Have you ever begun something that you feared would fail? List specific events. Did they in fact succeed or fail? Why, specifically? What conclusions for present action can you draw from these events?

6. What specific activities do you begin but have difficulty completing *(personal, family-related, job-related, church or other group-related)*? Why, specifically *(for reasons of money, time, personal energy; because of mixed feelings, external pressure, others' opinions)*?

7. What, specifically, do your reasons for beginning but not completing actions indicate about your personal values? *(No guilt permitted here, just an assessment of facts for your private consideration.)* Do the answers suggest that you need to adjust how you make commitments to others?

8. What projects do you have that make your heart sing *(personal, related to family or friends, job, social or church group)*? Do you ever have trouble beginning or completing them? How can you incorporate more things like this into your life?

9. What, specifically, do you do to renew yourself? List activities. How specifically, do each of these activities renew you *(in body, mind, spirit; in regard to physical energy, family or other relations, job, group activities)*?

10. Are your present activities for renewing yourself sufficient to correct the effects of stress in your life? What specific evidences in your actions or the present state of your body support your answer? Does your answer suggest specific new actions you should take?

11. What activities refresh and stimulate your mind? What activities help you feel connected to others or to the Mother? How can you incorporate such activities into your daily life?

A Healing Process for the Seed Moon

If you have never grown a plant from seed, try to do so, preferably indoors in a pot, where you can have an intimate relationship with the plant. If you have witnessed this miracle before, do it again, this time paying special attention to how uncertain and remarkable the birth of such new life is. I personally find growing a plant from seed a surprisingly difficult process. I can't seem to reliably do what's necessary to go from seed to seedling, all in the right order, and all at the right time.

I'm told, for example, that most seeds prefer to germinate in the dark, but I've never managed to find the right cupboard or closet for getting plants started. Seeds dry out easily, and will not complete germination if they have no moisture; however, if you make the soil too damp and put your little pot in a dark cupboard, you tend to grow wonderful molds and kill the seed, or you may forget about the seed and let the baby die of thirst. Other factors that are important are how deep you plant the seed, how warm a temperature it needs, and, for big seeds, how you orient it in the dirt.

Once you have a tiny plant actually growing, it needs light and water to thrive. Even a few drops of water can knock it down or uproot it. If you lack a sunny window, it may not get enough light to stay green. If you put several seeds in a pot, in case some don't germinate, you may have to pull up some of the seedlings lest the crowding spread the soil nutrients too thin for any of them to thrive.

Yet, with all the things that can go wrong, if you persist, in time you will have a plant that may grow as big as a tree, if it has enough time and its genes permit. Consider the profligacy of the Mother, that encourages plants to scatter millions of seeds, most of which fall in the wrong place, or are eaten, or die of any of the dozens of misadventures that keep those millions of seeds from overrunning the Earth.

The Mother's message is, as in the Birth Moon, to try and try again, for new starts are infinite, and what does not succeed this time may flourish tomorrow. If this day or this year or this life does not teach you what you need to know, in Her infinite womb your time will come again, and all the parts of you that are made today will live again, in some form, to some purpose.

10

Courting Moon

Mirror: The Courting Moon has no mirror.
Stage: Time-Out.
Range of Dates: The Courting Moon may begin as early as March 24 and as late as April 3. It ends as early as April 23 and as late as May 3. Total range of dates over which the Courting Moon may occur is from March 24 to May 3.

The Courting Moon is intercalary, and none of the seasonal festivals fall within its boundaries. Each nineteen-year cycle includes seven Courting Moons. Like intercalary periods in other calendars, the Courting Moon is considered a kind of "time-out" from the rest of life.

When the Courting Moon begins in April, Yule, the winter solstice, falls in the Death Moon in the following year, an event that occurs twice in the nineteen-year cycle.

Mood of the Mother

The Mother rests, a momentary pause between the first rush of spring's renewal and the forthcoming abundance of summer. It is an in-between time, sweet for being stolen from the workaday year. The weather is mild and life is easy. Gentle showers cleanse the air and make the world smell even greener. The fresh and subtle smells of spring have not yet given way to the more robust scents of summer.

Birds have laid their eggs but are not yet enslaved to the ravenous maws of their hatchlings. Young animals born in the spring are still mostly safe in their nests, not yet exploring the world and engaging their mother's energies in teaching and vigilance against predators. Trees that exploded in blossom and called the bees to the gargantuan job of fertilizing their flowers now settle back to producing leaves and gathering their energies for the work of making fruit.

Humans have sown their seeds. They have turned out their houses, exchanging the stale smell of winter for the fresh aromas of sun and new grass. Their bodies respond to a better diet, and their minds, dull from lack of sunshine and fresh food, perk up and look at the world anew. They have endured the winter once again, and, if the winter was hard, survived their retreat to the stubbornness of their animal will-to-survive. Perhaps they forget, for a little while, their non-animal purposes.

Soon they will be immersed in the labors natural to this time of year, weeding fields and repairing winter-worn houses and equipment, preparing for wedding feasts, and journeying to new places to seek additional community resources. For this year, the Mother has smiled and offers them a Courting Moon, a small idyll for enjoying her beauty and her bounty. Humans can take time to consider the meaning of life and how they might improve their lives. They have leisure to recognize, in their bones, that rest is the balance for work, and that repose is as sacred as labor, in its own place.

Images and Reflections

A freshly sown field, black in the sunshine. A spider resting in a finished web. Bread fresh from the oven, ready to eat. The new smell of the land after a spring rain. Rest after a day's hard work. The joy of watching the sun set or rise. Opening a new jar of last year's jelly. Sitting on the Earth and feeling the Mother's rhythms.

Sunday. All festivals and celebrations. Leap day. Utopia. "Thank God it's Friday." Discussing "life and God and art" with good friends. Recognizing the wonder of a butterfly and the miracle of the rainbow. The sudden, unexpected joy of love. Finding the perfection of the Order in all things.

Related Energies

Fasting Moon: balanced use of resources

Mother's Moon: trust in the universe

Zodiacal sign of Aries: spontaneity

Planet
   Chiron: ideal vision within reality

Tarot cards
   The Star: renewal
   Tens: hesitation between cycles

Primary Energies of the Courting Moon

Moderation/Excess

The ideal in reality/Fantasy

Freedom in/Slavery to time

Manifesting Courting Moon Energies

"To everything there is a season, a time for every purpose under heaven." The Courting Moon celebrates all such purposes. It is a time when we can look at all of them at once and recognize from them the patterns that are the Tao. In Courting Moon energies, we renew our connections to the Tao and to all the other lives that comprise it. This moon is a time to go beyond the concerns of mere physical survival, a time to unship the straining aspirations of our minds and spirits and to let them sail free. When they return to harbor, we can incorporate the insights they add into the processes of our everyday lives.

The Courting Moon is about the wise use of leisure, about learning to recharge our vitality by moving beyond the realities and immediate demands of our material lives to the secondary priorities of our mental functions and spiritual capacities. In this moon, we make a place to step outside our ordinary lives and look at them, to celebrate what is wonderful in our lives, and to discover, if we wish, new avenues for growth and joy.

The primary issue of the Courting Moon is learning to balance work and rest, but the moon's energies are also concerned with how humans use the multifaceted ideas that spring from their minds in a resting mode. We dream and design, we reframe how we view the world, we invent things and methods that might make our lives easier or more beautiful.

If we base our dreams on desire alone, without integrating the real limits and boundaries of our resources, our dreams will only produce dead ends, lost causes, and the futility of wasted effort. Even as the balanced energies of the Courting Moon invite us to try new visions, they remind us that, without a strong grounding in the realities of our lives, no ideal can be achieved.

Our minds can conceive an infinity of possibilities. As we integrate such conceptions with the actual resources we have available, we invent new ideas, new processes, new things. As in the process of biological evolution, some of these new possibilities work well, and move us forward. Some don't work, and go nowhere, but we can learn from failures as well as successes.

In either case, our new ideas must be tested and found good in the real world before we fully accept them. Those who reach for ideals without a firm grounding in everyday reality are the sources of cults and unbridled fanaticism, of religions that scour the soul instead of healing it, and of tyrants who bring those in their care to war and destruction.

Many of the ills of our world lie in the imbalances spawned by those who reach for ideals, lofty or selfish, that do not take into account the sacredness and balance of the divine polarities which inform natural law. We cannot make order without the creativity of chaos; we cannot nurture humans by solely material means; we cannot create from ideas alone without considering the limits of our physical reality.

When the enormous capacity of our minds to create is disconnected from our mind's moorings in the deep wisdom of our bodies, in the Mother, and in our connections to all that lives, we spawn "goblins and ghoulies and things that go bump in the night," either individually or as a society. The Courting Moon tells us that if we will take the time and effort to reconnect, we can realign our wandering spirits for healing and renewal.

Meeting Courting Moon Challenges

The challenges of the Courting Moon center around two issues: The first is our ability to use time for both productive work and for appropriate "re-creation" of our inner selves. The second is the problems associated with integrating the ideal and the real in our lives. Courting Moon energies seem to be difficult for our society. Both these issues manifest in personal problems and in the imbalances that we observe in our culture.

As a society, we spend a lot of money on "leisure" activities. We work as hard at many such activities as we do at our jobs. We are not always comfortable with gifting ourselves with true leisure, which I define as a "time-out" where we can be alone with ourselves and accomplish the renewal of true "re-creation."

If you feel stretched to the limits, unable to handle all your obligations in life, or feel that the harder you try, the less you produce, you are probably neglecting your needs for self-renewal. Our society does not make genuine recreation easy. Finding time to just "hang out" and to rediscover who we are can be a major challenge. Our only recourse may be to take time whether we seem to have it or not. When we do take time, our first order of business needs to be figuring out what activities we can neglect or eliminate so we can make time to renew ourselves again later.

Don't tell me there's nothing you can drop. If you had an emergency, a death in the family, or a natural disaster, you'd strip down to essentials in a heartbeat. I'm not suggesting so dramatic a re-evaluation. Just make a little time for yourself and for those you love, before you die of overwork.

The purpose for leisure is to renew our spirits and to improve our abilities to produce. "Recreational" activities that do not re-create are useless. Does watching five hours of television a day stimulate or stultify your mind? If your vacation requires a week of driving six hours a day, where is your source of renewal? Do you count a visit to a theme park for the kids, or a camping trip when you hate camping, as your recreational time? Evaluate how you spend your "leisure" and find a place for an activity that renews your spirits. Your value to others increases when you are more nearly whole.

The other primary source of Courting Moon challenges concerns the way we handle the relationship between the ideal and the real. As a society, we tend to profess high ideals and then act as though it's okay to behave in ways that violate what we say we believe. This discontinuity between what we say and what we do is often accepted as normal. We may hide our heads and feel guilty, but we seldom consider the possibility that our ideals are unbalanced and distorted when compared to the wholeness that is the Tao.

Our society is prone to split divine polarities, which naturally belong together, and to declare that the positive expression of each polarity is desirable and the negative, unacceptable. This dichotomy is the primary cause for the discrepancy between what we do and what we say we believe. In fact, both sides of these dualities are integral to all humans and to all human activities. Attempting to split them not only makes us dishonest, it also causes fundamental disruptions in our Selves and in our society.

For example, our society endorses logic, but puts down intuition; it encourages order, but not the chaos that is part of creativity; it lauds material success, but not spiritual success. We suffer the results of these imbalances, both personally and as a culture. When we conform to ideals that are based on this false dichotomy, we may feel incomplete. When we manifest the negative forms of the divine polarities, we tend to feel guilty for not living up to our ideals.

More seriously, when we approve of only one side of a sacred duality, we covertly feed the other side, and the qualities that we disapprove erupt in their most difficult and destructive manifestations. Thus, our "ordered" society is renowned for the violence of its citizens; our national unity is marred by our problems with human diversity; our material abundance is shamed by the almost inescapable poverty of our underclass, mostly woman and children.

When we base our worldview on the belief that one side of a divine polarity is "better" than the other, we basically spend our energies trying to make the tide run backwards. Looking through such a distorted worldview, we forget, or lose the ability to see, that everything is a balance of forces, and that there truly is a "time to every purpose under heaven."

When we bring such a false view of reality into our personal lives, we tend to load ourselves with guilt and self-blame for not working hard enough or for not meeting the impossible standard of avoiding the "evil" side of a divine polarity. We focus on how inadequate we are instead of how we can improve. Balanced Courting Moon energies would advise that we take a "time-out" and re-evaluate our personal standards to make them more nearly match the way the world is.

Such re-evaluation does not mean lowering our personal standards. In fact, when we plant our ideal visions in the fertile soil of what we can accomplish with the resources we have available, we free ourselves of both the guilt that accompanies unrealistic ideals and the failures that come from not doing reality checks.

The interaction between our visions of what may be and our actual ability to make things happen is the source of all human progress. When we take the time to modulate our ideals to fit within the realities of our lives, we gain a new wholeness. In the words of Native Americans, we "walk our talk," and learn to love ourselves again.

If You were Born in the Courting Moon

The great strengths of people born under a Courting Moon are likely to be their understanding of the need for balance and renewal and their lofty and creative visions for making the world better. A person who displays the balanced energies of this moon is likely to be good at having fun and to have a keener than average appreciation of those luxuries we call "the finer things in life." The weaknesses of those born under this moon are likely to be trying to accomplish too much with the time resources they have available and difficulty in dealing with people who don't meet their high standards. When Courting Moon people are unbalanced, they may make work out of having fun, or be over-concerned with "living the good life."

You who are born under a Courting Moon are, so to speak, born outside of time. Because your moon does not occur every year, you may tend to put yourself outside the flow of everyday life. Perhaps you are a natural party person, who wants to enjoy life and avoid responsibilities. Another direction you may take to remove yourself from normal human experience is to be a workaholic who can't detach from work or duty long enough for re-creation.

People whose reason for working is to make enough money to indulge in "outside of time" activities like hobbies, parties, or vacations make pleasure and self-fulfillment their greatest values. Those are worthy standards, so long as they are balanced by an understanding that life also carries responsibilities and duties. People born under this moon, who feel that work is drudgery, that responsibilities to family and friends impose on them, may miss the simple pleasures of a job well done or the warmth and pride of a united, healthy family.

If you have trouble settling into the "normal" activities of everyday life, you may wish to focus on bringing the unconscious values and priorities that actually drive your behavior to your conscious mind (see the chapter on the Seed Moon). Then, if you feel these priorities need adjustment, you can make whatever changes seem appropriate. Our society tends to disparage pleasure seeking, but when it is balanced by a productive life, it is a valuable skill that many people lack. Integrate rather than disregard your special gift for loving life.

The other position that may entangle people born in the Courting Moon is a kind of slavery to time, symbolized by clock and calendar. This imbalance manifests in workaholism or some other grinding devotion to "duty" that overrides any call to self-renewal. Where the "party person's" values are centered on self and pleasure, the "clock slave" is focused on service and production. This contrast is a good example of how an apparently "higher" standard can be as empty as a seemingly selfish motivation when it is not in harmony with the whole person.

The Courting Moon advice, that ideals should be validated in and through experience, applies here. This "slavery to duty" is often motivated by dedication to principles that were accepted without testing for how they fit into the balance of human physical and mental health. "All work and no play makes Jack a dull boy" is a cliché because it is so true.

If you tend to jump into a rat race and then feel you are personally responsible for keeping it moving, you may have to force yourself to make time to "re-create." You need to evaluate whether the benefits you derive from your hard work compensate you for costs such as stress-related disease, a sense that "life" is outside your schedule, or too little time with people you love.

Your birthright as a Courting Moon person is the "place outside of time" where humans can renew their spirits and consider how they run their lives. Rediscover that birthright, and teach it to the rest of us, who sorely need it. We don't have to give up productivity to have pleasure.

☾ Self-Discovery Journal: Courting Moon Issues

1. What, specifically, makes you feel renewed and refreshed (*regarding body, work, hobbies, home, family; church or community activities; spiritual or intellectual pursuits*)? How, specifically, does each of these activities contribute to your well-being?

2. Do you permit yourself to have leisure time? If not, why not? If yes, are you refreshed by what you do during this time? Do your answers suggest any specific changes in your behavior?

3. How, specifically, do you choose activities for any leisure time or vacations you may have (*personal enjoyment, meeting the needs/desires/opinions of others, "worthwhile" pursuits, "killing" time between more valued activities*)?

4. How do you represent the use of time in your life? (*Is time used, saved, wasted, worthwhile, killed; does it drag or fly?*) Does your experience of time change with what you're doing? How do clocks and calendars determine what you do? Do your answers suggest changes in how you think about time?

5. What, specifically, are your ideals in life (*material or spiritual success, personal or social values and standards of behavior, ideas about right and wrong*)? How, specifically, do these ideals relate to your behavior (*shape actions, determine decisions, possible/impossible to fulfill, have large/no relation to daily living*)? Do your answers suggest adjustments you should make? To your stated ideals? To your behavior?

6. A prophet named Baha'u'llah said, "The essence of faith is a fewness of words and an abundance of deeds." Which of your standards, specifically, regularly shape what you do? Which of your standards, specifically, are reflected more in your words than your deeds?

7. Concerning the personal standards to which you give more lip-service than action, which are reasonable standards for you to try to incorporate into your future actions, and which should you consider adjusting? How, specifically, do you tell the difference?

8. Where, specifically, do your standards for behavior come from *(experience, family, friends, job, books, society, a religious or other belief system)*? Which of these sources do you value most? Why, specifically?

9. Try to list as many of the principles that determine how you behave as you can. *(Try to list the principles actually reflected in your behavior, rather than principles you think you ought to have.)*

10. What, specifically, is the function of each standard you have identified? How, specifically, does each standard fulfill its function in your life and your actions?

11. How, specifically, have you tested the validity of each of your standards? Do your answers to these questions suggest any ways to make your standards more useful to you?

A Healing Process for the Courting Moon

Schedule a time-out to spend with the Earth. Go to some natural place, such as a park or a beach, and just enjoy what you find there. Go alone, at least the first time, and try to find a spot where you will not be interrupted. If you take a partner, choose someone who can be a companion without demanding your attention. Don't plan an agenda or any activity except sensing the particular qualities of the place. Don't take music, a book, or anything else to "occupy" your time. Your object is to learn to be alone with the Mother.

At first you may be bored. Our culture tends to teach us that inactivity is time wasted. Unstructured time can even be frightening. Many people in our culture have little or no experience with being alone without at least the noise of music or television. You may find yourself frantically trying to fill up the emptiness with self-talk. You may also mount a running internal conversation to interpret to yourself what is happening or what you see, working hard at getting "meaning" out of your experience.

Allow yourself to relax and let your inner voice be still. Focus on listening to your deep inner self, a soft, subtle voice that speaks in feelings rather than words. Listen to the Mother. You may feel her rhythms in the sighing of the breeze or the ripple of a brook. Perhaps you can sense the long, slow rise of an earth tide. You may feel your body change its breathing pattern to match hers. If you are still enough, and patient, you may observe small animals that decide that you are part of the landscape and safe to ignore.

Let yourself step mentally into a place outside your normal habitat. From this "outside" place, touch any plants that may be close by, with hand or mind, and feel their life. Try to go into their selves and perceive the world through their senses. Touch plants of different ages and lifespans and see how their feels differ. If you are near a tree, try to touch the dryad (life spirit of a tree) that lives within. If you are near a brook, let it run over your fingers and see if you can make contact with its naiad (life spirit of a body of water). Close your eyes and see whether you can see, out of the corners of your mind, other earth spirits that may dwell nearby.

Whatever you may find in your search, let the healing knowledge of your deep connection to the Mother in all Her guises and all Her other children enter your spirit and refresh your body. Be wise in this exercise and make a conscious decision not to lose yourself in what you find. Your first time, you may return with little more than a sense of renewal. If you try more often, over the course of time you will build a kind of separate place within yourself where you can discover how unseparate you really are.

The Courting Moon's mood, outside of "normal" time, offers us a platform for viewing the world from a different perspective. As a time outside Time, its special holiday ambience can renew our inner selves and help us to bring freshened minds back to our daily lives.

11

Mating Moon

Mirror, Waning Half of the Year: Sorting Moon.
Stage: Initiation.
Range of Dates: The Mating Moon begins as early as April 4 and as late as May 3. It ends as early as May 3 and as late as June 1. Total range of dates over which the Mating Moon may occur is from April 4 to June 1.

Beltane, the spring fertility festival, is the defining event of the Mating Moon. In the old calendar, Beltane is the beginning of summer. We still recognize this ancient festival in our celebration of May Day (May 1).

Mood of the Mother

Plant and animal hormones respond to longer days, and a new generation is moving from the proverbial gleams in their parents' eyes toward the beginning spark of manifesting in the world. Spring-seeding trees launch their babies to the wind in a rain of air-borne sails. Flowers, sexual organs of the plant kingdom, send scented messages on the breeze calling bees and butterflies to do their tasks in the plant version of "boy meets girl." After spring rains, winter-brown patches vanish almost overnight as dense mats of new seedlings fight for their places in the Sun.

Bees swarm, attending newly mated queens on their way to new hives. Species of birds that have not already started their families sing love songs at dawn, calling prospective mates, "Come to me, come to me." The bullfrog in his pond continues the song at dusk. The land sounds with challenges and roars as prairie chickens and other birds squawk and posture in complex mating dances, at once beautiful and alien.

Humans also look to mating. Spring greens and other fresh foods have cleansed and revitalized their bodies, and weather is mild enough to permit journeys to other villages to consummate marriages outside the village. Weddings bond men and women, but also communities. The same journeys that produce new families also permit the cross-fertilization of ideas.

Life renews itself. The wild chaos energies of the Mother strain toward manifestation in the world. The Father, gaining vigor with every day, becomes strong enough to encompass and give form to the Mother's unbounded potential. From this divine blending and sacred marriage, all life explodes in an astounding burst of creativity, following the divine command, "Be fruitful and multiply."

Humans celebrate the union of the sacred pair with flowers and dancing and sexual loving. In ancient times, people made love in the fields to remind the seeds to grow, and skipped around the Maypole to commemorate the Mother's receptivity and the Father's mastery. In the Mother's submission to Her other and opposite self, and in the new lives that their mutual love produces, we understand the mystery of the union of polarities, a union that mirrors the Tao and is the source of all creation.

Images and Reflections

The scent of apple blossoms. Mayday baskets full of flowers. Crimson roses leaping in an untrammeled spray of color over an Oklahoma chain-link fence. The moist, fertile smell of earth after a spring rain. Horseshoe crabs jockeying clumsily to mate in a moonlit tidal pool on the Florida coast. A praying mantis devouring her mate as he fertilizes her eggs. A peacock vibrating his tail to mesmerize his peahen. The mannered, mock-combat mating dance of prairie chickens. The bower bird collecting bright stones to decorate his love-nest. The caduceus.

A balance scale. Lovers of any age walking hand in hand. Robert Frost's line, "More than one and less than two." *(Meeting and Passing).* Chiaroscuro. The perfect order and underlying chaos of a Japanese print that depicts a tsunami wave. The "strange attractors" of chaos theory. An I Ching hexagram. The yin/yang icon. Aphrodite and Adonis.

Related Energies

Sorting Moon: choices

Mother's Moon: fertility

Festival of Beltane: fertility

Zodiacal Signs

Aries: pursuing desires

Taurus: sensuality

Planets
    Mars: sexual energy
    Venus: erotic love
Tarot cards
    The Lovers: erotic love, integration of
        complementary energies
    Temperance: balance and union of disparate energies
    Twos: lovers, balance, fertility

Primary Energies of the Mating Moon

Joining/Separating
Relationship/Isolation
Fruitfulness/Sterility
Acceptance/Non-acceptance of Self and others

Manifesting Mating Moon Energies

On the simplest level, the Mating Moon celebrates the mystery by which male and female come together in love and produce offspring. Humans may have other kinds of equally profound relationships, but lovers, especially lovers with whom we have children, have a way of turning our lives inside out.

On a philosophical level, our falling in love is a sequence of events. The "One" meets the "Other," and desires the otherness. As the two merge their mutual strangenesses, they transmute from "The One and the Other" (us and them) to "I and Thou" (we two, parts of one whole). The essence of the Mating Moon is this recognition that, however strange others may seem to us, they are bridges to the knowledge, "we are all one." New life comes from such a union of two individuals. New ideas spring from blending differences in a new way.

Peeling another layer off the onion of truth, we find that the acceptance of the Other into a union that makes it a part of ourselves goes beyond accepting another person. The Other also represents the parts of ourselves that we may wish to deny, sometimes called the shadow self. The Other may be the male within, for females, or the female within, for males. It can be the dark violence that lurks at the heart of the gentlest soul or the tenderness that the toughest people may nourish at their cores. The shadow self is all the parts of ourselves that we prefer not to acknowledge. Until we find, and love, the Other within ourselves, we cannot be whole, nor can we create.

The Mating Moon teaches us that all fertility is the merger of opposites that seed each other and, in merging, make something new. This is the lesson of the divine polarities, and of such folk wisdom as "opposites attract," and "two heads are better than one." As male or female, or any two persons, we stand alone. As mates or companions, we stand together, and, in sharing our bodies, our abilities, and our knowledge, we can bring something fine into the world, often something better than ourselves. In addition to children whom we hope will be better than us, true sharing also produces other good things, such as personal healing, and becoming a source of comfort and healing for those who encounter a truly united pair.

All creativity springs from unions of complementary opposites. An artist or poet merges the skills and linear knowledge of the left brain with the intuition and holistic vision of the right brain, and we have art. Creations that pull from only one side may persist for a while, but they never grow past their beginning point. Such persistent one-sidedness is, for example, the root cause of television series that lose their freshness in a season. By contrast, great artists can take stories that have been told a thousand times and enchant us by drawing anew from the wellspring of the ever-reseeding sacred dualities.

The balanced energies of the Mating Moon are expressed by our understanding that all life fits together in light and shadow, and that we must draw from both to make wholes. So long as we try to exclude one-half of what makes us alive and human, calling, for instance, our bodies shameful and our minds the highest value, or separating the material and the spiritual, we cannot draw on the wisdom of the Mating Moon or be truly creative, either for ourselves or for others.

Trusting in our own intrinsic value is the beginning of knowledge because to fully trust what we are, we must, on a deep level, accept all the parts of ourselves, from the mundane necessity to eliminate our body wastes to our loftiest visions. One of the components of "charisma" may be the quality of going beyond such self-acceptance to a willingness to use all of one's inner diversity. Our personal wholeness is easiest when we are able to celebrate the beauties of our own internal patterns. Each of us has a place on the circle, and all the qualities and components of which we are made have a place in each of us. The patterns of light and shadow we make are each unique, beautiful, and sacred.

We must begin with loving what and where we are, fully and unreservedly, before we can progress to somewhere else. The Mating Moon says it all. It celebrates erotic love and sexual appetite, complete with gamey smells and ungainly positions, as a sacrament, the human song of praise to the Creator for the gift of life, the material point from which our most profound spiritual instincts arise.

Meeting Mating Moon Challenges

Accepting diversity in others begins with accepting our own shadow selves without guilt or self-blame. Just learning to recognize what our shadow selves include is a difficult step. In my experience, you can't just sit down and list all the qualities that you don't like about yourself. The ones that do you the most harm, that come from behind and stab you in the back, are also the hardest to look at. You may have buried them so deeply that they are hidden from your conscious mind.

There are several techniques for discovering these hidden subversives. One of the best methods uses the "mirror" theory. The idea behind this technique is that when we look at other people, we do not see the whole of them, but a reflection of ourselves in them, and that the things we dislike most in others are often the very processes that lie in our own dark hearts. For example, a man who thinks women are intrinsically inferior to males probably denies the "female" qualities in himself. He may use anger to hide his sensitivity to hurt feelings, or use inappropriate smart remarks to conceal his fear that he is unacceptable to other people. Emotions and interest in relationships are traditionally feminine concerns. In the same fashion, fat people are often highly intolerant of obesity, women often put down other women, and members of certain cultural groups internalize and act out the stereotypical qualities which are the focus of discrimination and rejection by other groups.

When we are trying to bring light to our own dark corners, a good place to begin is to list what we most dislike in others. I found my own tendencies toward self-righteousness in my irritation at that quality in my husband. I found my inclination to "peace at any price" in my son's willingness to say what will get me off his back. I found my secret desires for power and glory in my envy of the successes of others.

Another method for discovering your shadow self is to look at patterns in your life. If certain patterns emerge again and again, almost certainly part of your shadow self lies at the center of those patterns, demanding your attention and acceptance. One of my recurring life tests has to do with trusting in the Universe for what I need. For years, I lived in fear of not having enough (a typical Harvest Moon concern). My family went through terrible financial difficulties over and over. We were homeless twice in a period of three years.

When I began to recognize that security lies in a conscious decision to endure, I faced my fears and accepted them. Once I acknowledged my fear and refused to let it drive my life, my family began to prosper. I still have spells of worry. Instead of allowing myself to be paralyzed by my fears, I try to find specific actions I can take to keep me safe. When I exhaust possible action, I remind myself that I have endured terrible times in the past and lived through them, and I promise myself that I will also live through this time. I release my fears and continue the business of my life. As I have gained skill in using this process, my personal prosperity and spiritual health have steadily increased.

When you discover your shadow self, or any part of it, accept what you find. I do not mean that you must approve of everything that lies within you, but that you see all your parts as facts, neither intrinsically good nor bad. For example, if you are greedy, you can always choose not to act inappropriately from greed. Nor is greed a quality without value. You can, for example, exploit that quality to help motivate yourself to a worthy material success. When you acknowledge the "little greedy" within, you can learn to tell the difference between what you want and what you need. You can even feed the "little greedy" where it will do others or yourself no harm, as when you buy something for yourself that you don't absolutely need, but which you can well afford.

Once you begin to accept the shadow parts of yourself, and such acceptance is a lifetime task, you will find yourself better able to accept diversity in others. I found, for example, that when I put false modesty aside and began to accept compliments for my achievements, I also learned to recognize that my every achievement rested at least partly on the contributions of others. In fact, as I learned to express public pride in my work, my true, rather than false, humility also increased, and I now find it easy to acknowledge how much of my successes derive from the help and input of others.

There is one caveat in this process. Accepting qualities in yourself and in others does not mean encouraging them. For example, we can accept that people have bad tempers, and love them despite it. We don't, therefore, have to accept behavior from them that demeans us or harms others whom we can reasonably defend. We do not have the right to judge how people should be. We do have a right to say what behaviors they may use around us.

There are two rules of thumb for evaluating uncomfortable behavior, either in ourselves or in others. One is to ask whether that behavior will have a harmful effect, to us or others. The second is to ask whether we can take effective action to prevent harmful actions. I believe that if the answer to both questions is "yes," I have no choice but to take whatever action I can to prevent the behavior. On the other hand, I am not obliged to act if I think my action will do no good.

Only you can judge how those two parameters apply to a specific situation; that is, make your decisions on your personal answers to the two questions, not on what others may think. We can accept that a rabid dog is not responsible for its disease, and love the dog despite it. We are not then exonerated from killing that dog if we have the means, to prevent its spreading its disease. Nor need we be shamed if we run from the dog or call for help when we are in danger from it.

If You were Born in the Mating Moon

The greatest strengths of people born under a Mating Moon are likely to be their appreciation for the values of diversity and their ability to integrate diverse elements into a creative whole. Balanced people born under this moon are good at relationships and teamwork. They often have a keen appreciation for sexual relationships and have unusually good teambuilding skills. The special weaknesses of people born in this moon are likely to be their difficulty in accepting their shadow selves and, consequently, difficulty in accepting diversity in others.

The obvious problems of people born under the Mating Moon have to do with relationships, especially sexual relationships. However, that almost hackneyed observation, while often true, is a symptom rather than a central issue. You who were born under this moon tend to be strongly focused on finding what completes you, and on recognizing how the opposing energies of the sacred polarities reverberate through all portions of your experience.

The likely place where this search for your "other half" to manifest is how you discriminate among people. One form of this search shows up as an apparent lack of discrimination, even promiscuity, in seeking partners or friends. Such behavior occurs when you search so diligently that you try a lot of different people, always looking for the one who is a perfect complement to you.

We all seek completion, and, in fact, no one is a perfect fit for any of us, because the completeness we seek is the whole of the Tao, and not just the union of two people. As we continue to search for the perfect mate or the ideal friend, we may sample many potential partners, each of whom falls short. One of the lessons of the Mating Moon is that we need both sameness and difference in our Others, so we can find a common ground for building something new. Finding a suitable mate is not so much a completion as the start of a process in which we can become more nearly complete.

The polar opposite of apparent lack of discrimination is too fine a discrimination. People with this strategy tend to exhibit self-righteousness and intolerance of what lies outside their personal standards. They are still looking for a perfect complement, but, instead of looking everywhere and making many trials, they set up a rigid set of parameters and avoid people who fall outside the parameters.

If you find that all the candidates who present themselves to you for perfect mate or ideal friend fall short, the most likely root cause for your problem is an unwillingness to turn within to confront and accept your shadow self. If you look, you may find that your personal weaknesses and your most unacceptable (to you) qualities are reflected in the people you consider for mates and friends. These same qualities may also be those which trigger your self-righteousness and rejection. Try working on discovering and accepting your shadow self, the Other within, and you may find the one with whom you can unite.

When you who are born under it balance the energies of the Mating Moon, you are likely to have a special talent for creating synergy, that extraordinary experience where humans blend diverse elements into a whole that is greater than the sum of its parts. Your birthright is understanding how to use the power that is released when such diverse elements are appropriately combined, and appreciating the value and beauty of all human diversities. Both these skills are sorely needed in a world that is becoming increasingly divided over ethnic, religious, or other points of difference among us.

☾ Self-Discovery Journal: Mating Moon Issues

1. What specific behaviors, values, or qualities do you associate with male and female *(physical, behavioral, emotional, intellectual, spiritual)*? Do all biological males or females necessarily exhibit these behaviors, values, or qualities, or do you see the behaviors, values, or qualities as generally male or female in the sense of the divine polarities?

2. What qualities that you associate with the opposite gender do you manifest? How, specifically, do you manifest these qualities?

3. Which of the qualities you identified, for your gender or the opposite sex, do you like? In yourself, in others the same sex, in others of the opposite sex? Which do dislike? Why, specifically? *(List specific examples, perhaps specific persons you know.)*

4. List the specific behaviors that annoy you most in others. How, specifically, do you manifest those behaviors?

5. Why, specifically, do you dislike these behaviors? What qualities or values do they spring from? Can you recognize the neutral point in those qualities or values, the place where they may be either good or bad in their effect?

6. What specific qualities make you feel that another person is so different that he or she is alien to you *(style, gender, race, moral standards, culture)*? Which, if any, of those qualities is essential to their humanity? What specific information do your answers give you about your own shadow self?

7. List the recurring patterns in your life, both successes and difficulties. *(List specific events.)* Can you find specific personal qualities or values common to any group of events?

8. How, specifically, can you build a bridge to accepting the qualities or values which underlie your undesired recurring patterns? How, specifically, can you work toward more healthful manifestations of those qualities or values in your life?

9. If you have a life partner, how, specifically, do the qualities of that life partner complement your abilities? How, specifically, have you used that potential for your mutual benefit? How, specifically, have you failed to use that potential or used it for your mutual harm? *(If you have had a partner, but do not presently, answer based on your experience. If neither is true, substitute "best friend" or "significant other" for "life partner.")*

10. If you do not have a life partner, is it because you feel complete or because you are unable to find the complement you desire? If the latter, what specific qualities are you seeking? Why, specifically? What do your desires tell you about your shadow self?

11. What have you created in your life? *(List specifics, include material, emotional, intellectual/ spiritual life; include children, home, relationships, business, ideas, art, community activities.)* How, specifically, do your creations reflect diverse elements?

12. How, specifically, are you different from every other human being *(body, mind, spirit, in abilities, outlook, potential)*?

13. How, specifically, are you like every other human being *(body, mind, spirit, in experiences, desires, values)*?

A Healing Process for the Mating Moon

Experiment with trying to understand something really different from yourself and with accepting it for what it is. I recommend that you start with a tree, but you could use some other plant, a rock, or an animal. You can even try a machine, but my experience is that machines are more alien than most natural forms of life. Human beings are too much like you for clarity in this exercise.

Find a tree that you like the looks of and hug it. Try to clear your mind of thoughts, especially of your preconceptions of what a tree ought to be like. Relax as deeply as you can and try to be receptive to the life rhythms of the tree. You may have to do this several times before you can detect a result.

If you get physically uncomfortable or are embarrassed by the position of hugging, sit under the tree with your back to it. Try to have contact between you and the tree over as much of your body as you can manage. Be sure your hands, or other bare skin, have direct contact. Closing your eyes and trying to blot out everything but the tree helps.

If you are impatient, as I am, this waiting for something to happen is the hardest part. I want immediate results, so I won't feel silly standing there with my arms around the tree. In fact, probably nothing will "happen." Whatever you get will be slow and subtle, a sort of bubble that floats to the top of your mind and dissipates almost before you can recognize it. What you are looking for is an inner recognition that the tree is alive, that its life is connected to yours, that the two of you share, however remotely, some common connection.

Trees have very slow processes. You may never get anything from your tree that you can put into a coherent sentence. Mostly, you may get a sense of personality and emotion, perhaps of age. I know disgruntled trees and satisfied trees and cheeky trees that don't much like me. Trees never move from their spot, so their experience is limited. They do have some experience, however. Scientists have established that they communicate with other trees and plants in their vicinities, although scientists have not yet established the mechanism for the communication.

Some plant species can take offensive or defensive action against animals that might harm them. (Consider the stinging nettle and poison ivy.) Trees contract diseases and grow old. Like us, their big life issues are getting enough to eat to stay alive, developing enough excess to provide for children, and managing to hang on during tough times.

I have a friend who hugs trees when he gets angry because the depth and wisdom of the trees overwhelm the pettiness of his rage. I know people who converse with dryads. All of us know people with green or "brown" thumbs, which is an index of their abilities to relate to plants. I can't tell you exactly what you'll find if you succeed with this experiment. I can only tell you that, afterwards, the most diverse humans will seem less different to you than they did before.

If you choose to relate to life forms other than trees, the process is about the same. Rocks move even slower than trees. Animals are easier to connect to, but the experience is more complex. You'll find it especially hard to avoid projecting your own ideas of how an animal feels into the experience, because we ourselves are animals. However, at some level, animals are as alien to humans as trees. Reach for that portion in your experience. Find what is different from you and recognize its right to be as it is, and, by extension, your right to be as you are.

12

Journey Moon

Mirror, Waning Half of the Year: Death Moon.
Stage: Cycle Change.
Range of Dates: The Journey Moon may begin as early as May 3 and as late as June 1. It ends as early as June 2 and as late as July 1. Total range of dates over which the Journey Moon may occur is from May 3 to July 1.

Litha, the summer solstice, usually falls in the Journey Moon in years with a Courting Moon.

Mood of the Mother

Conditions for travel are ideal. Days are long and nights are warm. Food is plentiful, and many plants are near their peak of production, after spring rains and before the searing of the summer Sun. Migratory animals move to summer feeding grounds. Humans journey to see new places and to bring back exotic commodities for their communities. Fairs and gatherings take advantage of the weather and set up at central locations.

In the life of small agricultural communities, the crops are sown and it is time to move the herd animals to summer pastures and away from the growing grain. Work to maintain the fields is relatively light, and the next big cycle of heavy labor, harvest, is months away. It is time to consummate the marriage plans made during the Mating Moon and to visit one's relatives in other villages.

Communities are enriched by input from the world outside their boundaries. Now the Mother makes life easy enough to allow travel to marshy lands for certain medicinal herbs, to salt licks to gather that essential substance, to stands of wild fruit that ripen in early summer. Gatherings, where many communities meet, are a good place to sell the excess product from winter-made crafts or to barter for goods that cannot be locally produced. Other goods, such as extra spring lambs or cheeses made from the spring-fresh milk of cows and goats, can be exchanged for luxuries and materials that may make life a little easier.

If a community has grown beyond its ability to support its population, this is the time of year to send out explorers to find new places to settle. Restless young men scratch the itch of their wanderlust and set out to satisfy their curiosity about what lies beyond the far horizon. Travel, for specific purposes or for exploration, spreads news of all sorts: new places to find materials, new and improved ways of doing things, new tales to keep minds active and questing during the long months of winter.

The Mother smiles on Her restless sons and daughters, who will not stay put or rest content with what they possess. Those who dare and dream may find new and unexpected riches.

Images and Reflections

Weeds colonizing a lawn. Escaped day lilies growing in a roadside ditch. "Volunteer" wheat growing between the fence and the road. The American dandelion, immigrant from Europe and Asia. A vee of birds flying. Animal migrations: buffalo, lemmings, army ants. A fiddler crab looking for a new home. Spiders taking up housekeeping in quiet corners. Young animals just venturing out to explore their environment.

"The grass is greener on the other side of the fence." "The bear went over the mountain to see what he could see." Conestoga wagons strung out across a prairie. The entire mythos of Western movies. The Oklahoma land runs. Einstein's "thought" experiments. Space exploration. The Fool's journey in tarot. Jason and Odysseus, Columbus and Magellan, astronauts.

Related Energies

Death Moon: change

Mating Moon: seeking new experiences

Birth Moon: love of what is novel

Festival of Litha: celebrating Father energies

Zodiacal signs
    Taurus: practicality, persistence
    Gemini: curiosity

Planets
    Venus: relating to others
    Mercury: curiosity, seeking variety

Tarot cards
    The Chariot: movement
    The Hermit: seeking
    Sevens: exploring new options

Primary Energies of the Journey Moon

Love/Fear of the unknown

Risk/Safety

Innovative/Traditional

Unorthodox/Conforming

Progress/Stagnation

Time/Eternity

Manifesting Journey Moon Energies

The Journey Moon tells us that we may aspire to more than we have if we can but find the courage to dare new places and new directions. Humans have always been explorers, both of the land and of new ways to accomplish what we desire. There are human settlements above the Arctic Circle and at all latitudes below to just north of the Antarctic Circle.

Humans have adapted to extremes of hot and cold, wet and dry. They have explored mountaintops and ocean deeps, outer space and inner universes. We have extended our muscles with automobiles and other machines, our senses with instruments that can look at both galaxies and atoms, and the powers of our minds with computers. The great challenge of our era may be to manage the escalation of technical innovation in a balanced fashion that will not destroy the stability of the planet on which we live.

The energies of the Journey Moon deal with balances between the new and the old, the unknown and the familiar, change and permanence. If our present society seems overbalanced in its love of technical innovation, we also see movements to overbalance in the opposite direction, in backward-looking fundamentalists of all persuasions, in luddites who would destroy all technology since 1850, and in quasi-cults like the Flat Earth Society, which categorically deny any facts that contradict what they desire to believe.

In our personal lives, one practical and balanced way to handle Journey Moon energies is expressed in the old adage, "Be not the first by whom the new is tried, nor yet the last to lay the old aside." The only constant in our world is change, and if we cannot adapt to new ideas and facts, we stultify in stagnant pools, dying by degrees as we deny the renewal that should be our birthright as humans. On the other hand, if we chase pots of gold at the ends of rainbows beyond every distant hill, and never stop to examine the riches on the hill we presently occupy, we will never garner enough energy and grounded knowledge to produce something worth having. We can die of having no roots as surely as we can of not moving.

Our challenge is, as always, to find the balance. This time the balance lies between, on the one hand, being open and taking risks, and, on the other, appropriately valuing what we already possess. The Mother offers us both green valleys and far horizons, the renewal of change and the stability of safe harbors. It is our task to find the best use for both and all that lies between.

Meeting Journey Moon Challenges

We do not interact with the real world; our brains are wired to filter out most of what happens in our environment, to protect us from data overload. In the early days of our species, our brains learned to store all non-essential data below the level of consciousness. We still operate that way. The unconscious mind processes such data and brings important information to our attention as we need it. Our unconscious decides what's important according to our models of the world, which in turn reflect what we believe to be true, based on what people have told us and what we've actually experienced.

The effect of this process is that we tend to notice only the things that fit in with our models. In other words, once we decide something is true, we practically have to be hit on the head to notice any evidence that contradicts it. In simpler times, when most important information was concrete and directly related to survival, this tendency to edit out new information was less serious than it is in our present environment. Now what is important and what is not is a difficult and complex issue.

We may forget that the maps we make that show us what to pay attention to are just symbol sets, and not complete descriptions of the territories we travel through. That is, sometimes we confuse our models with reality, and decide that anything that's not in our model has to be wrong, maybe even evil. For example, the scientific establishment has no place for psychic phenomena in its model of how the world works. Therefore, despite a large body of evidence that psychic phenomena do occur, many scientists not only deny their existence, but dismiss anyone who attempts a serious study as a charlatan, not a "real" scientist.

We can't afford to have totally inflexible models of the world, although some people do aim for that, because if we keep out all new data, we lose our ability to adapt to changing conditions. Whether we like it or not, we have to deal with change, and we have to accept new data. The style we use to deal with these Journey Moon issues is directly related to other traits in our personalities.

Humans display a full range of strategies for dealing with new data and the changes it brings. On one extreme, we find conservatives and reactionaries who try to freeze time and hold their models of the world stable and intact. Such people include fanatics who terrorize anyone who does not conform to their ideas of the world, and also people who stubbornly, and often self-righteously, demand a return to "old-fashioned" values. On the other end, we have liberals and radicals, who may move so eagerly to incorporate new data into their models that they can fail to properly validate the new information and make sure it is consistent with other data in their model. In their scurry to live on the cutting edge, the people who express this side tend to lose continuity in their lives and in their models of the world. Like the rolling stone, they gather no moss.

Beyond the immediate issue of change, the Journey Moon also addresses how we respond to the infinite variety we may find "over the far horizon." Again we find the paired polarities of stability and variety. In nature, all life is infinitely varied and new. Nonetheless, underlying this variety are basic and unvaried repeating patterns. For example, depending on the level at which we compare, we can easily see how all domestic cats are alike, we can see how that species shares a pattern with lions and tigers, and we can recognize what cats share with dogs and bears, and how they differ from worms and insects. At each level, we find both stable, common points, and special, unique characteristics that differentiate one group from the other.

In a similar fashion, humans are unique individuals in how and why they respond to particular situations, yet we are all the same in what we feel emotionally. The stimuli that make me happy are peculiar to me, yet the quality of my happiness is no different than yours, even if you and I choose to act in vastly different ways. The Journey Moon teaches us to respect and value both the uniqueness and the sameness of all life, and to discover both renewal in old experiences and the comfort of the familiar in new experiences.

Many Journey Moon challenges can be met by learning to look beyond the surface of both the things we would keep and what we wish to bring new into our lives. For example, some of us try to hold onto what is beautiful and valuable in our experience long past the time when that beauty and value have worn away. If the essence of what we loved once was worth loving, that essence remains, perhaps under a new guise, in the here and now. If we look, we may find the quality we so love expressed in a new form and we can reaffirm our love. When we learn to "recognize" this essence, we can reconnect to it at will, both now, and then again later, when the present form, inevitably, also loses its ability to contain that essence we value.

For those of us whose Journey Moon challenges manifest as a restless boredom and a continual seeking after new experiences, we also need to recognize the essences that change form but not substance. For us, the questions are whether a new form truly holds the essence, and whether the new expression is valid. We may also need to ask ourselves whether we have sufficiently plumbed the value of the form we already possess. Those who search for newness sometimes forget to finish what they begin, and they often miss the real treasures beneath the surfaces they have barely scratched.

The Journey Moon teaches us that we need both the renewal of new horizons and the security of a homebase to return to after our adventures. Without new experiences, we cannot adapt when changes occur, as they inevitably do. Without a still center from which to evaluate those new experiences, we will become disoriented and make mistakes, perhaps even fatal mistakes. When we risk new horizons, we are rewarded with renewal. When we build permanent bases, we are rewarded with a place to rest and to integrate our renewal while we await the next cycle.

If You were Born in the Journey Moon

The special talent of those born under a Journey Moon is to create an inner stability that frees them to explore new places. People born under this moon who are balanced in its energies tend to be experimental and inventive, but they move with caution, always aware of what is safe and what is risky. They have a discerning appreciation for the interplay of pattern and variety. They may be natural pattern finders who seem to have an almost preternatural ability to find the common points between systems. The greatest weakness of people born under the Journey Moon is a tendency to hold their inner stability too firmly, and to taint the value of their questing by failing to make appropriate and timely changes to their inner homebase.

Your challenges, as one born under this moon, typically center on how you handle new ideas and experiences. People born under this moon may gravitate to one side or the other of variety and stability. They may be easily bored, always trying new things, or they may spend their energies in trying to hold the world still around them. Sometimes they express both poles at once, as when they start many new projects and then make exactly the same mistakes every time. It's as though they exhaust their willingness to take risks in their many new starts, and then balance that risk by using familiar patterns of behavior, even when they know those patterns have never worked before.

The "backwards, inside-out theory of reality" says that what we think we're doing is often the exact opposite of what we're actually doing. Thus, people born under the Journey Moon who are always looking at new ways to do things often have a core of rigid ideas about the world that is the real mediator of their behavior, however forward-looking they think they are. On the other pole, people born under this moon who seem to be curmudgeons, and who hate change so much you wonder how often they put on new underwear, may find abiding personal renewal in the experiences that they have fixed on. The key is not whether you like new things or old things, but whether you are stagnant or become new within.

People born under this moon may spend a significant portion of their life's energies looking for the balance between a need for roots and a need for growth. Ignoring either leaves them unfulfilled. Whatever we don't acknowledge in ourselves is likely to sneak around and stab us in the back. So we have the paradoxes of inflexible inventors and of collectors who spend their resources to fill their houses with things they dare not use.

If you can't seem to find a comfortable place for living your life, consider whether you are filling both sides of the equation: a place to be and a reason to be. Discover what makes you feel safe and connected, then look for what stimulates your questing mind, and put the two together. New for new's sake is ultimately as boring as the same old place, which may have new aspects you never happened to notice. Safe for safe's sake will ultimately leave you vulnerable, like the dinosaurs that died out because they couldn't adapt when their environment changed.

In real experience, the most lasting progress is that which builds on a tested foundation and adds new components in small increments, usually from tested sources. Do not lose your vision because you are tired of traveling. You can bring what you learned in your travels to one spot, and use it to build a home. If you have a home, but it's empty of meaning, invite in a traveler, in the form of new people and new ideas. Your safe harbor and the seeds of their new ideas may grow the best of all possible worlds.

☾ *Self-Discovery Journal: Journey Moon Issues*

1. Where, specifically, do you prefer something new over something familiar (*styles, jobs, relationships, projects, ideas*)? Why, specifically?

2. Answer question 1 again, and substitute in turn the word pairs, "unknown/well-known," "progressive/obsolete," "innovative/traditional," "unorthodox/conforming," and "risky/safe," for the words "new/familiar."

3. How do your answers in question 2 differ from those for question 1? What do these differences say about your personal ideas and values regarding change and stability?

4. How, specifically, do you judge progress (*in personal growth, relationships, business, society—how do you know progress occurred?*)? What do your standards for progress reflect about your personal values?

5. In what specific parts of your life are you willing to take risks to learn/experience new things (*health, family, relationships, job, business, values, belief systems*)? In what specific parts of your life do you build your homebase, your safe harbor?

6. Think of several things you have begun but have not completed (*hobby, home, school, business, community project*). Why, specifically, did you fail to follow through? What can you do in the future to assure that you complete projects you begin (*be more careful what you undertake, change approach to projects, develop system/rewards for completion, get others to help*)?

7. When you have too many things to do, how, specifically, do you prioritize them (*at home, work; social obligations; personal goals like health, education, recreation*)? Do those priorities reflect your personal values? If not, what specific

strategies can you use to bring your priorities into alignment with your values?

8. Have you ever tried to "freeze" a place, a relationship, or a set of values so that it would not change *(at home, at school, in business, in social groups; your own values, your family's, those of other relationships)*? What, specifically, happened? What did you learn from such experiences that you can apply to your present actions?

9. Have you ever tried to force a change on a place, in a relationship, or in a set of values *(home, school, business, social groups; your own, your family, other relationships)*? What, specifically, happened? What did you learn from such experiences that you can apply to your present actions?

10. What specific strategies do you use to make yourself feel safe *(physically, economically, emotionally, intellectually; prepared for change, the unexpected, emergencies)*? How effective are those strategies? How do you know? Do your answers suggest any changes in your strategies?

A Healing Process for the Journey Moon

Go someplace you've never been before. Choose somewhere you can commune with nature, a park, a place in the country, or even a friend's backyard. Try to come to this new place with new eyes and to see it through the uncluttered perceptions of a child who does not know enough to be distracted by all the concerns that turn us aside from knowing the Mother and our connections to Her.

Begin in this new place by sitting quietly, preferably on the bare ground, with your eyes closed. If the setting is safe, do this barefoot and barelegged. Breathe slowly and deeply. Stretch your nose into the air, so your air passage is as nearly vertical as possible. Try to identify the smells around you, both natural, as plants and soil, and artificial, as car fumes or cooking smells. Open your mouth and taste the air, using your tongue to move it around. Can you discern a taste?

Touch something in your environment, such as tree bark, leaves, or soil. Crush a leaf or blade of grass and put it under your nose. Brush it with your tongue. If more than one plant is available within your reach, compare the smells and textures and tastes of each. If you're not certain of the safety, leave out tasting.

Feel the texture of the soil. Is it dry or moist? Is the texture fine or coarse? Is it sandy or sticky? Rub it between your fingers and smell it. Explore by touch and smell and taste whatever you can reach without moving. How does the ground feel beneath you? What thoughts and feelings come to the surface as you do so? Do the smells or other sensations take you back in memory? Where?

After you have explored touch and smell with your hands, see what you can learn from the rest of your skin. Is there a breeze? Can you sense it on your cheek? What direction does it come from? Is it warm or cool, dry or moist? Does it move your hair? How does the sun feel on your face? Can you tell a difference between light and shadow? Can you see light through your eyelids? How do the feel of these things differ between where you have bare skin and where your skin is covered? If you turn your head, do you smell different things, or does the quality of the smells change? What can you deduce from this difference, if any?

Listen. Can you hear the wind? The rustle of leaves and branches? Animals or insects? Man-made sounds? What are they? What direction are they from you? Can you feel vibrations in the ground? Can you hear your own breath or heartbeat? How does your body feel? Does it vibrate in rhythm with the Mother?

When you have explored both your environment and of yourself as much as you can without moving from your place, open your eyes, but do not move your head. How large is your field of view? How does the restriction on movement affect what you experience?

What can you discern within the limits of this restriction? Can you distinguish two noses as your eyes see the tip separately? Can you see your shoulder? What other parts of your body? What colors does the Mother present in the picture before you? Are there flowers? How many plants can you identify? Do you see insects or other animals? Do you know what they are? If you have animals in your view, observe them for a while. Look at them as a moving art form.

Look at the scene before you in sections, carefully and fully examining each section in turn. Do you see things you did not see before? Before you leave your new place, try to list all the things you experienced that were new to you, the things you had forgotten, and the things that seemed the same.

The newest things in the world are those we have never seen before, even though they are right in front of us. The infinite variety of the Mother cannot be exhausted. In the same way, our experiences and what we produce are infinitely varied and splendidly beautiful, if we will only look.

13

Mother's Moon

Mirror, Waxing Half of the Year: Birth Moon.
Stage: Beginning.
Range of Dates: The Mother's Moon begins as early as June 2 and as late as July 1. It ends as early as July 1 and as late as July 30. Total range of dates over which the Mother's Moon may occur is from June 2 to July 30.

Litha, the summer solstice that celebrates the peak of the Father's energies, is also the peak of the Mother's abundance. Litha falls in the Mother's Moon in thirteen years of the nineteen-year Sun-Moon-Earth cycle. In the old calendar, the summer solstice was the midpoint of summer, and was also called Midsummer.

Mood of the Mother

The Mother opens Her arms and spills forth the cornucopia of Her bounty. Even lazy lifeforms can find food for the asking, with few limits. The Father reaches His greatest power and pours forth His life-giving warmth upon the land. Days are long and soft, full of the melodies of insects and birds, and the rustle of summer breezes through full-leaved trees.

In this easy time of year, young animals have grown enough to emerge from burrows and nests and to learn the skills that will permit them to make their own livings. We can bless the generosity of the Mother in making many babies, for even during this easy time, there are tests. Young animals, not yet experienced in evading enemies, make life easy for predators also. Nor are plants, which have their greatest growth at this time, exempt. The greedy and ungainly teenagers, who will delight us in their adult butterfly form, leave devastation behind them as they gorge in their caterpillar stage. They in turn fall to birds and other insectivores, and to parasites who are to them as they are to the plants.

The bounty and the dangers come to all, for the Mother limits none of Her children. All that live have the right to live, if they can. In this moon, the Mother's glory is the rich variety of life, a symphony of changing/unchanging forms for moving through the stages of birth, reproduction, and death. Each individual sings a unique series of notes within the signature that defines its species. In a meadow of flowers, we may see a thousand buttercups, each a little different from the other, yet each is clearly a buttercup. When their season is past, we see them no more, but we know that, in the fullness of time, they will come again.

The Mother teaches us, in the canvas of our world, that Her love is unbounded. All who live have their opportunities. The Father, at His height, also brings a lesson: For each individual, there are limits and boundaries, in what they are, in where they live, and in what they share/compete for with other life forms. The unconditional love of the Mother enables us to live. The conditional love of the Father enables us to grow.

Images and Reflections

Summer. High noon. A field of golden wheat waving in the wind. The unbounded joy of a fine summer's day. Mosquitoes and dragonflies, prairie dogs and rattlesnakes, deer and wolves. A bird feeding its chicks. A mother hen spreading wings over her chicks. The fierceness of a mother bear defending her cubs. Love and youth under summer moonlight. A full larder and a safe harbor.

"You've got the whole world in your hands . . . ." The Cornucopia, the ever-renewing horn of plenty, which is an icon for the womb of the Mother. Spaceship Earth. The "survival of the fittest." The mysteries of love and meaning. Demeter's joy at the return of Persephone. The persistence of life, in weeds that will not die and humans who will not give up.

Related Energies

Birth Moon: children

Father's Moon: fatherlove

Mating Moon: fertility

Festivals
    Litha: celebrating the abundance of summer
    Lammas: harvest

Zodiacal signs
    Gemini: versatility
    Cancer: children

Planets
  Mercury: pushing limits
  Moon: motherhood
Tarot cards
  The World: having it all
  The Moon: spiritual growth through
    acceptance of material reality
  Sixes: peak experiences

Primary Energies of the Mother's Moon

Motherlove/Fatherlove (unconditional/conditional)

Abundance/Scarcity

Trust/Lack of trust

Relationship of material and spiritual values

Hope/Manifestation

Security/Insecurity

Dependence/Independence

Manifesting Mother's Moon Energies

When we are born, our mothers are the center of our lives. They provide all we need without demanding a return. For the rest of our lives, our ability to thrive rests at least in part in our recreating the sense of security we had in our mothers' unconditional love. All the components of that sense of security—our means to live, our health, our homes, our feelings of worth, how we relate to the people we live and work with, and our sense of belonging to community—rest on having the experience of motherlove.

Our sense of security is our material base, the foundation on which we build our emotional and spiritual growth as we mature from infancy to adulthood. A starving, homeless person seldom produces art and philosophy. The person who lives at subsistence level has no energy for finding the Other, either within or without. To become whole, we must build on the most secure material base we can manage: enough money to live, healthy bodies and safe homes, jobs we can be proud of, and families and communities where we can find mutual respect and support. Above all, we need to feel that we are worthy, as our mothers found us worthy.

The spiritual issues of the Mother's Moon lie in recognizing our intrinsic self-worth and in trusting that, if we try, we can find what we need to fulfill our lives. The lesson of motherlove is that we are all sacred and perfect, that each of us, no matter where we are on the circle, has the right to strive for life and growth. With that assurance, we can learn to handle the limits and boundaries against which we struggle in that process.

It is important to understand this interaction. Unconditional motherlove gives us the security we need to achieve those qualities that fatherlove, which is conditional on what we do rather than what we are, demands. These sacred polarities are not related to gender. They are the balanced components of all love, expressed and needed by all humans.

The Mother loves all that lives equally and impartially. Her love is unconditional, but it is also impersonal. We are loved and provided with the opportunity to get what we need, not because we are "special" or unique, but because we are Her children. The balanced energies of the Mother's Moon teach us that we are each intrinsically valuable and worthy of life, and that the abundance of the universe is available to us as it is to all others.

The balanced expression of these energies produces people who have a healthy self-esteem and the wisdom to understand that they "deserve" neither more nor less than other children of the Mother. Such people are able to fully enjoy the abundance that comes their way without becoming slaves to their material needs. They are able to ask for and to work for what they need, with the assurance that they will receive it, and without fearing deprivation or succumbing to greed for more than what they require.

Meeting Mother's Moon's Challenges

The challenges of the Mother's Moon are connected to our feelings of self-worth, especially in regard to what we achieve as we live. In our culture, we tend to believe that, as George Orwell said, "All animals are equal, but some animals are more equal than others." Thus, we are prone to judge our own and other's worth by degrees of material success. We tend to believe that people who are not materially successful are inferior, and that people who have money are somehow essentially superior, even when they display unbalanced and unhealthy lives, as, for example, some entertainment or sports stars do. Note that "superior" and "inferior" are qualities mapped on a vertical line rather than a circle.

In a climate where everyone is "one up" or "one down" from everyone else, we may find it difficult to believe that all people are intrinsically sacred, including drunken bums lying on the street and serial killers. We confuse the intrinsic worth of all that lives, the value loved by the Mother, with the value that individuals may acquire by their actions. That is, a serial killer has the same intrinsic value as you and I do, the same right to unconditional love.

However, motherlove is only half of human love. It is appropriately balanced with fatherlove, which is conditioned on what we do and how we use our resources. Beyond our intrinsic value as living beings, we also have an acquired value, to ourselves and to our communities, which is based on our actions. As individuals or as a society, we have the right to refuse approval and continued freedom to serial killers because their acquired value to us is destructive rather than constructive.

I often say that all that lives is sacred and perfect, as it is, where it is. I use the word "perfect" here in the sense of complete, congruent with the time and place particular beings have chosen to be. I do not mean by that statement that all the "perfections" of others are, or should be, equally acceptable to me. I have the same right to live, if I can, as others who would infringe my right. I can apply motherlove to recognize their essential worth, and fatherlove to reject, and, where I can, restrict their behavior that impedes or harms me.

We can meet most challenges of the Mother's Moon by internalizing the fact that we need both motherlove and fatherlove, both to judge ourselves and to judge others. We need to recognize that our essential value is not changed by mistakes, or unwise actions, or even by what we own or have achieved. We are perfect where we are. If we desire different perfections, we can change our behavior, but nothing we do changes the intrinsic worth that is the foundation of any value we may acquire by our achievements.

We are not what we do. What we do affects the network that interconnects all members-in-process of the Tao. What we do is encouraged or impeded by what others in this net choose to do. We're all in this together. If our actions are not in accord with the needs of the whole, we are likely to have a difficult life. That is, our happiness and sense of self-completion lie in bringing what we do into harmony with those around us. The Mother's Moon tells us that we are all cells of the single body that is the Tao.

As a body's health is affected by the well-being of every cell within it, so this harmony on which our own happiness rests requires that we esteem ourselves enough to provide for our own physical and spiritual wholeness. That wholeness can then be a resource to other beings who are members-in-process of the Tao. How we choose to make our personal resources available to others, and to partake of their resources in turn, is the foundation of our own prosperity and growth. By balancing motherlove and fatherlove in the processes of our lives, we optimize not only our own development, but those resources of our community that are available to us for such development.

If You were Born in the Mother's Moon

If you want to feel cherished, find a person born under the Mother's Moon who is balanced in its energies. The greatest strength of those born under this moon is their ability to look beyond the idiosyncrasies of individuals and to find and love the underlying essence in those they choose to love. They can be unswerving friends and lovers, always there when you need them. People born under this moon tend to like material comfort, and to appreciate the "good things in life." Their greatest weakness is their tendency to neglect cherishing themselves as much as they cherish others. Sometimes they have difficulty taking responsibility for their own needs, and they may manifest material greed.

You who are born under the Mother's Moon tend to focus strongly on material security and on acquiring, or not acquiring, material resources. The problems you may have with handling this moon's energies derive from your willingness to trust the universe to provide the means you need to live and from your evaluation of your own worth.

You understand at a very deep level that abundance is available to us all, but you may have trouble with the other half of that equation, that we must enable receiving such abundance by a process called working for a living. If you struggle with taking full responsibility for your own sustenance, you may be operating on the hope that you will be provided for if you manifest sufficient neediness. Someone will surely take care of you, whether it be relatives and friends or the welfare state. In our society, the price for letting others provide for you is a low level of competence in dealing with the world.

In the opposite direction, you may have almost no trust that your needs are likely to be met from sources other than yourself. You may not feel that you are valuable enough to receive help from others, and you may bolster both your sense of self-worth and your concern for having "enough" by an unhealthy accumulation of goods. As one born under this moon, you naturally recognize that material security is a necessary foundation for spiritual growth; however, when you try to build the whole house from material security, you end up living in a fortress that isolates you from the life and growth you desire.

If you are afraid that you may not have "enough," you may display that fear as miserliness or by overfilling your home with things, often things you do not need and cannot easily afford. You may also tend to hold onto outworn and obsolete items "in case you ever need them," or you may gather massive collections of anything from comic books to clothes for no clear reason other than to possess them.

The origin of both these Mother's Moon imbalances is low self-esteem, and if you manifest either or both of these patterns, you need to begin by strengthening your sense of self-worth. If you never quite manage the means to full independence, a sneaking suspicion will lurk somewhere inside you that, if you ever actually leave the protection of family or Big Brother, you will discover you are not good enough to make it in the real world. You may believe that your "secret" inner fears, which in fact are felt by us all, prove that you are unworthy.

If you are one who clutches at and accumulates possessions, you may also have a self-image problem, even though you may seem arrogant and full of yourself to people who don't know you. In this pattern, you may feel that your possessions add to your consequence, and you may hope that an impressive pile of goods will distract others from seeing what you feel is the minuscule person within. You may have trouble believing anyone would love you for yourself.

The solution to these challenges comes from two directions. The first is to recognize that we are all frail and incomplete, and that all of us live in fear. The differences among us are the degree to which we let the fear keep us paralyzed. Those of us who keep moving do so despite our quaking knees and pounding hearts. The way out always begins with a decision to find a way, whether out, around, or through. Sometimes our ways out aren't elegant, but at least we're moving. Every time we fight our own way through a difficulty, we bolster our sense of self-worth.

The second direction for healing is to consciously recognize and internalize the love of the Mother. She loves us for what we are and values each of us because, together, we make the whole that She and the Father created. Each of us is a note in Their universal song. Every note has its place, and the beauty of the music rests not on the sweetness of individual sounds, but on the harmony of the whole. We need to accept that all we have to do to deserve the Mother's bounty is to sing our note. Only silence is unrewarded.

The Mother's Moon assures us that each of us is worthy. There's no magic formula for instant self-esteem. We have to operate "as-if" we're valuable if we wish to acquire value to ourselves and others. The good news is that we're not alone in this task. All of us have this problem; some of us just hide it better than others. But when we behave as though we're valuable, even when, in our heart of hearts, we're not sure, we somehow discover that our "big lie" is actually the truth. The Mother loves us. Dare we say She is wrong? We can open our hearts to Her love, and let Her heal our fears of unworthiness.

☾ Self-Discovery Journal: Mother's Moon Issues

1. How, specifically, do you determine your self-worth *(by health, money, relationships, social status, skills, talents, job, education, material or spiritual success)*?

2. Which specific components of your life are most important when you assess yourself as successful or unsuccessful? Which are least important *(health, money, relationships, social status, skills, talents, job, education, material or spiritual success)*? Why do those specific components indicate your success or lack of success?

3. Which specific components of your life do you take responsibility for *(health, material support, relationships, skills, talents, job, education, material or spiritual success)*? Which components do you expect someone or something else *(as family, friends, spouse, school, job, government)* to provide? Do your answers suggest any specific changes in your actions or attitudes?

4. Which specific relationships in your life are examples of balanced motherlove/fatherlove? *(They both open potential and provide boundaries in regard to parents, life partner, children, friends, teacher, employer.)* Which relationships are unbalanced in this regard? How, specifically?

5. How, specifically, do you relate emotionally to material things *(comfortable, uncomfortable, greedy, detached, value, devalue)*? Do you relate to different material things differently *(your body, your clothes, your home, possessions, necessary tools, "unnecessary" items as art)*?

6. How, specifically, do your material resources relate to your spiritual strivings *(directly, not at all, enable, get in the way)*?

7. Do you trust your ability to meet your own material and spiritual needs? If not, what specific personal resources do you require to be able to do so? How, specifically, can you acquire them?

8. When, specifically, is it appropriate for you to ask others to help you *(discomfort, survival requirement, personal desire, for self alone or for others in your care)*?

9. When, specifically, is it appropriate for you to offer or refuse help to others? Does it matter whether they ask directly or you perceive a need?

A Healing Process for the Mother's Moon

Imagine that you have an hour to pack up yourself and your family in a car, and that whatever you leave behind will be destroyed by fire or flood. Do not allow yourself to be disturbed by this thought. The purpose of this exercise is to help you recognize what is most essential to you and yours and how much of your personal well-being rests on a material base.

We have many layers of need. When survival is the issue, we can strip almost all the layers away and find our most central needs and values. What are you going to take with you? Food and clothing? Tools? Cooking utensils? Bedding? Medicines? Personal items such as jewelry and toys? Family records? Treasured books and art works? Your VCR or computer?

Begin by deciding that you and your family will survive, and that, no matter how tough it gets, you'll find a way to make it through the disaster. If the thousands of people who experience natural disasters every year can endure and recover, so can you. With this resolve in mind, decide what you must have to make it through the next few days and what you need to form the seeds of recovery when the crisis is over.

Clothes and bedding, non-perishable foods, and containers of water are obvious. So are necessary medications and basic household utensils. What about family pictures and records? How about your child's teddy bear? What about your favorite books or objects? Think about emotional as well as physical survival. Think about what you will tell your children or your spouse to help them survive and recover later, how you can explain that the disaster is impersonal and not an expression of their personal worth. Make sure that you understand the truth of what you say.

After you complete your list and have stripped down to absolute necessities that will fit in the car, walk through your home in your mind and celebrate all the objects and qualities that sustain you and your family. Recognize the bounty in your life. Discover how an old chair that fits your body comforts you. Acknowledge that an ugly lamp annoys you every time you see it. Consider how the cleanliness, neatness, and good condition of each object affects your sense of comfort and well-being. Count your blessings and take joy in what you have.

14

Father's Moon

Mirror, Waxing Half of the Year: Milk Moon.
Stage: Growth.
Range of Dates: The Father's Moon may begin as early as July 1 or as late as July 30. It ends as early as July 31 and as late as August 29. Total range of dates over which the Father's Moon may occur is from July 1 to August 29.

The Feast of Lammas, the harvest festival, falls in the Father's Moon sixteen years of the nineteen-year cycle. In the old calendar, Lammas marked the beginning of autumn and the first harvest, of grain.

Mood of the Mother

After the abundance of the Mother's Moon comes the realization that such plenty cannot last. The Father, at His height of power during the solstice, so warmed the soil that now, as the Earth releases that stored heat, we experience the searing of deep summer, "the aftermark of almost too much love." We still bask in His life-giving energies, but the Father is clearly losing strength. Each day is shorter than the one before it. We have His light and warmth for the present, but the wise notice the shorter days and announce the sobering news that winter is on its way.

In the great story, the Father chooses to sacrifice Himself before he succumbs to the weakness of old age. His death opens the way to transformation, for He will return in the Divine Child He sired on the Goddess, the child that even now grows in Her womb. We see this sacred drama in the cycle of the Sun, and also in the grain that ripens and dies and also represents the Father. We transform the body of the God (the harvested grain) into the bread that sustains our lives, and we will use the seed grain saved from the harvest to plant next year's crop. The Father dies, is transformed, and comes again to provide us with the means to live.

The heat of deep summer has a bittersweet edge. The Mother already begins to mourn the inevitable loss of Her lover. Vegetation that burgeoned earlier now goes dormant and lies dry and sere, brown patches that will grow like cancer until they cover the entire landscape of winter. We have little rain, and the dry earth thirstily sucks up what falls. We are brought hard upon the fact that all life exists within limits and boundaries. We bless the bounty of the Mother, the fruit of Her union with the Father. We harvest that bounty as the body of the God, John Barleycorn, an avatar of the Father, and hone our own edges against the coming trials of winter.

Images and Reflections

An August day, hot and cloudless, merciless in its brightness. Bound sheaves of grain marching across a harvested field. The smell of fresh-baked bread. A bird thrusting her young from the nest. The dry smell of earth thirsting for rain. The growing independence of spring-born animals. The seeds and fruits of mature plants. The wonder of growth and the cycle of the year.

All-Father Odhinn hanging from Yggdrasil for nine days, pierced by His own spear, then sacrificing His left eye as the price of knowledge. The sharp blend of pain and joy in a child's growing up and away from us. The sorrow and need in the punishment of a child. The sense of helplessness with which we watch those we love struggle with their human limits. The bittersweet acceptance of the truth that for every joy there is a price, for every sorrow a lesson. In the words of Robert Frost *(To Earthward)*, "Now no joy but lacks salt that is not dashed with pain . . . ; I crave the stain of tears, the aftermark of almost too much love."

Related Energies

Milk Moon: education

Nesting Moon: limits of resources

Death Moon: transformation

Feasts
    Lammas: sacrifice and transformation
    Mabon: harvest

Zodiacal signs
    Cancer: protection
    Leo: the healthy ego

Planets
    Moon: parenthood
    Sun: passion and vitality

Tarot cards
> The Hanged Man: knowledge gained at a price
> The Sun: enlightenment after struggle
> Fives: struggle, adjustment

Primary Energies of the Father's Moon

Sacrifice and transformation/Self-indulgence
> and stagnation

Fatherlove/Motherlove (conditional/unconditional)

Knowledge of limits/Unlimited potential

Learning/Ignorance

Manifesting Father's Moon Energies

The task of fatherlove is to shape and encourage our potentials by teaching us how to become effective adults. The archetypical father is respected first and loved second. His job is to teach his children how to survive, and some of his lessons can be painful. The child who reaches toward the pretty fire feels hurt and angry when its hands are slapped. It does not yet know enough to realize that the slap is a protection and an act of love. Fatherlove is necessarily constrained, for it can give approval only for success. To offer false praise or reinforce wrong behavior is to risk the child.

Humans tend to resent fathering processes, both those we receive from our parents and other teachers of either gender and from interacting with the natural limits and dangers of the wide world. Our brains are wired to learn more readily from mistakes; the punishment of failure is often more productive than the rewards of success. We learn more efficiently from restriction and pain than from freedom and joy. Motherlove alone would never make us fit to live independently. Without tests, we do not learn. Without difficulty, we do not grow. Without tempering, we will not survive.

We manifest the energies of the Father's Moon when we impose limits on ourselves and on others for the purpose of accomplishing something, or when we choose to sacrifice something we value to meet the needs of another. The earliest lesson of the Father's Moon is that everything costs something. TANSTAAFL (There Ain't No Such Thing As A Free Lunch) is a key to all the secrets of the universe. Yet, while everything costs something, everything contains its own gift as well. From the pain of separation from the security of motherlove comes the priceless gift of freedom. The mystery of sacrifice is that, when we choose freely to give up something we value, we may be transformed by our act into something better than we were.

The costs and lacks that limit us are also the boundaries against which we discover who we are and what we can do. When we have exhausted the possibilities of one set of limits, it is time to change to another place on the circle. The purpose of fatherlove is to assist in such change and help us make the change as growth-enabling as possible.

The Tao is always moving and changing. Nothing lasts forever. No matter how hard we try to hold onto something, it will swirl away from our grasp. If we think we have succeeded in holding on to it, it changes and becomes a distortion of what we loved. The Father's willing sacrifice shows us that, by actively accepting change, we can make the best of what we cannot prevent.

All change implies the sacrifice of what we must leave behind, including things we may value highly. The decision to change is a risk, for what we gain could prove to be less valuable than what we lose. However, if we do not risk change when it is time, we will surely stifle and wither in the coils of the safe and familiar to which we try to cling. We manifest balanced Father's Moon energies when we sacrifice our fear of pain and loss to gain the joy of growth and renewal.

Meeting Father's Moon Challenges

The challenges of the Father's Moon relate to how we take and carry out responsibilities to ourselves and to others. First, we must make wise choices about the responsibilities we accept. We are always limited in how much we can do for others. No matter how much we love someone, we cannot protect others from the consequences of their own actions without harming them or ourselves. We are each accountable for our own growth and sustenance and may not neglect it, even to help others. Our first challenge is to discover our own limits and to set suitable boundaries for our own actions, especially those related to our care of others.

Fatherlove responsibilities of caring for, protecting, and supporting others usually involve helping them to recognize and accept their own limits or to "push the envelope" so that they increase the boundaries within which they can operate. We play this kind of role in many places. In addition to our own children, we have opportunities for "fathering" with spouses or other relatives, with elderly parents or neighbors, as employers or workers in social welfare or healthcare, as teachers or ministers, as youth or political leaders.

The role of fatherlove requires that we command respect; it may not include receiving love or even being liked. The challenges of the Father's Moon sometimes mean accepting the unpopular role of taskmaster or bearer of bad news. No one likes to accept limits. Almost everyone resists the effort required to expand limits. In order to get the job done, the person manifesting fatherlove may have to sacrifice the joys of personal recognition and gratitude. The first reward of the Father's path is more often the growth of others than a tickling of personal ego. But, by the mystery of transformation, our sacrifices on this path almost always enable our own growth and renewal as well.

Helping others to define their limits and to discover their capabilities is a sacred task, full of both rewards and difficulties. Rewards include learning from those we teach and minister to, often as much or more than we give. Difficulties include giving up our attachments to, and control of, those we care for when the time comes for them to be independent of us. Worst of all, this task includes our accepting that we are helpless to prevent the pain that arises when those we care for make mistakes.

The way of the Father can be full of difficult choices, and we don't always make the right decisions, no matter how mature and wise we may think we are. Our own limits restrict what we can do. The limits of others or of our environment further constrain the possible outcomes of our actions. For ourselves or for those we love, all we can do at a specific time and place is the best we can with what we have available at that time and place.

For ourselves and for those to whom we give fatherlove, we must learn self-forgiveness, even for the disasters that we may create. Part of learning our limits is not to blame ourselves because we have them. Part of accepting errors is to turn them into knowledge, that we may act more wisely in the future. The cost of such knowledge is often pain, but when we focus on the gift instead, the pain diminishes. When we learn these lessons, we are transformed into new persons whose limits now define a larger space.

The final lesson of the Father's Moon is that such transformation moves us to a new part of the circle. The price of change is that we cannot go back and recapture who we were and what we had before we changed. We sacrifice a safe and familiar set of limits for new and perhaps frighteningly undefined boundaries. Our choices are to take joy in exploring what our new environment offers or to spend our energy mourning what we have lost.

Consider the butterfly. The caterpillar who provides the energy for the butterfly's metamorphosis is itself ugly and greedy. It is earthbound, often limited to living on a single plant of a specific species. It sacrifices its initial form to become a butterfly, which is beautiful and free to fly. However, the butterfly has no capacity for growth, only for reproduction. Each form in its turn has its limits and its capacities, even its special beauties. We "can't go home again" after we turn an existential corner. The turning changes us forever.

If You were Born in the Father's Moon

The greatest strengths of people born under the Father's Moon are their willingness to accept responsibility and their generosity in sharing what they know with others. They are natural accumulators of knowledge, and are often unusually competent at directing activities and assuring that everything is done properly and on time. The greatest weakness of people born under this moon is their tendency to undertake inappropriate responsibilities, either in an unnecessary self-sacrifice, or as a means to control people in their lives.

You who are born under a Father's Moon tend to ride Duty as though it were the only steed available for traveling through life. Those who walk the Father's path as parents, teachers, and helpers often feel worn down by the burden of their responsibilities to others and by the lack of gratitude their service brings. When those born under this moon are not balanced in its energies, they may tend to martyr themselves.

If you fall easily into parental behavior, you may relish the special respect and deference that this behavior evokes. You may also enjoy the control that "playing papa" gives you over those who often willingly surrender responsibility for their lives, if you will only consent to take care of them. The downside of this pattern is that your pride may be hurt when your probably superior wisdom and competence are not acknowledged and deferred to. You can also be hurt when you do too much for others and then find that they are not only ungrateful, but perhaps even resentful at your taking over.

A hurt feeling and a sense of being undervalued for what you sacrifice for others is a clear signal that you have been pushing your help on someone, help which is either not needed or not wanted. The saddest part of a parent's experience is the fact that we cannot take our children's hurts away or make their mistakes, and bear the consequences, for them. Whoever we try to take over for, our assuming unreasonable responsibility for others leads only to our hurt and to their failure to learn necessary lessons. People born under the Father's Moon may need to take special care to recognize and respect the rights and needs of others to make their own mistakes and to learn their own lessons.

In another direction, the result of taking all this responsibility for others is that your sacrifice is mostly wasted. It not only prevents those for whom you sacrifice from learning what they need to know, it is also a distraction from the requirements of your own life path and your personal self-development, which you may have put on hold while you take care of someone else.

Consider the possibility that you put yourself in service so that you will not have to confront your shadow self, those hidden portions of your inner self that you prefer not to acknowledge. Spending your energies helping others also gives you ample excuse for not succeeding, and for not developing your own potentials.

Duty is usually an uncomfortable steed. If you don't pay attention, you can be so diverted by the metaphorical pain in your backside that you fail to notice you haven't traveled very far. Your special talent for fulfilling responsibility to others does not excuse you from fulfilling your first and primary responsibility, to become the person you are meant to be.

The special challenges of the Father's Moon revolve around the issues of individual growth and independence. Individuals each have unique paths with tests and difficulties that they must surmount. The requirements for navigating such paths are not satisfied by giving the load, all or in part, to another, or by taking up the load of someone on a neighboring path. When we stand up and accept our own struggles, however difficult, and allow those we love to do the same, we manifest the essence of the Father's Moon growth-enhancing energies.

☾ Self-Discovery Journal: Father's Moon Issues

1. What specific limitations do you consider yourself to have *(physical, emotional, intellectual, skills, talents, relationships, social or business connections, education, cultural background)*? What evidence, specifically, do you have for defining these personal boundaries at the place you do? *(List specific events.)*

2. Which of these limitations would you like to extend? What specific actions can you take to extend them?

3. What specific strengths do you have that help you get what you want in the world *(physical, emotional, intellectual, skills, talents, relationships, social or business connections, education, cultural background)*? What specific evidence do you have for possessing such strengths? *(List specific events.)*

4. Which of your strengths would you like to increase? What specific actions can you take to increase them?

5. Common wisdom says that every weakness has its own strength, and every strength its weakness. What are the specific advantages to each of your limitations? What are the specific disadvantages to each of your strengths?

6. What kind of benefit do you require before you sacrifice something you value *(sacrifice of time, personal energy, money; benefit to self, others; benefit is physical, emotional, monetary, spiritual; level of benefit relative to cost of sacrifice, who receives the benefit)*?

7. Where in your life, specifically, do you make or have you made inappropriate sacrifices of your resources *(played the martyr)*? *(This may include sacrifice of time, personal energy, money; sacrifice for spouse, children, friend, job, religious or other group, community at large.)* What specific evidence do you have that these sacrifices are or were inappropriate? *(List specific events.)*

8. How many of these sacrifices that you make are requested by those you make them for? How many do you volunteer without being asked? Are all of these sacrifices welcome to the recipient?

9. Where in your life, specifically, do you demand or have you demanded inappropriate sacrifices from others *(sacrifice of time, personal energy, money; from spouse, children, friends, employer/employee; religious or social group, community resources)*? How, specifically, do you know that such demands are or were inappropriate?

10. Do you give others the opportunity to refuse such unsuitable demands? What kinds of pressure *(emotional, moral, monetary)* do you bring to bear to get such sacrifices from others?

11. What specific actions or situation in your life do you accept appropriate responsibility for, and where do you try to pass such responsibility to others? *(Hint: where do you say of your own actions, "It's not my fault.")*

12. Where in your life, specifically, do you take inappropriate responsibility, or try to avoid appropriate responsibility, for the lives of others? How, specifically, do you know which are appropriate and inappropriate?

A Healing Process for the Father's Moon

Make a sacrifice of your time and energy for the benefit of the Earth, directly or through one of Her children. You might consider picking up all the trash along a stretch of road, or your block, or even your own yard. Perhaps you have an elderly friend that needs a garden weeded, a lawn mowed, or help with landscaping. You can do these things alone or with a group, but whatever you choose, do it with the conscious intent that your efforts will help you to renew your sense of connection to the Mother.

Choose a task that engages your body. Even people in wheelchairs or with other physical disabilities can find suitable tasks. They can use a "grabber" to pick up trash on the ground, or, with help from others, plant seeds in pots that will grow into plants that can be used in landscaping. The important criteria are that you choose physical tasks, something that gets your hands dirty, and that you have a clear intent to act for a benefit beyond your personal needs.

Set a specific amount of time to do this task, preferably an amount of time that pushes you a little. The "pushing" can be the duration of the task, the physical difficulty that strains your body, or a commitment to repeat a specific task several times. Be wise. Don't press yourself to the degree that you damage your body or neglect other obligations. What you want is the sense, all the time you are doing your chosen task, that you are expending effort to reconnect to the Mother and to Her children. Physical effort translates into that connection more readily than other kinds of activities.

As you work, think about how the boundaries of time and your abilities affect what you are able to accomplish. Think about how you could stretch those boundaries. Think about how much you can accomplish within them.

If you chose a task you normally dislike doing, like weeding or picking up trash, notice how different the experience of willing sacrifice is from acting out of duty or obligation. Does the task become more fun? Do you feel an increased connection to the person or cause you are serving? To the Mother? Do you feel a sense of accomplishment, even a mild exhilaration, when you finish?

What happens to us is less important than what we tell ourselves about what it means. If we tell ourselves that what we are doing is dreary and unpleasant, it becomes so, even for tasks that are supposed to be fun. On the other hand, if we can find something good about what happens to us, no matter how difficult, we tend to handle it better.

We may not be able to control everything that happens to us or what other people in our lives do, but we can control how we let events affect us. The words we use to represent our experience are among the most restrictive of all the limits we impose on ourselves. When we learn to use different words, words that find the growth potential in the event, we can transform our experiences for the better. We can give ourselves the benefits of fatherlove.

Nesting Moon

Mirror, Waxing Half of the Year: Fasting Moon.
Stage: Testing (Challenge).
Range of Dates: The Nesting Moon may begin as early as July 31 and as late as August 29. It ends as early as August 29 and as late as September 27. Total range of dates over which the Nesting Moon may occur is from July 31 to September 27.

Lammas falls in the Nesting Moon three times in a nineteen-year cycle, each time in a year before a Courting Moon. Mabon, the autumn equinox, also falls in the Nesting Moon three times during that cycle, each time in a year with a Courting Moon.

Mood of the Mother

Shorter days stimulate changes in living things. All plants that have not yet produced fruit or seed rush to complete their cycles in a last flurry of activity before the cold. Plants begin to set seeds or cache minerals and sugar in their roots, preparing to jumpstart new plants the following spring. Fruits and nuts ripen, preparing to embark another generation toward its place in the sun.

Bees busy themselves filling honeycombs. Birds form flocks and fitfully begin their long journeys to the south. Ants scurry to accumulate underground stores. Squirrels and other rodents begin to bury acorns and other durable foods. Animals eat heartily while food is still plentiful. The layers of fat they build now will make the difference between life and death in the cold reaches of the year.

The Mother's children prudently use the last warm days in autumn to prepare for winter. Humans repair their dwellings, checking roofs and stopping up chinks in the walls. Green wood is cut and stacked to season for winter fires. New baskets and other containers are completed to hold the food still to be harvested. Medicinal herbs and roots are gathered and dried to remedy winter illnesses. Animal shelters and pens are constructed or repaired. Tall grasses that ripen in the late summer heat are cut and stacked for winter fodder.

The first signs of fall appear in cooler mornings and occasional thundershowers that prefigure the changing weather patterns that will bring autumn rains. Some vegetation that died back in the heat of deep summer greens a little and resuscitates in a pale imitation of spring's abandon. Crisp mornings bring a special autumnal scent to the air.

The landscape adds gold and purple and the bright oranges and reds of fall flowers and fruits to spring's green and white palette. The leaves on some trees begin to lose chlorophyll and show their true colors of red, brown, or yellow. The final harvest of the year is nearly upon us. The Mother whispers, "Make your nest soft and warm. Spring is a long way off."

Images and Reflections

Haystacks and newly thatched roofs. Butterfly cocoons and neatly wrapped spider eggcases. A shelf of fresh-canned fruit and vegetables in mason jars. The smell of jelly boiling. A root cellar stacked with garden produce. The rich smell of a silo heaped with new straw and fresh grain. A lean-to filled with cords of wood. Putting up storm windows and airing winter bedding in the sun. The smell of mothballs and new school clothes. The first crisp morning that requires a sweater, followed by a hot afternoon.

Insurance policies and retirement plans. "Winterizing" a home or car. Fallout shelters and emergency supplies. A warrior girding for battle. Leading a good life to store up good karma. Valkyries choosing heroes to live in Valhalla until it is time to fight at Ragnorak.

Related Energies

Fasting Moon: wise use of resources

Harvest Moon: gathering resources

Feasts
    Lammas: first harvest
    Mabon: second harvest

Zodiacal signs
    Leo: self-interest
    Virgo: methodical, practical

Planets
    Sun: lifeforce
    Mercury: planning

Tarot cards
> The Emperor: worldly success, order
> The Devil: limitations and boundaries,
>   especially those caused by self-bondage
> Fours: order, manifesting in the material world

Primary Energies of the Nesting Moon

Preparation/Unreadiness for trial

Wise/Unwise use of resources

Focus on now/The future

Protection/Vulnerability

Concern for others (guardianship)/Self-centeredness

Manifesting Nesting Moon Energies

The balanced energies of the Nesting Moon celebrate joy in present riches and the wisdom of husbanding those riches against tomorrow's lacks. We are reminded that life is not perpetual summer, that every interval in the Sun is followed by a period of trial, where we must validate our individual rights to survive again and again.

Our present culture isolates most of us, somewhat, from gross fears for our physical survival, but we face many other kinds of threats to our survival, both material and spiritual. We may at any time lose a job, be disabled by accident or age, change our family status in death or divorce, or undergo any of a myriad events that could impair or destroy our "normal" means of making a living. We are bombarded by advertising, by political and social propaganda, and by calls to particular spiritual paths. We must judge among these many choices for where to spend our money or our personal energies, and where to lend our support both for personal benefit and for the common good.

The specific circumstances of our modern challenges may be different than those our ancestors faced, but we have not escaped the need for trial. Humans survive only when they are prepared, physically and emotionally, to weather whatever changes and chances may befall them. We grow and we learn by surviving trials, which in turn prepares us to face still greater trials further down the road. The purpose of the journey is the journeying, and tests are always part of the trip. How wisely we prepare determines the comfort of our travel, and, to some degree, where we may go.

Prudence is the watchword of the Nesting Moon. Now, while we have resources, let us become strong. Save money and other resources against emergencies. Exercise our bodies and eat the right foods before the stresses of work and age threaten our lives and mobility. Join with others who can help when trials overtake us. Prepare our minds to outlive disaster if it comes. Most of all, prepare without overspending our energy in preparation, and without forgetting to enjoy the pleasures of today.

On another level, the energies of the Nesting Moon are expressed in our commitment, as individuals or as a society, to protect children, the elderly and the sick, and all others who are vulnerable to damage and destruction. These energies are reflected in the existence of police and fire departments and in programs for disaster relief and vocational rehabilitation of injured workers. They manifest also in our personal actions to protect those in our care and to provide for their continued physical and emotional sustenance.

The lessons of the Nesting Moon are both somber and hopeful. We will be tried, but we can find the means to meet our trials and to overcome them. This moon suggests that our preparation needs to be both personal and communal, for some tests are beyond the capacity of any individual to handle alone. In the balanced energies of this moon, we accept this need to prepare ourselves—physically, emotionally, spiritually; personally and as a community—without fear or undue distraction from the daily business of our lives. As we integrate a deep understanding that we can, at need, find the means to meet whatever comes, we are able to turn our attention to the pleasures and labors of today.

Meeting Nesting Moon Challenges

How to feel safe in the world is the primary focus of Nesting Moon energies. Almost all the challenges of this moon are connected to making mistakes about where safety lies. We may accumulate material resources or goods in the belief that security is based on having "enough." We may retreat to the home as castle and fortify ourselves in the bosoms of our families and friends, letting the rest of the world go by. We may decide that security is having strong principles to guide our every action, and then, once we have selected these standards, we may refuse to adapt those principles to changing circumstances.

As a society, we put a lot of energy into the components that traditionally make security. We value steady employment. We tend to punish those who fail to meet that standard, and make procuring public welfare a humiliating experience. Major portions of our national economy are based on "defense" industries. Many recent social and political trends in our country derive from the failure of old strategies that sought to build national security on a mostly military and industrial economy and to represent our nation to others as the "biggest, baddest" country in the world.

True safety is, paradoxically, founded on the recognition that there is no such thing as perfect safety. None of us—no matter how healthy, wealthy, or wise—are exempt from sudden disaster. There is nothing any of us own that cannot be ripped away from us tomorrow. We have only our character and our education, which cannot be taken from us while we are of sound mind. All physical security, and the emotional security that is based in it, must begin with this one fact.

We can build a strong point for handling change from accepting that we may at any moment lose our goods, all that we hold dear, even our lives or health, and from deciding that, if such things should happen, we will not give up. When we are mentally prepared for loss, if and when it comes, we need not waste energy on mourning what cannot be recovered, but can break free to find a way to survive and recover from our trial.

Preparation for trial is an essential component of successfully passing tests. We must recognize the probability of trial before we can prudently prepare to survive it. The Nesting Moon teaches us to save money against job losses or financial disaster, to seek education against the need to change jobs, and to cultivate friends to help us when we need emotional support. It also teaches us to recognize that we cannot anticipate all possibilities, so we should also exploit the joys and pleasures of the present. The memories of such present joys can themselves provide a store of strength to motivate us to endure when times are tough.

Above all, we must, consciously and specifically, decide that we will find a way to meet our lives' challenges. The key to true safety in the world is our renewed and repeated determination to survive, somehow, and also our willingness to abandon whatever will not support that determination. Such determination cannot be taken from us.

If You were Born in the Nesting Moon

People born under the Nesting Moon are ideal choices to be in charge of mounting a complex operation. People balanced in this moon's energies have a special talent for discriminating between what is essential and what is not, and for keeping to a plan based on their understanding. They keep their heads in a crisis, and, if they choose to stand at your back, you can ask for no better protector. People born under this moon also have well-honed instincts for how to be comfortable and how to make those around them comfortable. The greatest weakness of people born under this moon may be a tendency to get caught up in the process of making a nest, and to emphasize owning things rather than creating results.

You who are born under a Nesting Moon may have a hard time finding a place where you feel secure. You are probably a practical person who works hard and seeks earnestly for the means to give yourself and your family a fortress of well-being. The most obvious distraction you may stumble over is the matter of acquiring possessions. If you have a house so full of things that you can hardly move around, if you are a survivalist who bases security in owning stores of guns and freeze-dried foods, or if you spend most of your energies on accumulating economic tokens (money and other material resources), you may need to consider whether you own your property or it owns you. The Eastern concept of being bound to the wheel of life is an apt image for the encumbrance of too many possessions.

Surprisingly, some forms of asceticism are another paradigm for this same acquisitiveness. Instead of racking up material goods, you may try to accumulate spiritual stores, the kind not subject to moths and rust. You may feel that your security is based on not letting material possessions or needs gain a hold on you. In this permutation, the pattern is the same; only the tokens change. In some ways, the tyranny of possessions is greatest for those of us who strive hardest to avoid possessing.

If you feel burdened by either what you own or by your stringent disregard for material possessions, take a step back and consider what you can divest yourself of. You know you have a problem with material things if installment debts consume your paycheck, if you have to move furniture and boxes when you want something you haven't used for a while, or if you can't find things you need among the clutter. Look at every item you own and decide whether its usefulness is greater than the cost of storing it. This weeding of unnecessary possessions can be painful, but we also gain a blessed freedom when we manage to do it.

Weeding spiritual "possessions" is a little harder to delineate, but well worth trying for. By spiritual possessions I mean your principles and values, the guidelines you use to make decisions for yourself and your family. The danger signs are fairly clear. Do you often decide on an action solely for the sake of principle, when the action itself does not benefit anyone? Do you play "holier than thou" and take pride in how detached you are from material needs? Do you believe that enjoying the material or physical is shameful? Any of these suggest an unhealthy aversion to the material side of human experience. The "weeding" procedure for non-functional standards is the same as for unneeded material possessions. Ask yourself what advantage, or harm, each of your standards bring to you or others.

If you find that your "spiritual" closet can do with some cleaning, be sure to exercise the prudence that is your birthright. Don't just throw out your principles, like "the baby with the bathwater." Modify your guidelines where it seems appropriate. Make the modifications small and test each change before you commit to it. Probably the standards that are causing you trouble are perfectly good in themselves, but you may need to apply them differently. Moderation is an important aspect of prudence.

You who are born under this moon may benefit from consciously recognizing that your central concern is likely to be security. Whether owning things or accumulating spiritual merit is your preferred style, consider applying a crucial question, "Does owning this or believing this make me more secure in my life?"

Your answers may surprise you. You may find yourself making wiser and more useful decisions about both material possessions and spiritual standards. With each wise decision, your real personal security increases. Ultimately, our safety is not founded on what we possess or on the correctness of our belief systems, but on our own characters and inner resources.

☾ Self-Discovery Journal: Nesting Moon Issues

1. What, specifically, do you desire to make yourself feel safe in the world? What, specifically, do you need to feel safe in the world *(money, goods, family, friends, home, skills, job, knowledge, faith, police, armed forces, social programs)*? How do you know the difference?

2. How, specifically, do the things you have identified actually make you safe? What conclusions do you draw from the differences between what you need and what you desire to make yourself feel safe?

3. Intelligent preparation for disaster is a matter of playing the odds. For example, nothing you can do will make your house safe from a tornado, but good safety practices can reduce the likelihood of fire, and smoke alarms can increase the likelihood that your family will get out in time to save their lives if a fire occurs. What specific preparations have you made for disasters and other crises *(accident, natural disaster, personal loss)* in your life *(money, firearms, stored food, relationships, safe practices for car and home, skills, education of children and self, specific plans of action, insurance and retirement programs, spiritual support)*?

4. How, specifically, will each of these preparations help you and your family to survive or to recover in the event of disaster? Are there additional preparations you can reasonably make to increase your odds for survival and speedy recovery?

5. Who, specifically, can you turn to for help when you need it *(in physical, economic, emotional, spiritual crisis; from family, friends, co-workers, religious group, social agencies)*? What,

specifically, can you do to increase your network of resources for such help?

6. Who, specifically, are you willing to help in a crisis *(family, friends, co-workers, religious group members, ethnic group, strangers, the community)*?

7. What specific kinds of help can you give *(money, goods, equipment, skills, time, personal energy)*? What specific kinds of help are you willing to give? What limits do you place on your help *(of first aid, your labor or skills, transport, loans or gifts of money or goods, emotional support, knowledge)*?

8. What specific kinds of crises do you believe you can survive and recover from *(physical injury or illness, loss of material goods or job, loss of family or friends, natural disaster or war)*? How does the possible severity of the crisis change your evaluation of your ability to survive and recover from it?

9. Are there any kinds of trials *(physical, emotional, spiritual)* that you believe you cannot survive and recover from? Why, specifically?

10. What, specifically, would it take for you to be able to survive and recover from such trials? Can you acquire or should you try to acquire the means that you might need?

11. How does your evaluation of your ability to survive and recover from a particular trial affect your likelihood of survival and recovery?

A Healing Process for the Nesting Moon

Our bodies have resources and ways of perceiving that we normally do not fully utilize. Select a site, indoors or out, where you can experiment in moving around with one or more of your senses blocked. Choose a place in which you feel reasonably safe, but which represents a potential for getting into difficulty. A natural place is preferable to a room in someone's home, because you are less likely to know it intimately, and because it offers more evidence to your senses than most indoor locations.

Ask a friend to observe you in this exercise and to help you if you get in trouble. Ask the friend not to intervene unless you are in danger of serious injury, and agree on what that phrase means. If you feel confident enough to do it by yourself, ask someone to check on you at specific time intervals. Do not do this exercise without some oversight.

Begin by covering your eyes. Block out all light if possible. Stand in the middle of the area and rotate your body until you are no longer certain of your orientation. Use your hands and feet, and, if you desire, a stick, to explore the space. Focus on the clues you use to know where it is safe to go. In addition to touch, do you use smell or hearing to explore? Experiment with singing or other sounds and how they echo off what surrounds you. Are there sounds in the environment that give you clues to where obstacles are located? Can you feel changing air currents on your skin?

After you have explored with only sight blocked, block your ears and continue your exploration. How does your experience differ? Are you more disoriented, more hesitant to move? Strive to capture the sense of self that exists beyond your physical senses. Do you have senses you had not noticed before, as a recognition of the location of a large mass before you touch it, or the ability to recognize light and dark on the skin of your face?

If the site permits, wear as little clothing as possible and go barefoot. As you explore your ability to navigate safely without the information you ordinarily use, add shoes, gloves, and other clothing to feel how your experience differs. Consider trying the exercise with nose plugs in addition to eye and ear blocks. Experiment with not using one or both of your hands. Focus on the information that remains as you obstruct your normal sources of information for moving safely in your environment.

As you explore, you will find that you are more able to handle yourself safely than you expected. You may wish to continue adding levels of sense deprivation until you exceed your personal safety limits, just to discover how able you are. The key component of your safety is not the body you wear or the environment in which you live, but the intelligence and heart that are at your center. The essential you is beyond the body, beyond education or job or friends, beyond anything that can be taken from you.

16

Harvest Moon

Mirror, Waxing Half of the Year: Seed Moon.
Stage: Maturation.
Range of Dates: The Harvest Moon may begin as early as August 29 and as late as September 27. It ends as early as September 27 and as late as October 27. Total range of dates over which the Harvest Moon may occur is from August 29 to October 27.

Mabon, the autumn equinox and celebration of the second harvest, falls in the Harvest Moon sixteen years of the nineteen-year cycle. In the old calendar, Mabon is the midpoint of autumn.

Mood of the Mother

Cold nights and shorter days signal that the year is winding down. Perennial plants commit their resources to their roots. Autumn temperatures push procrastinating fruits and other seeds into final ripeness. Deciduous trees, preparing for winter dormancy, withdraw circulation from leaves and outer branches. Chloroplasts, which color the leaves green, die, and the unmasked true colors of red and orange, brown and yellow, give us a brief autumn glory, a farewell to the growing season.

Animals marshall for the coming winter. Some grow denser fur and thick layers of fat, both insulation for cold and stored calories against the lean times of the coming season. Many species, especially birds, migrate to warmer climes. Others, fat with the final bounty of the year, grow torpid, and begin to settle into a drowsing, fitful hibernation until the world awakens again. Some animals, their bodies at the peak of fitness and vitality, mate to beget the early births of spring. The biological clock of the year announces a slowing. It is time for the Mother and Her children to think of rest. The Mother drowses, heavy with child, awaiting Her time to deliver a new Sun/Son and a new year.

The second harvest, fruits of tree and vine, has arrived. As though to compensate for shortening days, the full Moon rises near sunset, extending the day for busy humans who labor to complete their gathering before deeper cold sets in. Its golden, blessed light seems an extra bounty of the Mother. Humans reap what they and the Mother have sowed, accepting with joy Her gifts for their winter sustenance.

The Sun reaches Mabon, the autumnal equinox, the perfect balance between the powers of the Mother and the Father, an appropriate time to celebrate the production that arose from their union in spring. From now until the spring equinox, night shall have dominion over day. What is not reaped before frost, and put by safely, will spoil in the fields. Those who have not prepared may perish. Within the joy of harvest celebrations lies a somber undertone; the easy times are over until spring.

Images and Reflections

Grapevines heavy with ripe fruit. A field of orange pumpkins vining among shocks of golden grain. A honeycomb dripping gold. Trees heavy with ripe apples or pears. A threshing or husking bee for wheat, corn, or beans. A wine festival.

The crunch of dry leaves under foot. The crisp smell of an autumn morning. "October's bright blue weather." Octoberfest. The scent of woodfires and burning leaves. The silence of birds and insects. Shrill sunshine on red leaves. The nubby feel of a wool sweater. The diamond glint of dew on grass through the thin sunlight of a brisk morning. The silver dust of early frost on plants that have not yet turned brown.

The rosy glory of a sunset and the magic light of dusk. The "golden" years of humans. Grandchildren. The bittersweet memories of youth and foolishness. The comforts of a warm fire, good friends, and a full belly. The joyous fulfillment of one's labors. The wisdom and sorrow of experience. Herne the Hunter. The Wild Hunt.

Related Energies

Seed Moon: commitment to action

Death Moon: endings

Sorting Moon: discrimination

Festivals
 Mabon: second harvest
 Samhain: third harvest

Zodiacal signs
 Virgo: service to the community
 Libra: sharing, justice

Planets
>   Mercury: thought, legal matters
>   Venus: cooperation

Tarot cards
>   Justice: karmic justice
>   Nines: completion
>   Queens: releasing

Primary Energies of the Harvest Moon

Gathering/Releasing

Endings/Beginnings

Responsibility/Irresponsibility for actions

Fulfillment/Incompletion

Manifesting Harvest Moon Energies

The Bible says, "Whatsoever a man soweth, that shall he also reap." The Harvest Moon brings us up against the truth that we get what we earn. The easiest way to express the mood of this moon is to contrast it with its mirror, the Seed Moon. In the spring of our lives, we anticipate and dream, looking forward. We planned to work hard, to do great things, and to bring in a fine harvest.

In the autumn of our lives, we look backward, and evaluate what we actually achieved. Weather and the other vagaries of nature had their part, as always, but the harvest we have reaped also reflects our actions, and our failures to act. We cannot go back and repair the damages from weeds we did not pull or from birds and other creatures we did not chase from our fields. What we have is what we get, the often bitter recognition expressed in The Rubyiat of Omar Khayyam:

The Moving Finger writes; and, having writ,
Moves on: nor all your Piety nor Wit
Shall lure it back to cancel half a line,
Nor all your Tears wash out a Word of it.

The balanced energies of the Harvest Moon teach us to embrace the harvests we have sown and grown, both to enjoy the fruits of our labors, whatever they may be, and to accept responsibility for any shortfall in our production. We come to terms, not only with what we have achieved, but with what might have been and was not. When in balance, we neither feel guilty for what we have nor blame others for what we do not have. The Harvest Moon is the recognition of reality, an acceptance of what is, sweet or bitter, and the recognition that when we move on from here, we will do so only with what we have in hand.

Our personal riches or poverty, material or spiritual, are not caused by the riches or poverty of others. They are directly related to the choices we have made in life. If we are reluctant to enjoy what we have earned because others have less, our reluctance does not thereby improve the lot of those others, not even if we were able to give them all that we have. Harvests not earned rot the heart, as surely as harvests not taken timely rot in the ground.

When we mourn the harvests we might have brought in, but did not because of the choices we made, we neither improve our present circumstances nor affect the status of others. Harvests not earned because we failed to sow, or failed to cultivate what we sowed, do not exist, and have no place in the realities of our lives or any others.

In the same fashion, when we envy others who have what we desire, we do not thereby gain what we desire. What others own has nothing to do with us. We must earn our own way, and learn to make the most of our own resources. Energy wasted in envy would be better used to work toward some new harvest.

As we evaluate our lives and individual actions, the Harvest Moon counsels us to focus on the harvest we have at hand, rather than on what did not grow in our fields. The reason for any deficiency is now immaterial. The reality is that we have only what is available. What we did not achieve brings its own harvest, if we will but own it. Sometimes, when we choose to reap the knowledge from our failures, that harvest of experience may turn out to be more valuable than all our previous successes.

Meeting Harvest Moon's Challenges

The challenges of the Harvest Moon revolve around timing—when to take a harvest, and ownership—taking the benefit of our own or other's harvests. Harvesting late fall crops always has a timing component. If you wait too long to pick the tomatoes, frost will kill them and you get no use of them; however, every day they ripen on the vine improves their quality. In our own affairs, we must let relationships and business deals "ripen" to the most favorable point before we take decisive action, yet waiting too long is likely to sour the deal.

The other issue—who rightfully owns a harvest—relates especially to taking credit for work. Many of us, especially women, are taught to refuse the rightful fruit of our labors. We work hard to produce something, and it is successful; then we say "It is nothing." Even worse, we give the credit to someone else who reaps the benefit without deserving it.

On the other side of the coin, we see people who steal credit (claim the harvest) for the work of others. Managers who fail to acknowledge the contribution of the workers who implemented their plans are an example. Another is people who expect to be taken care of without having to give anything in return. The enablers who allow themselves to be exploited by such parasites are the mated half of this imbalance.

The best approach to handling timing difficulties is to become more aware of our own unconscious processes. (See the chapter on the Seed Moon.) If we tend to make mistakes by acting too soon, we need to pay attention when we begin to feel uncomfortable about an unresolved situation. When we recognize that discomfort, we can step back and consciously identify why the situation must, or must not, be resolved "right now." Giving an ultimatum to a lover or business partner forces the other person to make a commitment. Wisdom says that if the other were ready to make a commitment, he or she would have done so, and that forcing it will likely assure that we reap either an undesired ending or an improper commitment, one not thought completely through. An "unripe" commitment is likely to produce a harvest of pain, and, in the end, of loss.

When we put off making necessary decisions, we are usually afraid to act for fear of irreparable loss. We need to consider it a danger sign if we find ourselves enduring inner pain with the hope that, if we last long enough, the pain will go away and everything will be all right. Without some clear evidence that our patience will be rewarded, we risk living in a painful and unsatisfactory situation for a prolonged period, and then reaping only the pain, with little benefit. We reap the pain we sow, which may very well be greater than the pain of the loss we fear.

Justice is the sword that helps us make appropriate decisions on both timing and claiming harvests. Justice says we should get what we pay for. The wisdom of the Harvest Moon says to be careful what we pay for. A central issue of the Harvest Moon revolves around our internalizing both an acceptance of our own rights to life and happiness, and a companion recognition that the only way to get life and happiness is to earn them.

Justice is a difficult virtue to apply, and often the only way to apply it is to strip all the issues down to (a) what we actually have, (b) what we really want, and (c) what we can practically do. For example, if we are in a relationship that causes us pain, the first question is whether its benefits exceed its costs. The net benefit or loss is what we have. The second question is, what outcome do we desire? How we represent our desire has an effect. Saying we want a better relationship, or saying we want to feel less pain, makes a difference in what we decide to do.

Finally, determining what we actually can do clears our minds of all the distractions and feelings that get in the way of our acting. In this example, we have only two choices: terminate the relationship or change our behavior. Generally speaking, changing our own actions is the only way we can cause a change in someone else's behavior. Justice tells us that truth, also. When we take the map of where we are, define the location we want to get to, and assess the means we have to get there, our appropriate choices usually clarify and we are freed to act for our own best interests.

The process of applying Justice to determine when and how to act takes some practice. The hardest part is stripping off all the non-essential material that confuses us. Once we know what to do, our actions determine our harvest. We will get our just harvest, whether we choose to act or to dither. Justice, who will not be silent, patiently repeats Her truth: we get what we earn, whether we like it or not. The good news is that the choices are ours. We can harvest whatever we desire, so long as we have the means to make it, the will to earn it, and the courage to act.

If You were Born in the Harvest Moon

The great strength of people born under the Harvest Moon is likely to be their ability and willingness to "sow and grow." They often take responsibility for initiating projects with easy courage, and cultivate those projects efficiently and with appropriate input of resources. Those balanced in this moon's energies have a keen sense of justice, and an unusual ability to consider all sides and contingencies. The greatest weakness of those born under this moon may be a tendency to have problems bringing projects and relationships to a productive closure.

The question of responsibility is key to many people born under a Harvest Moon. This issue surfaces when we take an unwarranted burden of responsibility for others, when we refuse to take reasonable responsibility for others, and when we refuse to take reasonable responsibility for ourselves. Harvest Moon people tend to be either suckers for economic and emotional parasites or practiced and skillful parasites themselves. I use the word "parasite" here to mean a person who unjustly uses another's resources, or "harvest," in preference to developing resources of his or her own. The injustice derives not from the use of another's resources, but from an unwillingness to give fair return for the resources used.

Some parasites are easy to spot. There is the emotional "bottomless well" who, no matter how much love and support we give, always needs more. There is the person who frequently borrows money or other things from us, and is both careless about returning the loans and reluctant to reciprocate, or the person who hits on us to babysit or do essential errands, but never has time to help us. Dealing with such people is mostly a matter of reminding ourselves that we have no responsibility for them, and learning to tell them "no."

There are other parasitic relationships that are more subtle and more difficult. Consider the employer who allows an employee to take responsibility for important work but does not give the credit or compensation that should go with it. How about the spouse who lets us do more than our share of housework and parenting, the sibling who lets us take full responsibility as caretaker for mom and dad, or the group leader who won't act unless we make the decision, and then takes credit for the group success or blames us for its failure?

These are examples where we do have natural responsibility, and where our actions make a difference in the outcome of something we care about. We can't just opt out of the situation and let the people who are unjustly trying to profit from our efforts hang.

Our society often fails to support justice in such situations. We are told that we should be content with our moral superiority in these situations and are advised not to make an uncomfortable fuss about who should get credit for what. In some situations, as when an employer exploits workers, demanding our just return may even be dangerous. There are no easy answers for this kind of parasitism.

Begin by recognizing that when we fail to claim our just harvests, we harvest injustice instead. We have a right to consciously make such a choice, but not to complain of it afterwards when we have chosen that path. The Harvest Moon teaches that we get what we earn, including bad treatment.

Another possible tactic is to scale back our efforts to the level for which we do receive a just return. The secretary can refuse to cover for the boss, the child can give only his or her fair share of time and money to parents, the group can fail for lack of leadership. Here the Harvest Moon says that we must all bear the consequences of our actions. If the people from whom we withdraw our uncompensated support fail, that failure is their consequence. However, we may also suffer unwanted consequences by losing a job, having parents go without necessities, or losing a social connection that we value.

Each situation has its own cost/benefit ratio. Perhaps the job in which we are exploited offers opportunities for advancement. Perhaps we care more about meeting our parents' needs than getting a fair share of help from siblings. The important criteria are that we knowingly choose to do more than our share because we wish to, not because we must, and that we accept the consequences of our choices, including any unfairness.

Probably the most successful strategy for dealing with others who exploit us is to loudly claim the credit or value due us and to openly ask for our just return. Surprisingly, many people, when an injustice is brought to their attention, will correct it. We are all a little lazy about doing our fair share when others will pick up the burden for us. People born under the Harvest Moon have a tendency to pick up loads for which no one asked them to take responsibility. Unless we offer to those who are slacking the opportunity to make amends, we are also treating them unjustly, depriving them of their opportunities to learn and to gain the benefits from their own efforts.

This brings us full circle to the people born under this moon who tend to engage in parasitic behavior. These people also reap the harvests of their inaction, whether in not learning necessary living skills that they will need when their hosts abandon them, or in not experiencing the joys of earned harvests.

We Harvest Moon people live cheek-by-jowl with Justice and her sharp sword. We cannot escape her. We may try to beat the system now, and then pay later. We may try to take over the system, and then pay in bitterness when our contributions are not valued and recognized. If we would live happily with Justice, we must recognize the beauty of her directive, that we get what we earn, and change our course to earning what we want.

☾ Self-Discovery Journal: Harvest Moon Energies

1. What specific harvests, good or bad, are you presently reaping in your life *(in regard to health, relationships, skills, knowledge, job, social, or ethical benefits or costs)*? How, specifically, do you feel you earned, or did not earn, those harvests?

2. Where in your life, specifically, do you hold "overripe" harvests that you should consider abandoning as unusable *(clothes, furnishings, other possessions, relationships, economic enterprises or job, ideas, or ethical standards)*? How, specifically, do you know they are "overripe" or unusable?

3. Where in your life, specifically, have you failed to claim harvests justly due you *(harvests of money, loss, love, hate, respect, disrespect, credit, discredit, understanding, or knowledge)*? Why, specifically, did you fail to claim the harvests that were an advantage to you *(fear, self-effacement, inattention, love of another)*? What have been the consequences of your failure to claim them? *(Try to list specific events.)* What did you lose by not claiming the harvests that you felt would be a disadvantage to you?

4. What, specifically, have you sown for future harvests *(health, material goods, marriage and children, other relationships, education, economic enterprises, creative or intellectual projects, service to the community)*?

5. How, specifically, are you shaping (cultivating), or failing to shape, your expected future harvests *(with money, work, love, attention or energy, thought, education)*?

6. Where in your life, specifically, do you build on the harvests of others *(harvests that result from ancestors' genes; economic, cultural, intellectual heritages; money, love, work, ideas of others)*? What benefits, specifically, do these others derive from your use of their work? Do you use any of these sources unjustly?

7. Where in your life, specifically, do you allow others to build on your harvests *(family, friends, co-workers, social or religious groups)*? What specific benefits do you derive from this sharing? Do any of these recipients unjustly exploit your efforts or resources?

8. How, specifically, do you determine what you deserve *(from self, family, friends, co-workers, society; in regard to your health, relationships, job, moral status, social benefits)*? What, specifically, do you do to deserve these things?

9. How, specifically, do you determine what others deserve from you *(economic or emotional support, material goods, trust, information, labor, allegiance; to family, friends, employer, co-workers, community or country)*? What, specifically, must they do to receive these things from you? Do your answers suggest any changes in your future actions?

A Healing Process for the Harvest Moon

Start a plant, either indoors in a pot or in a garden, with the express intent of gaining a harvest. The harvest may be flower or fruit, a savory herb for cooking, a pretty plant to cheer you, or even a seedling that can grow into a tree. If you have experience with plants, choose a plant that you have never grown before.

Before you begin, learn all that you can about the plant you have chosen. The public library, a knowledgeable friend, the staff of a nursery, or your local county extension device are all good sources for information. Does your plant propagate best from seed or cutting? What temperature range does it prefer? What kind of soil works best? What kind of soil do you have? Does the plant need full sunlight or shade? How much water?

How long does it take for the seeds to germinate? Do they germinate better in darkness? If you can use a cutting, how do you prepare it? Do you start it in water with plant food, in vermiculite, in soil, in a mixture of the two? How can you tell whether the cutting "takes"? Does the season in which you are doing this exercise have an effect on your success? Is the plant prey to any disease or parasite? How can you protect it from such harm?

What is the history of your plant? Where did it originate? How did it come to this country if it is not native? What varieties of it are available? Does it occur in the wild, or is it strictly domesticated? Is it edible, medicinal, or ornamental? Is it grown for color, scent, or other value? Why did you choose it?

Having harvested knowledge, put the knowledge to work as you start your plant. Find a good location for it, with appropriate amounts of light and correct temperature. Consider keeping a brief journal of your interaction with the plant, recording how often and how much you water it, whether you feed it, perhaps measuring its growth weekly. Develop sound methods for knowing when to water it and when and how to protect it from too much or too little water or heat and from any parasites or predators.

As the plant grows, notice not only how it thrives on your attentions, but how you come to feel about it. When it is time to harvest? If your plant is a culinary herb, does its flavor in your cooking make the food special? If you grew a flower, what pleasure does it give you? If your plant is ornamental, how does its beauty lift your heart? Is your harvest worth the effort?

We harvest things every day of our lives, mostly without much thought. What we give our conscious attention to tends to thrive and give us good returns. The harvests of neglect and inattention are always disappointing. Be aware of what you sow and grow, and give blessings for your good harvests.

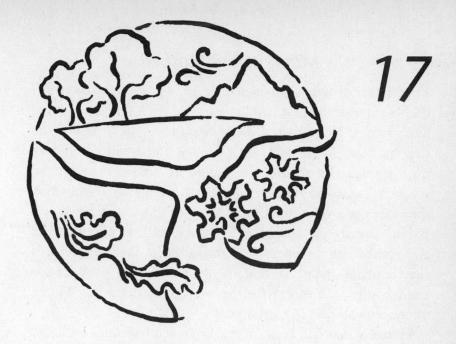

17

Sorting (Culling) Moon

Mirror, Waxing Half of the Year: Mating Moon.
Stage: Initiation.
Range of Dates: The Sorting Moon may begin as early as September 27 and as late as October 27. It ends as early as October 27 and as late as November 26. Total range of dates over which the Sorting Moon may occur is from September 27 to November 26.

Samhain, the traditional festival of the dead, occurs in this moon twelve years of the nineteen-year cycle. In the old calendar, Samhain was the third harvest, of animals, and the beginning of winter. We celebrate a version of this festival on Halloween.

Mood of the Mother

The Mother drowses, gravid and sleepy in this interval between the splendor of the first two harvests and the coming joy of the Sun's return. Her children, beginning to feel the cold and the decreased supply of food, grow uneasy. Some will not endure until spring. The sorting has begun, as predators catch the weak and unwary, plants die back into dormancy from which they may not awake, and death looms for those who are ill-prepared. Already the seeds that fell where plants cannot thrive, the bruised fruits that now rot, too soon to benefit the seeds they bear, and the plants that are diseased, or too small, or too shallowly rooted to survive the winter, are doomed. Winter, which tests all that lives, is upon us.

Humans also cull their stores. Damaged fruit and withered vegetables are set aside to eat almost immediately, for they will rot the sound food if they lie in the same container. The processes of preserving what can be kept in syrup or salt or by drying are now almost completed. The last harvest is come. There will be no more this year.

The third harvest, of animals, arrives. Livestock herds are thinned to a number small enough to crowd under available shelter during the worst of winter storms, and few enough to feed from the laid-in stores of hay and grain. Those culled from the herds are slaughtered, their carcasses hung in smokehouses or packed in salt for winter meals when hunting grows thin. The weather is cold enough now to process such meat without undue spoilage.

In households, the final provisions all stowed, other goods are sorted for winter work. The skins of butchered animals are tanned to provide materials for leatherwork. Fibers are gathered and combed to be spun into thread and woven into cloth by winter fires. Mending of clothes and other gear, which has gone begging during the busy autumn, is sorted into what may be repaired and what, past mending, needs to be salvaged for material and parts.

This is a comfortable time of year. Storerooms are full from recent harvests, and the bitter cold of deepest winter is still to come. Humans have time to sit by the fire and dream. Now, at the end of the year, they evaluate what went well, and what they will do differently when spring comes again. They think of those who have passed to the otherworld, and honor their lives. They welcome the thought of babies soon to be born from spring marriages.

Humans recognize that the culling that is part of the Mother's way will take its toll of them also. Some, too old or too young to endure the coming period of cold and the lack of fresh foods, will not see another spring. Lack of exercise and vitamins, and the poor hygiene of groups confined in close quarters, will breed illness and infection that may carry off others.

The veils between the worlds seem very thin. The cycle of all living things—birth, growth, and death—is stark and clear in the minds of humans. None escape that cycle; all are bound to the wheel. Now, as the year dies, humans feel their chains. When will the Tao call them? What will they have left undone? It is a time for self-evaluation.

Images and Reflections

The seed fallen on stony ground. A tree branch broken by the weight of ice after a winter storm. A Bush Hog clearing a right-of-way. An old buffalo, straggling behind the herd, pulled down by a pack of wolves. The clash of horns as two male deer contend for a harem of females and the right to reproduce. A rabbit that escapes safe into its hole from the snapping jaws of a coyote. A fish that refuses the lure.

Forks in a road. "The Road Not Taken" that "makes all the difference" (Robert Frost). The many choices in the labyrinth, with only one true path. The Norns, three old women who weave the thread of our lives and dwell beside Mimir's Well under the roots of Yggdrasil, the world tree. The three Fates—Clotho, who spins, Lachesis, who measures, and Atropos, who cuts the thread—weaving the web of human life in strands of light and shadow.

Related Energies

Mating Moon: choices

Nesting Moon: preparing for winter

Fasting Moon: wise use of resources

Festival of Samhain: sorting

Zodiacal signs
    Libra: balance
    Scorpio: preserving

Planets
    Venus: life and loving
    Pluto: death

Tarot cards
    Judgment: awakening for evaluation
    Eights: sorting for evaluation

Primary Energies of the Sorting Moon

Discrimination/Acceptance

Choice/Failure to choose

Analysis/Synthesis

Specialization/Generalization

Free Will/Fate

Order/Chaos

Manifesting Sorting Moon Energies

What we are at any moment is a cumulation of thousands of choices, good and bad, each with consequences that have moved us inexorably to our present state. Every act expresses a choice. We get out of bed in the morning because we choose to go to work rather than choose to suffer the consequences of staying at home. Even doing nothing is a choice. And every choice implies a hierarchy, one possibility we deem better than its alternatives. For weal or woe, we choose the branches that form our paths.

When we make our choices by default, without conscious consideration of what we do and why, our results vary. Because we make such choices unconsciously, we may or may not link our decisions to their consequences. We may fail to repeat our good choices, or may repeat the bad, because we did not trouble to learn from our mistakes. If we become confused and uncertain, because we do not understand the full meaning of our choices, we may act randomly, without thought, or we may become paralyzed by fear of making the wrong decisions. Unconscious choices make us slaves to external forces.

The balanced energies of the Sorting Moon are expressed by making choices easily and wisely. Choices come easily when we make our decisions consciously, and when we base them on clear parameters that we have developed from experience. We make such choices, accept their consequences, fair or foul, and go on. As we choose and learn, our choices become wiser. We discriminate between what works and what does not. We are able to extrapolate from the outcome of one choice to help us make similar choices later on.

The Sorting Moon is about decisions and how we make them, free will and how we use it. The process of decision is based on knowledge. We determine, over a lifetime, what helps and hurts us and other people, what works for us and what does not. We learn both from our own experience and that of others. As the hillbilly proverb says, "It's a wise man learns from experience, but it's a darn sight wiser man lets the snake bite the other fellow."

Despite the knowledge we acquire, every decision point in our lives is unique and complex. Our choice to get out of bed today and go to work is similar to a choice we have made thousands of times before. We hardly think about its parameters. However, today we are different than we were on any other day. Our responsibilities to others are a slightly different mix, and, as always, our free will gives us the opportunity to choose not to get up and go to work. The difference between a conscious recognition of free will and an unconscious choice is immense.

The wisdom of the Sorting Moon suggests that when we fail to notice that we have a choice, we tend to feel trapped, at the mercy of external forces beyond our control. We have no freedom, no dignity, just our bonds to the wheel of life. On the other hand, when we go to work because we actively decide to go, our freedom remains intact, and we have once again acknowledged our ability to act as we choose.

I often tell people that the reason my marriage is strong is that I seriously consider booting my husband out once or twice a week. By that consideration, I acknowledge my right and my ability to end a relationship that, as in all marriages, sometimes gives me pain. Because I recognize my freedom to choose, I am not trapped in a hopeless coil. Each time I reaffirm my free choice to stay partnered with this particular man, my bond to him grows stronger, for it is forged in conscious choice and not from necessity. In the words of William Ernest Henley, in *Invictus*:

> *It matters not how strait the gate*
> *How charged with punishments the scroll,*
> *I am the master of my fate;*
> *I am the captain of my soul.*

The Sorting Moon teaches us that we cannot live without making choices, even if our only choice is to avoid making conscious decisions. This moon also teaches us that, when we accept our own accountability for making choices, we also gain our freedom. We are never truly without recourse. We may not be able to choose all that happens to us, but we can always choose how we will respond. In taking charge of whatever choices are offered us at the decision points of our lives, we manifest our human birthright.

Meeting Sorting Moon Challenges

I believe that everything in the universe interconnects in a vast network, and that the action at any node in that net affects the whole network, like the ripples that spread out when we toss a stone into a pond. Even if you are unwilling to accept the full extent of my idea, your own experience shows you that you are interconnected with a local network of people, and that your actions affect, a little or a lot, many other people, some of whom you do not know personally. Almost all the challenges of the Sorting Moon are rooted in a failure to consider how our actions, or inactions, and the choices they reflect, affect our local networks and the overall shape of our personal lives.

When we procrastinate making a choice, or try to avoid taking responsibility for our choices, we severely restrict our personal ability to shape what happens around us. There are a broad range of styles for putting off decisions. Obviously, closing our eyes and hoping the boogerbear before us will go away is one form. Another less obvious strategy is to get so caught up in gathering and analyzing information that we never quite get to taking action. Making choices without discrimination or a specific direction is still another pattern of trying to avoid responsibility for our actions. The outcome is the same. We put ourselves at the mercy of circumstances.

Please note that there is a vast difference between consciously deciding that our best choice is not to act, and avoiding a choice that needs to be made. In the first case, we are in control of our actions and shape the consequences. In the second, we abrogate responsibility for controlling the course of our lives.

Our failure to take decisive action is a major cause of our frequent perception that we are at the mercy of fate, that our lives are constricted by other people's desires, by social or legal pressures, or by other external forces over which we have no control. Unless we take responsibility for trying to shape our lives in accordance with our desires and our values, we are indeed pawns of fate. When we stand up on our hind legs and try to tame the world to our specifications, we become magicians.

I define magicians as those who act from the idea that they have the power to shape the world. I do not mean that they have any absolute power, or that they are necessarily successful in all they do. The problem of the magician is twofold: to construct an achievable vision of what he or she desires, and to acquire the knowledge or skills to make that vision manifest in the real world. Both processes operate over a long term. We gradually, over time, develop increasingly accurate ideas of what can be done, as well as increasing levels of skill and knowledge to accomplish what we desire. Ideally, a magician's vision always exceeds his or her grasp by just enough to motivate further striving.

The most effective way to meet challenges associated with the Sorting Moon is to teach ourselves to become magicians. That mode of operation has risks, which are the natural companion of freedom to act, but, as in any business venture, the potential reward is proportional to the risks. As we learn to step forward and actively shape what happens in our lives, within the constraints of necessity, we become more skilled in matching our actual accomplishments to our visions. As we accept responsibility for our choices and their consequences, we exchange slavery for freedom.

If You were Born in the Sorting Moon

People born under a Sorting Moon are likely to have a special talent for analysis and evaluation. When they are balanced in this moon's energies, they are exceptional at making reasoned decisions that reflect a range of parameters and values. They tend to classify things, and one of their special joys is bringing order out of chaos. The special weakness of people born under this moon is their tendency to get so caught up in classifying all the factors that may affect a particular decision that they may lose sight of the need to make a decision.

The pitfalls for you who are born under the Sorting Moon are likely to be overanalysis and overgeneralization. The process of choice may be so important in your life that you become entangled in the mechanism and sidetracked from the primary product of making decisions, which is taking action. Depending on your personal style, you may dissect things into so many pieces that you lose the beauty of the whole, or find so many analogies between disparate data that you lose the peculiar delight of what is unique and special about the things you encounter. In either case, you may spend your energy on side issues instead of the main points, which are to make a good decision and act on it.

In paleontology, these two styles of dealing with data are called "lumpers" and "splitters." Paleontologists are like detectives. They use incomplete specimens and painstaking study to try to decipher the history of life. For their results to be useful, they need to incorporate both the differences and the coincidences between the remains of ancient animals and living species. Both lumpers and splitters tend to obscure the essential patterns that paleontologists need to make valid conclusions from their data.

Lumpers focus on similar structures and lump as much as they can into one pot. They set descriptive parameters so broadly that wildly disparate animals may be shoehorned into a common class. A lumper might, for example, catalog a bat with birds because both have wings, and overlook some of the profound ways in which bats and birds are different.

People born under a Sorting Moon who overgeneralize do the same kind of thing and for the same reason. They go for the easy surface analogies and do not take the time to look deeper, or to validate their early intuitions. When that happens, their choices may be based on too little data, and they may make mistakes. The counter to this tendency is to doublecheck any sweeping generalization you come up with. Ask whether the generalization is both valid and useful all the way down to the specific level of your proposed action.

Splitters, on the other hand, lovingly catalog every tiny detail. Any disparity among specimens may be a cause to set up a new species or genus. I heard of a case where a splitter classified the male and female of the same animal as separate species due to size differences and other sexual dimorphism.

People who overanalyze often feel that they cannot make a decision without knowing every detail. They split hairs and catalog distinctions that make no difference. They often fail to make timely decisions because they are still "studying all the angles." The counter to this practice is to set up decision criteria beforehand. That is, make a list of questions that have to be answered to make a proposed decision. Check frequently to see whether any particular information bears directly on what is to be done, and ruthlessly weed out any line of thought that addresses a side issue.

People born under a Sorting Moon are often brilliant at manipulating data, but this important talent works best if you learn to steer between the devil and the deep blue sea. When you squeak by the "devil" of overanalysis, your recommendations for decisions are often based on solid, well-researched analyses of appropriate data. When you avoid letting the "deep blue sea" of overgeneralization swallow you whole, you may come up with breathtaking intuitions that reveal useful inter-connections among data that everyone else has overlooked.

The way to escape the dangers of navigating around these two hazards is to concentrate on where you're headed, and stay in the middle of the channel. Steering too close to either peril can delay you from making landfall. Homing in on your end goal keeps you from becoming entangled in trivia or fluff. In this age of information explosion, your skills are greatly needed. People balanced in Sorting Moon energies are among the best for helping the rest of us know which data we need to pay attention to.

☾ Self-Discovery Journal: Sorting Moon Issues

1. Try to list all the choices you have made over the last three hours *(what you did or did not do, how you did it)*. How, specifically, did you make each decision *(conscious or unconscious, routine or considered, your desire or another's request)*? What are the consequences of each decision *(please yourself or another, something done or not done, short-term or long-term benefit or disadvantage)*?

2. Name three choices you have made in the last year that have improved your life *(relative to body, emotional or economic state, relationships, job, spiritual or ethical principles—don't limit yourself to formal choices, also consider choices that you can infer from a subsequent change in your life)*. How, specifically, did they shape where you are now? How, specifically, did you make those decisions?

3. Name three choices you have made in the last year that have made your life more difficult *(relative to body, emotional or economic state, relationships, job, spiritual or ethical principles; don't limit yourself to formal choices)*. How, specifically, did

they shape where you are now? How, specifically, did you make those decisions?

4. Name a choice you made, formally or by default, that you believe had more influence on where you are today than any other such choice in your life. What makes this choice so influential? Was it, in the long-term, helpful or detrimental? How, specifically, did it shape your life?

5. Name a choice made by another that you believe had more influence on where you are today than any other such choice in your life. Did you have input into the choice? Was it, in the long-term, helpful or detrimental? How, specifically, did it shape your life?

6. How would you characterize your usual style of making important decisions *(active or passive, impulsive or considered, fast or slow, on your own or with input from others, responsive to specific circumstances or based on principle)*? Consider specific evidence in your life that shows the effectiveness, or ineffectiveness, of your style. Do your answers suggest changes you can make to improve the choices you make?

7. What specific choice could you make right now that you believe would make your tomorrow better than today?

8. What specific choice could you make today that would bring you nearer to what you most desire *(materially, emotionally, spiritually)*?

9. Where in your life, specifically, are you a slave of circumstances and where are you free *(material, emotional, spiritual life; with self, home, family, friends, job)*? Do you desire to make changes based on your answer? If so, what choices do you need to make to accomplish such changes?

A Healing Process for the Sorting Moon

Keep a log of all the money you spend in a week or a month, or try to reconstruct the money you have spent in such a time period. If you are part of a family, try to include family expenditures as well as the money you personally spend. Keep your list as specific and detailed as you can. Keep grocery store receipts, for example, so you can differentiate between money spent for food and non-food items, and for staples and "treats." You can do this exercise with general information and estimated amounts, but it works better with a list of specific items.

Take your original, primary list and sort the items on it onto three new lists. Label your first secondary list, "essential," your second, "necessary," and your third, "non-essential." Begin with the "essential" list, and complete it before you go to the next list. While the amounts you spent for each item are useful data, they are not essential to this exercise. Write your lists in pencil to allow yourself to make changes as you go along.

As you put items on these three secondary lists, separate them into two subsections, things that apply to you personally, and things that apply to those who live with you. Use the additional second subsection for items that do not impact you personally, but are necessary for someone else, as, for example, diapers or baby formula.

On the first, "essential" list, put all the items that you must have for physical and economic survival. This list might include most of the food, prescription medications, house rent, transport expenses to go to work, basic clothing or equipment, essential cleaning supplies, and anything else you feel you cannot survive without.

On the second, "necessary" list, put those things that are necessary to your life, but whose lack is not life-threatening. This list might include some utility bills, food items like snack foods, clothing duplicates, over-the-counter medications, most toiletries, and anything else you consider necessary for living, but that you could, under emergency circumstances, do without.

On the third list, put all the remaining items that, however desirable, are not necessary to either your physical survival or to normally comfortable living. This list might include your cable TV subscription, junk food, clothing that was bought for style rather than protection, cosmetics, and jewelry.

Look at your three secondary lists and reconsider each item, beginning with the third list and ending with the first list. Does working from the other end cause you to change some items? Sort your lists again, on a fresh piece of paper, this time adding the parameter of what you need for emotional and spiritual survival. How does that make a difference?

Make your choices on how you feel, and not on what others might think. For example, some women consider cosmetics necessary to their mental health, and a bedridden person might need the stimulation of television. The important thing is to sort by your own ideas of what is necessary or not in your life.

How do the lists reflect your values? If you feel that they do not, what would you add to them to make them reflect what you consider important? What would you remove? Do the lists make a statement about the wisdom with which you spend your money? About the influences of our culture on your purchases? Influences of friends, family, co-workers?

This exercise will probably surprise you. Had you thought about how much of what you buy is necessary to live? Did the number of items on your third list startle you? How many items reflect a conscious choice? How many are things you just bought, without considering why you wanted or needed them? How would your life change if you could only have the items on the "essential" list? The "essential" and "necessary" lists?

When you complete your lists, consider adding to each one the other items that are normally part of your life but which you did not happen to purchase during the time period you are using. How do you sort between what goes on the first list and on the second list? Do you have a feel for what portion of your total resources go to items on the third list?

This exercise is also interesting if you log how you spend your time over a certain period. Whatever values we may claim to have, we always spend our available time and money on what we value the most. When you have trouble knowing your own heart's desire, this parameter will reveal it to you more readily than almost any other criterion.

Your primary logs, of what you buy or spend your time on, are raw data. They are a record of choices you actually made. The secondary lists reflect a lot about how and why you make the choices you do. With both lists, you have a map of what you think is important, what is in your secret inner heart, and a snapshot of how your choices shape your life.

18

Short Takes

The following are offered partly for fun, and partly to show the universality of the spiritual journey represented by the moons in this lunar calendar.

The Year as Business Plan

The Death Moon declares the present business plan is obsolete,
The Birth Moon has a new idea,
The Milk Moon develops the plan,
The Fasting Moon streamlines the plan,

The Seed Moon wants to play with the concept,

The Courting Moon wants to put the plan on hold,

The Mating Moon wants to integrate material from another source,

The Journey Moon wants to take an entirely different tack,

The Mother's Moon implements the plan,

The Father's Moon keeps it on schedule,

The Nesting Moon assures that resources are available,

The Harvest Moon completes the plan,

The Sorting Moon does the post mortem,

And the Death Moon says, this plan is complete, now let's go up a level and make a new plan. We can build something new on this success.

The Year as a Human Life

In the Death Moon, a soul decides to end its sojourn in the Summerland and to become carnate. A human child is conceived.

In the Birth Moon, the child is born.

In the Milk Moon, it is nurtured.

In the Fasting Moon, it begins to explore its environment, and to discover that it is not the center of the universe, that there are limits and boundaries to what it can achieve.

In the Seed Moon, this human reaches puberty.

In the Courting Moon, it explores the idea of human love.

In the Mating Moon, it is married.

In the Journey Moon, it discovers the new lessons and perspectives that accompany going from being single to being a family.

In the Mother's Moon, this human has children of its own.

In the Father's Moon, this human teaches its children how to get on in the world.

In the Nesting Moon, this human accumulates resources to launch its children into the world and to prepare for its own retirement from active life.

In the Harvest Moon, this human enjoys the fruits, both material and spiritual, of its life work, the "golden years" of wisdom and, often, prosperity.

In the Sorting Moon, this human, in the retrospect of old age, ponders the lessons of its life.

In the Death Moon, this human chooses to end this turn of life and returns to the Summerland.

The "Great Story" in a Year of Moons

In the Death Moon, the Goddess, gravid in late pregnancy, rests and mourns the death of Her lover.

In the Birth Moon, the Goddess gives birth to the Divine Child.

In the Milk Moon, the Goddess nurtures the young God.

In the Fasting Moon, the Goddess teaches the God His purpose, which is to sacrifice Himself in the vigor of His manhood for the good of Earth children, for, unlike the Goddess, who endures and renews Herself forever, it is the task of the God to be born, to grow old, and to die.

In the Seed Moon, the young God reaches puberty, and achieves the capacity to aid in producing the bounty needed for the lives of Earth children.

When there is a Courting Moon, the divine couple take time out to explore their growing love.

In the Mating Moon, they love each other as male and female, and engender the fertility of summer.

In the Journey Moon, the God and Goddess find new ways to express their love for each other in the infinite diversity of life.

In the Mother's Moon, they celebrate the bounty that comes from their union.

In the Father's Moon, the God accepts his responsibility to Earth children, to return His vitality to the Earth at the height of His powers, before the inevitable enervation of His aging body diminishes the power He has to give.

In the Nesting Moon, the God and Goddess prepare for His sacrifice, in love and sadness.

In the Harvest Moon, the God dies in a blaze of autumn glory, that the Earth and Earth children may not be diminished in the store of life.

In the Sorting Moon, the God travels the Great Spirit Road to the land of the dead, along with all others who have died in the past year. In this time, the Goddess and all Earth children cherish with her the memories of His gifts and His sacrifice, and of the lives of all Earth children who accompany Him.

In the Death Moon, the God ends His sojourn in the otherworld and incarnates once again in the womb of the Goddess,

. . . and the story continues, now and forever, world without end.

Moon Mirrors:
Similarities and Distinctions

When we look in a mirror, we see an image of ourselves that is accurate except that it is reversed from the way we look to others. The twelve moons that are the basic year of this calendar also mirror each other, forming six pairs. Each moon of a pair expresses the same essential energy as its partner, but with a twist or reversal relative to the other, like the reversal of our images in the mirror. If we discount the Courting Moon, which is outside this part of the system, the pairs occur six moons apart, one of each pair for the waxing and waning halves of the year.

239

The six pairs of moon mirrors also seem to me to describe a sequence of processes that delineate the fundamental course of human life. I have defined this sequence by these words: "beginning," "growth," "testing," "maturation," "initiation," and "cycle change." This pattern seems to me to be a pattern of human life as a whole, and of many events within human lives. Each sequence repeats twice in a year. The moons in the waxing year express these basic processes more nearly in the direction of "Mother" energies, while the moons in the waning year express the same processes more nearly in the direction of "Father" energies.

Looking at the mirror moon pairs adds another dimension to this lunar calendar. Comparing the pairs enriches our understanding of the individual moons in each pair. The sequence of the pairs also seems to suggest enhanced meanings for the separate moons. As you might expect in a lunar system, the meanings from this point of view don't quite match the ideas we've already encountered, but are still somehow the same, rather like a photographic double exposure.

A Word about Mother and Father Energies

Using the terms "Mother" and "Father" energies sounds a bit awkward, but it is commensurate with some of the other ideas in this book. Each of the mirror moons tends a little more strongly in the direction of Mother or Father energies. The moons in the waxing half of the year, from the Birth Moon to the Journey Moon, lean toward Mother energies, those in the waning half, toward Father energies. When I talk about the "negative" form of the divine polarities, I mean Mother energies, while Father energies are in a "positive" direction.

Let me remind you that positive and negative are not value judgments. No place on the circle is intrinsically and always "better" than any other place. Also, the best balance is not always in the center, where the two energies are exactly equal. Each possible "mixture" of the dual energies is suitable for some time and place.

In our lives, our best balances shift and change from one side of the circle to the other, but hardly ever rest at the center. Even when we reside at the midpoint between the poles, we could be unbalanced relative to our circumstances. The central, equal balance of the divine polarities is generally attributed to the Tao as a whole, rather than to individual members-in-process of the Tao.

Most of our personal challenges in life come from local imbalances between divine polarities that we express in our values or behavior and the place we are on the circle. For instance, a person who is too emotional to think clearly is tending toward Mother energies, while a person who is too aggressive to relate well to other people is tending toward the Father side. Both examples may be considered imbalanced because they specify dysfunctions, but not because "being emotional" or "being aggressive" are themselves inappropriate. Within an entire person or a system, either expresses many different polar balances; even apparently dysfunctional qualities may fit into the balance of the whole.

Beginning: Birth Moon/Mother's Moon

Beginnings happen when something moves from an unformed, unlimited potential to a particular form with specific limits. All new things are born at such moments, even as the potential of the ovum is limited and fulfilled by the particular sperm that wins the race among millions of its fellows to make a baby. The infinite number of pictures that might be painted on a blank canvas rapidly diminishes with every stroke of the artist's brush, moving toward a particular picture. The universal experience of happiness, once captured in the words of a particular language, can only touch the hearts of those who know what those specific words mean.

The Birth Moon celebrates physical birth and the renewal of hope. The Mother's Moon celebrates spiritual birth and the fulfillment of hope. The new mother loves her child because it *is*. She has little sense of what that child may or may not become, only a hope that it will be a good person, or beautiful, or successful. The mature mother loves her child despite what it is, despite years of changing diapers and wiping snotty noses and experiencing all the disappointments and difficulties of parenthood. Indeed, one of the mysteries of parenting is that dealing with the dirty diapers and the snotty noses is part of what endears our children to us. The older child, who recognizes that it is not perfect, is not everything that its mother might wish it to be, is renewed in hope because its mother continues to love it unconditionally, despite its inadequacies and imperfections.

The juxtaposition of the two moons expresses the difference in direction of Mother and Father energies rather well. In the Birth Moon, the acceptance of a new baby, or, symbolically, any other new human enterprise, is impersonal and without form, which is consistent with the Mother's tendency toward generality. In the Mother's Moon, the child, or a partially completed project, is accepted with the Father's tendency to specificity. The offer of hope is in the direction of Mother energies. The fulfillment, or completion, of hope is in the direction of Father energies.

We start all human enterprises with hope and a potential for making something. If we remain at the initial stage of greatest potential, we never move on to an actual result. The lesson of this mirrored pair is that we must renew our hope at intervals throughout the life of a child or a project. If we allow ourselves to lose hope when, inevitably, our "baby" starts showing qualities we wished to avoid, we will never reach a completed product.

We must sustain hope through the realities of our experiences, which include the fact that nothing ever turns out exactly the way we expected. We must work through our disappointments to the achievements that lie beyond them. As our children grow, they reveal both defects and miracles. They are not all we hoped for, but what they are is often richer and more fulfilling than we could have anticipated. The Birth Moon tells us that a newborn baby is absorbing for its potential. The Mother's Moon tells us that a growing child is enchanting for who it is becoming.

Growth: Milk (Nursing) Moon/Father's Moon

Human growth has two tasks: we must discover how we are like all our fellows, and we must understand also how we are unique. The Milk Moon expresses general growth that follows a pattern. The Father's Moon expresses specific growth that makes its own pattern.

The newborn child, at its mother's breast, does not distinguish between itself and its mother. Its security lies in being an integral part of a system that can protect it and nurture it. With such security, it can address itself to following the program encoded in its DNA and grow, first its body, then the other components that make us human.

As we grow, we gradually learn both the anguish and joy of being separate beings. Our capacity to be useful lies in our peculiar combination of the generality called "human" and of the speciality called "self." Our task in life is to learn the limits and boundaries of "self" that allow us to function within human potential.

The same pattern of moving from the general to the specific characterizes all human experiences. We decide to make a clay pot, and we begin with an idea and a shapeless lump of damp earth, which as yet does not hint what final shape we may wrest from it. As our vision grows, and we come to understand the limits and possibilities of both the clay and our own skills, we create a specific form. The purpose of growth is to reach that form.

To achieve growth, we must have or give nurture. At beginnings, we give relatively undifferentiated energy or other resources to get our projects off the ground. Once we overcome the inertia of starting, we "feed" our projects with increasingly precise kinds of energy and resources. We shape what we make to specific ends, within the general patterns of its natural potential.

The Milk Moon tells us that we are all connected, all part of the same "stuff," and that we can thrive, because we are not alone. The Father's Moon tells us that we are also separate, both limited and empowered by the unique qualities we bring to our lives, and that our growth is not confined, because we are special.

Testing (Challenge):
Fasting (Weaning) Moon/Nesting Moon

Each day we make dozens of choices because, at each fork we encounter in our paths, we can take only one of the roads that meet there. Which way we go tests our personal values and abilities. The decisions we make shape our paths. Our selection of a path also determines what kinds of choices we may encounter in the future. The Fasting Moon tells us how we may shape ourselves by choosing to suppress our desires for a greater good. The Nesting Moon tells us how we may fulfill our desires by prudent planning and the help of the community.

The infant at its mother's breast recognizes the power of its desire. When it cries and demands, it receives food when the mother has milk. Weaning may be the first time that a child's power over its mother is challenged. Weaning is also a place where the child encounters useful limits to its desire. Weaning is necessary both for the child, so that it may move into the next stage of individuation, and for the good of the family. The mother cannot indefinitely continue to provide the necessary calories for the growing child, and if another child is on the way, its needs will soon take precedence.

Humans whose desires are never thwarted do not grow beyond infantile behavior. The natural position of the infant is, "I am the center of the universe." So long as that position is not challenged, the child's ability to achieve is limited by the resources within its physical reach. When the child learns, sometimes by painful means, that it is not all-powerful, that lesson also gives the child its first clue that meaningful power to shape the world can be gained by enlisting the help of others.

The child builds on this intuition. A group of people always has greater resources available than an individual, but one of the costs of gaining cooperation is that one must give precedence, at least some of the time, to the needs of the group, above one's own desires. As the child matures, it is tested on its courage to give up what it wants for some greater good, and on its ability to wait for satisfaction. It is also tested on its wisdom in planning to meet its own needs, and to help fulfill the needs of others.

The Mother and Father qualities of this moon pair are not obvious. At first glance, the stringency of learning to deprive oneself that is associated with the Fasting Moon seems more in the direction of the Father than the Mother; however, the focus here is not on self-deprivation, but on the benefit to the community, which is a Mother perspective. The child is weaned, and adults fast, to eke out family or community resources. Any benefit to individuals is a side-effect rather than the central thrust. One person's desires are immaterial beside the survival of the whole.

The Nesting Moon emphasizes the benefit that the community offers to the individual, which is an approach in the direction of Father energies. Individuals improve their abilities to survive by enlisting the help of others, especially for big jobs like harvest and constructing or repairing large structures. The testing indicated by these two moons is the ability to modify one's immediate desires to meet community demands for a long-term benefit to the group, and also the ability to meet one's personal needs by paying a certain amount of community service, for maximum benefit to both the individual and the group.

The Fasting Moon tells us that we will be tested by not being able to have all we want when we want it, that we must learn to curb the greed of the infant if we wish to grow to maturity. Once we have recognized the relative unimportance of our personal desires in the continuance of our species, we are ready for the lesson of the Nesting Moon, which says that we may have our desires, or at least many of them, if we learn the rules of the road. Our choices to act in the community make us better and abler individuals. Our choices to improve our personal abilities make us more valuable to our society.

Maturation: Seed Moon/Harvest Moon

Making courageous choices to live as members of the human community affords us the wisdom and strength to make timely and effective choices. "To everything there is a season, a time for every purpose under heaven." The reasoned, mature person knows these times from having seen the cycles and observed their turns. This knowledge translates into the wisdom to use the forces inherent within the cycles effectively.

The Seed Moon concerns knowing when to act so that we catch the force of the cycle on its upward leg. The Harvest Moon is about knowing when to reap the benefits from the downturning wheel, the point where we can harvest the optimum output available, before impetus is lost as the wheel crosses its zero point and begins a new cycle.

Maturation is the stage of human growth when we are poised at a resting balance between the rapid growth of our bodies as children and the deterioration of our physical processes as we advance into age. Maturation represents the force of inertia in our lives, the point where the force applied to move us forward and the force applied to hold us still exactly and equally balance. Note that the vernal and autumnal equinoxes ordinarily occur in these moons.

We see inertial force mirrored precisely in this pair of moons. The Seed Moon must overcome the inertia of a place at rest to start things moving. The Harvest Moon must apply a force to arrest the motion of growth before it moves past usability into death and decay. The cycle demands both motion and rest, in their appropriate places. Only those in the mature vigor of life have the will to start and the strength to stop this endless succession.

As the Mother represents potential, the ability and energy required to create, so the Seed Moon celebrates the potency of beginning, of having the courage to act. As the Father represents knowledge, the ability and energy required to create a specific form, so the Harvest Moon celebrates the limits that unfold and reveal themselves in completion, of having the judgment to set appropriate boundaries.

There are an infinity of ways to begin and end projects and enterprises, but only a few that have the power to make something new and valuable in the world. All the ways that work require maturity, with its components of experience and courage, knowledge and wisdom. The Seed Moon reveres the experience necessary to know when to begin a successful enterprise, and honors the courage to act on that knowledge. The Harvest Moon honors the knowledge required to wrest the optimum gain from the work we do, and honors the wisdom to know when to call it quits.

Initiation: Mating Moon/Sorting Moon

In this context, the word "initiation" refers to those life passages in which others recognize that we have arrived at a level where we are fit to make decisions. This initiation is analogous to initiation into a society where one moves from being an aspiring member with few or no privileges to becoming a full voting member with all privileges. The whole purpose for humans to accumulate resources, material or non-material, is to have wider fields of choice. The Mating Moon is concerned with our choices to unite with or adhere to people, groups, or values. The Sorting Moon is concerned with our choices to accept or reject resources, actions, and values.

The first rite of initiation celebrated in primitive societies was the passage from minor child to full adult at the onset of puberty. This passage signalled that the one presented for initiation was fit to take his or her place in society. Our culture no longer celebrates this biological milestone as a discrete rite of passage, but in earlier societies this event was important, the true signal that one had become an adult and now deserved full adult privileges, and had achieved the ability to discharge full adult responsibilities. The menarche of girls signalled their ability to bear children, and adult women welcomed these girls into the mysteries of life and birth, growth and death. Male puberty rites tested adolescent boys for courage and strength and then pronounced them fit to support the needs of the community and to undertake responsibility for a family. Such initiations were not pro forma. Children were hurt or died in the course of trying to pass such tests.

Our modern marriage rites echo this process, but faintly. Today, we emphasize choosing the person with whom we will mate, and we focus less on the responsibilities of mating, both in regard to the new family and to the community at large. I do not suggest that marrying for love is wrong. I do suggest that it is the wrong primary focus. A successful marriage, which is of value to both individuals and society, rests on the commitment and responsibility of the parties to each other rather than on a fleeting erotic attraction. Cherishing a mate and the children that result from mating goes far beyond the self-involvement of new lovers.

The phrase, "falling in love," which is a major theme in our popular arts, implies that we do not have a choice in whom we love. It indicates that lovers sustain their relationship with this particular emotion. In fact, the institution of marriage, a union of two people who may or may not be "in love," persists by the daily choices of the individuals involved to continue to work together. Where those choices are built on mutual values and mutual respect, we have healthy marriages that provide support to the partners and produce useful members of the community. Divorce reflects a change in focus from such daily choices to work with another to a greater concern for personal needs and the fulfillment of personal values.

The choices of the Mating Moon center on uniting with others for the purpose of meeting community needs for, among other things, families and children. The emphasis is in the direction of Mother energies, toward material gain, the potential for fertility, and the needs of the group.

The Sorting Moon moves in the direction of Father energies, toward spiritual gain, achievement of goals, and the needs of the individual. This moon celebrates another kind of initiation and life passage, the point in life where our individual accomplishments have earned us the right to make choices for our private needs and pleasure.

The equivalent state in our present society is that of materially successful people who, when they reach middle life, can indulge themselves in luxuries. In an earlier society, this status would include the wise old men or women who are forgiven eccentricities and other self-indulgences because of their value to the community. Their material contributions to the community weaken as they move toward codifying the wisdom of a long life. Their value to the community increases as they succeed in this endeavor.

We all make choices every day, and every choice we make is based on the resources available to us, and on values that we have developed through experience and maturity. When we make wise choices, we acquire additional resources and refine our values, and the number and range of our possible choices widens. When we make unwise choices, we may limit future choices by decreasing our resources. However, if we pay attention, we can improve the guidelines we use to make our decisions. No choice and its consequences are without value unless we refuse to learn from it.

The Mating Moon advises us to increase our resources by joining with others and doing what we can to support our families and the community. The Sorting Moon suggests that we use our personal needs and preferences to develop valid guidelines for choices. The Mating Moon helps us have more choices. The Sorting Moon helps us make better use of the choices we have.

Cycle Change: Journey Moon/Death Moon

When we have achieved the mastery implied by initiation, it is time to begin another cycle, and to move once again through all the stages, to a new level of mastery. In human life, no place will satisfy us indefinitely, no achievement endures forever, and no victory stays won without renewal.

As humans are born, grow, mature, and die, so do all human activities begin, expand, reach an optimal level, and then either start the cycle over again, or die of stagnation. The Journey Moon shows us how to travel to new places to discover new possibilities for our material success. The Death Moon takes us through the spiritual world, to new levels of consciousness.

With the miracle of satellites and television, sometimes it seems we see enough of other cultures in our own living rooms to give us the benefits that other ages acquired by long and arduous journeys to "faraway places with strange-sounding names." With the speed of travel and the popularity of western culture, we can now travel most of the world and never know the discomfort of a truly "foreign" environment. I know people who eat at American fast food restaurants all over the world and think they are sophisticated travelers.

The First Awful Truth is, "It don't work the way you think it do." Specifically, the value of travel is not in seeing exotic sights or even in standing in exotic locales. The value of travel is discovering new ways to look at the world, ways that can enrich and correct our ideas about how the world works. We change and are renewed by such journeys, and that renewal is the difference between mere travel and true journeying.

Cycle change comes after initiation because the essential precursor of a useful journey is a certain stability and maturity, a still place from which to view the turning world. That is, we cannot profitably explore new things unless we have a foundation on which to build. We have to maintain a balance between being sure of what we know, and being willing to consider new ideas.

This balance is the key to success in the world. Those who admit nothing new to their lives fail from stagnation, for the world will not stop for them. Those who run after new things without building a strong base of tried and validated data fail from lack of stamina, for the world will not sustain them. Only the balanced blend of old and new has the potential for the renewal we seek in our journeys.

In a spiritual sense, some of us seek new ways, but others have new thoughts thrust upon them, often by the irretrievable loss of something they value. The bitter pain of loss makes us re-evaluate. What, in the face of inevitable change and death, is worth doing? Where we strive for material profit in the Journey Moon, in the Death Moon, we are confronted with Jesus' question, "What is a man profited if he shall gain the whole world, and lose his own soul?"

The recognition that no thing, person, or institution is immune to transformation or death sends humans journeying through their inner ways in search of meaning. No one who undertakes this journey into the labyrinth comes back unchanged. With new ideas of how the world works, we inevitably change the way we act, for all our actions are conditioned by our values. Such changes of mind and heart, and the actions that follow them, mark transitions to a new stage, another cycle in a human life.

Cycles are part of the experience of life. We see them as the year turns from the green of spring and summer to the colors of fall and winter. We see them in our children as they grow from infants to independent persons. We see them in ourselves as the young, questing person within us is increasingly trapped in a body whose capabilities diminish, and we find ourselves too tired to listen, one more time, to the same hopes of youth that we ourselves once entertained.

In the Journey Moon, we learn to focus on the value of what greets us beyond new horizons rather than on what we have left behind. We celebrate the joy of the love we will find in the town over the hill, instead of mourning the poignant joy of first love that we will never know again.

In the Death Moon, we learn to recognize that the apparently transitory nature of all we love is an illusion, disguising an eternal cycle whereby all that dies shall come again. We celebrate the beauty of the butterfly before us, secure in the knowledge that, when this particular butterfly is no more, its children will return next year to delight us once again.

The Seasonal Festivals: The Wheel of the Year

The eight seasonal festivals I cover in this chapter were so widely celebrated in northern Europe during ancient and medieval times that many echoes of them still survive, in major festivals we still celebrate, or in local folk practices. Covering these festivals with any depth could easily fill a book, so I will confine myself to a few remarks on the history of each festival, a discussion of the energies and themes that I believe each represents, and the date range of the festival as it occurs in the luni-solar calendar represented in this book.

The histories of and lore associated with these seasonal festivals are rich and complex. They were celebrated in a variety of permutations all over northern Europe, and are widely celebrated today by modern Pagans. Four of the festivals, the quarter days, have certain dates. Yule, Ostara, Litha, and Mabon are the winter solstice, the spring equinox, the summer solstice, and the autumn equinox, respectively. The other four festivals, the cross-quarter days, are less firmly fixed and the dates in ancient times probably varied by place, depending on local conditions. The cross-quarter days were the beginnings of the seasons in some calendars, and some of these festivals were originally celebrated over a period of several days.

The calendar in *Earthtime Moontime* sets the cross-quarter days at the second full moon after the nearest solstice or equinox. As you may discover by studying the tables in appendix C, this method means that these festivals can occur as quickly as about four weeks or as late as almost eight weeks following the related solstice or equinox. In a world less obsessed by clock and calendar than ours, that kind of uncertainty was less distressing than it would be to us moderns who sometimes forget that organizing human events primarily by time and date is a relatively recent way to do things.

In this calendar, having the festivals fall in the moons that most closely reflect their spirits was more important than having a time pattern for the festivals that is perfectly neat by modern standards. Most modern Pagans celebrate the four quarter-days on a specific date (a date certain), a practice that forms a regular pattern of alternating six- and seven-week intervals between the eight seasonal festivals. Although the cross-quarter festivals now usually have specific dates associated with them, the original celebrations certainly varied somewhat from place to place in accordance with the growing season and the weather patterns for particular localities.

The method for setting dates for the seasonal festivals in this calendar is neither more nor less valid than the better known pattern of eight specific dates. The important ideas of the seasonal festivals are that they mirror the changes in the Earth and Sun through the cycle of the year, and that they mark times for appropriate human celebrations. In a real Bronze Age village, the pleasure of interrupting workaday tasks for a party was probably at least as important in the lives of the inhabitants as celebrating the deep spiritual truths that are encoded in this "wheel of the year." Let me say once again, the line between the ordinary and the exalted, between everyday material concerns and the deepest spiritual experiences, is not well defined. We get to the mountaintop by walking up a path, step by step, through smooth places and stony. We can discover our spiritual selves in our material celebration of these festivals. They are not the only path, but they are a tried route to knowing the Mother.

Yule

Yule is the winter solstice, the day when the Sun seems to stop its journey to the south and return toward the north in ever increasing strength, until the summer solstice, Litha, where the process is reversed. Yule is the longest night of the year. In astronomy, the solstice is defined as the moment when the sun moves from Sagittarius into Capricorn. The specific date varies a little from year to year, but the most common date is about December 21. The name, "Yule" is thought to be derived from the Norse word "Iul," which means "wheel," and to signify the wheel of the year which, in the Norse calendar, begins a new turn with this solstice. Its Roman equivalent was the Saturnalia, also a new year celebration.

In ancient calendars, Yule was the midpoint of a winter that ran from Samhain to Imbolc, and the midpoint of the dark half of the year that ran from Mabon to Ostara. Indeed, Yule has the alternate name of Midwinter. Our own Gregorian calendar is based on the Norse pattern, rather than the Celtic practice of beginning and ending years at Samhain. Our present New Year begins almost immediately after the winter solstice.

Cultures throughout the world celebrate the birth of a Divine Child at the winter solstice, although in the southern hemisphere the date is in June instead of December. The correspondence between this birth and the Christian celebration of Christmas is obvious. Many other religions have celebrated similar births, including the Egyptian birth of Horus and the Middle Eastern birth of Mithra. In some Pagan traditions, Yule is when the Oak King or the Lord of the Light defeats the Holly King or the Lord of the Dark. Many of the traditional symbols of Christmas, including the yule log, evergreen trees with lighted candles, and decorations with holly and mistletoe are survivals of Pagan practices that celebrated the return of the light and the persistence of life. In the year as a day, Yule is midnight. It is associated with the direction of north. In the wheel of the year, Yule represents the planting of the seed.

The theme of Yule is the joy of birth and of all beginnings, and the enlightenment and freeing of humans from the dark of ignorance and fear. The Sun's journey into darkness, with the withdrawal of the Father's life-giving light and warmth, prefigures the deaths of all that live. His return prefigures not only the rebirth of individuals, but also the hope of renewal throughout our lives. The image of this feast is best captured in the ancient words, "Let there be light."

Imbolc

Imbolc comes from the Celtic word for lamb because it occurs about the time spring lambs are born. This holiday celebrates the day when the Goddess comes to the sacred well of the world as the Winter Hag, the Death Crone, old and clothed in black. She drinks of the well, and, in a single night, is transformed into the Maiden, the Virgin Bride who brings the spring.

In some ancient calendars, this feast is the beginning of spring, which runs to Beltane. This festival is also called Oimelc and Brigantia, the last meaning the day of Brigit, the Bride. Its Roman equivalent was Lupercalia, which was a rite for fertility.

In the lunar calendar of this book, Imbolc may occur over a range from January 20 to February 18. In most years, it occurs in the Milk Moon. When Imbolc comes in the Fasting Moon, it is time to add a Courting Moon to put the moons back in sync with the changing seasons.

In many Pagan calendars, Imbolc is celebrated on February 2. This date also corresponds to the Christian feast of Candlemas, which commemorates the purification of the Virgin forty days after her delivery of Jesus. The return of Persephone in Greek mythology has a similar meaning. This feast is associated with the "washing of the Earth's face" in preparation for spring, and with lighting candles to signify the growing light of the Sun. In the year as day, Imbolc is dawn. It is associated with the direction of northeast. In the wheel of the year, Imbolc signifies the stirring of the seed.

Imbolc's primary theme is the promise of renewal and the purification associated with renewal, where the residue of our old mistakes falls from us as the Crone aspect falls from the face of the Goddess at the sacred well, and we are made new. This is the feast in which we mark our certainty that the days are indeed growing longer, and that we can safely prepare for the beginning of spring. We also mark our movement from inner darkness to outer manifestation in light. Imbolc is the beginning of the regeneration that derives from what we learned in our winter's journey into darkness and the otherworld.

Ostara

Ostara, the spring equinox, is named for a fertility goddess, Easter, who liked to appear in the form of a white rabbit. In astronomy, the equinox occurs when the Sun moves from Pisces into Aries, and it marks one of two days in the year when day and night are of equal length. The date varies, but is most often around March 21. It is the midpoint of spring and the transition point where the dark half of the year yields to the light half of the year.

The Christian feast of Easter, which is named after the same goddess, celebrates the resurrection of Jesus, and through that event, the resurrection of all humans. I find it interesting that Pagans celebrate Ostara as a specific date, set by the Sun, while Christians celebrate Easter as a movable feast, set by the Moon. In addition to Easter, the Christian calendar also celebrates the Annunciation on March 25, the date on which the Virgin conceives the Divine Child who is born nine months later at Christmas. In other mythologies, the spring equinox is associated with the resurrection of Osiris and the return of Adonis. The Roman equivalent of Ostara was the Bacchanalia, which also celebrated resurrection.

Here, in the midpoint of spring, we see that life that seemed dead only a few weeks earlier, can and does come again. The traditional symbols of Easter—eggs and rabbits—are associated with fertility and new life and with the symbolic pregnancy of the Earth that is manifested in the greening land. In the year as a day, Ostara is sunrise. It is associated with the direction of east. In the wheel of the year, the seed sprouts.

Ostara celebrates resurrection and the balance of energies that result in the triumph of life. We have the renewal associated with rebirth, and the burgeoning potential of physical and spiritual creativity. Our lives quicken when we permit the fertilization of energies from both sides of the divine polarities.

When we participate fully in this balance, we will, in time, bring forth something new. What has existed only in potential begins to achieve form, in us and in the Earth.

Beltane

Beltane, or Bealten, is Celtic for the magic of flowers. This feast is a celebration of fertility, as spring gives way to the summer that will last until Lammas. The Goddess as Maiden yields to her Lover, and from their union comes all the production of summer, and the Goddess enters her phase as Mother. The Roman equivalent was named Floralia, which celebrated the fruits implicit in flowers.

Traditional symbols for May Day, which has no equivalent in the Christian ecclesiastic calendar, are flowers and the weaving of ribbons on a maypole. The maypole represents both the physical instrument of the God's triumph and the renewal of Yggdrasil, the World Tree. The weaving signifies that even as the God masters the Goddess, she binds him to her in turn by her yielding, as the World Tree depends for life upon the Mother's love.

In the lunar calendar in this book, Beltane may range from April 18 to May 18, and it belongs in the Mating Moon. The fixed date that is used for this feast is May 1, or, from a time when days ran from sunset to sunset, the evening of April 30, which is called May Eve or Walpurgisnacht. Beltane is a joyous festival, full of raucous fun and sexual hijinx to welcome in the summer. It is a night of wild energies, and one where the chaos energy of the Mother reaches its peak. In the year as a day, Beltane is the freshness of mid-morning, and is associated with southeast. In the wheel of the year, the seed flowers.

Beltane expresses the wild magic of a burst of creativity that is the outcome of properly balanced and blended divine polarities. Metaphorically, the chaotic and formless potential of the

Mother is mastered by the forming and limiting knowledge of the Father for the purpose of creating life. Beltane is expressed both by open delight in sexuality and also by the mature acceptance of the consequences of fertility. It is also associated with the responsibilities to family and community connected with bringing babies into the world.

Litha

Litha is the summer solstice and the longest day of the year. Astronomically, it is the moment when the Sun enters Cancer, usually about June 21. It is the midpoint of summer, marking the maximum energy from the Sun. The waxing year turns to the waning half of the Sun's cycle. In some pagan traditions, Litha is when the Oak King or the Lord of the Light is defeated by the Holly King or the Lord of the Dark. The Roman equivalent was called Vestalia, a rekindling of hearth fires. In some traditions, all fires in a village would be extinguished, to be relit from the Midsummer bonfires.

This festival may also be called Midsummer's Day, a festival which, in the Christian calendar is associated with the feast of St. John the Baptist on June 24. June 23, St. John's Eve, also called Midsummer's Eve, is associated in old folktales with fey creatures and the possibility of weird and unusual events, some of which are dangerous. Herbs such as mistletoe and St. John's wort are supposed to be gathered on Midsummer's Eve for their highest potency. In the year as day, Litha is high noon. It is associated with the direction of south. In the wheel of the year, the seed sets fruit.

Despite the sobering news that the Sun's energies have crested, the primary themes of Litha arise from the abundance and diversity of life at this time of year. The Sun is at his peak of power, and the Earth, at her most fruitful. The cornucopia of her bounty and his warmth are available to all without qualification. Its usual home is in the Mother's Moon.

We bask in the Mother's unconditional love. The energies of Litha are analogous to the euphoria of a woman late in pregnancy. As her body prepares to deliver, a pregnant woman becomes detached from the worries and irritations of daily living, waiting dreamily for her child to be born. She may recognize the work and difficulty awaiting her after delivery, but, for now, she basks in a sense of well-being.

Lammas

Lammas, also called Lughnassad or Teltane, is the festival of the first harvest, when grain is harvested and the first bread is baked from the new wheat. It is the end of summer and the onset of autumn, which will continue until Samhain. The Father, personified as the God of Grain, John Barleycorn, dies in his plant form and, in dying, produces seed that is the means by which He shall come again next year.

In this book's calendar, Lammas occurs as early as July 21 and as late as August 18, and almost always in the Father's Moon. Traditions that put a particular date on this festival usually say August 1 or August 15, but obviously the actual date of grain harvest varied by latitude.

The equivalent feast in the Christian calendar is the assumption of the Virgin into heaven on August 15. While this designation is relatively recent, this date was a feast of Mary, the mother of Jesus, from earliest times. In other mythologies, this time of year brings the deaths of Adonis and Tammuz, and the murder of Osiris. In an alternative version of the great story, this is also when the Goddess descends to the underworld to negotiate the return of her dead lover the following year. The rape of Persephone by Pluto and Demeter's mourning is an analogue of this version. In the year as a day, Lammas is the burning heat of midafternoon. It is associated with the southwest. In the wheel of the year, the seed's fruit ripens.

The themes of Lammas, like the Father's Moon that is its natural home, are sacrifice and transformation, signifying the sacrifice of the God's life in both the dead grain and the waning Sun. While the mood can be somber, Lammas also celebrates the joys and rewards of willing sacrifice. This sacrifice is accompanied by the transformation of the grain into nourishing bread, and by the mystery that the harvested seeds will bring the God to life again next cycle. This festival has both the joy of harvest and the sorrow of the God's sacrifice, the promise of rebirth and the bittersweet recognition that, as the year wanes, so nothing that lives endures forever.

Mabon

Mabon is the autumn equinox, the second time of the year when day and night are of equal length. Astronomically, it occurs when the Sun moves from Virgo into Libra, usually around September 21. Mabon is the second harvest—of fruits and vine, especially of grapes for making wine. The equivalent Roman feast was a wine festival. Mabon is the midpoint of autumn, and marks the beginning of the dark half of the year.

The closest feast to Mabon in the Christian calendar is September 21, St. Matthew's Day, which is associated with the wine harvest. The red leaves of autumn are sometimes related to the cremation of the sacrificed God's body. In some versions of the great story, the God's sacrifice is also associated with Mabon. This idea is echoed in the stories of maenads who tore young men limb from limb in their Dionysian revels at wine-making time.

The mood of Mabon is a diminished, sober joy, where the happiness of having completed this harvest is balanced by the knowledge that the trials of winter are coming soon. In the year as a day, Mabon is sunset, and associated with the west. In the wheel of the year, the seed ripens and falls.

The theme of Mabon is justice, the message that we reap what we have earned. From this day, dark will have dominion, in the sense that nights are longer than days, until Ostara. The resurrection and hope of the spring equinox have come full circle and we recognize that, in the balance of all things, shadow must equal light. Before we may be renewed, we must first sacrifice what we are; before we can be reborn, we must die.

Samhain

Samhain (pronounced SOW-WAIN) was the Festival of the Dead in the Celtic calendar. It was both the end and the beginning of a new year, a time of letting go of the past and looking forward to the future. Samhain marks the third Harvest, when all the animals that had been culled from the herds were slaughtered and the meat prepared for winter storage.

Samhain is the beginning of the winter that will remain until Imbolc. The Goddess dons Her dark aspect, as the Crone who cuts the thread of life, or the Dark Sow who eats the dead. In this calendar, Samhain occurs as early as October 23 and as late as November 21, and it usually falls in the Sorting Moon. It is associated also with the Death Moon, and it falls there in years when the calendar needs a Courting Moon the following spring to adjust the moons to their proper seasons. In the year as a day, Samhain is the first deep dark after the final colors of sunset fade. It is associated with northwest. In the wheel of the year, the seed falls into dormancy, a little death, that it may rest until its time to be reborn.

The date certain for Samhain is October 31, Halloween, or the Eve of the Feast of All Saints in the Christian calendar. As in the Celtic feast, Halloween is associated with a thinning of the veils between this world and the otherworld, and with the presence of ghosts and goblins abroad. It is a time to divine the future and see what the coming year will bring. Despite its wild reputation, Samhain is in fact the height of the energies of order, even as its counterpart, Beltane, is the peak of chaos energies.

The fundamental order of life, by which we are born, abide for a while, and finally die, is the central motif of Samhain. Symbolically, this festival recognizes that untrammeled life must be limited by death, for growth without a balancing restriction ends in total destruction for all, even as one of the most effective herbicides we have is a growth hormone that encourages plants to grow themselves to death. Cancer, which some of us fear more than any other disease, is also a malady in which cells multiply out of control, beyond the benign parameters of normal growth. By limiting the unbounded creativity of the Mother, the Father's energies succeed in assuring that life as a process will continue.

The primary themes of Samhain are death and rebirth. This festival celebrates death as the fulfillment of life, the end to which we all will come. What cannot be avoided becomes the avenue to renewal, the transition between an ending and the beginning that lies within it, waiting to be born.

As we accept the turning of the wheel, and the inevitable changes that accompany it, we transcend our bondage to the wheel, for freedom lies in knowing that in every death there is a beginning of life, and that a part of every birth is the death that awaits the one being born. The purpose of the journey is the journeying, and he travels easiest who follows the flow.

Afterword

The eight seasonal festivals are a rich soup of symbols and archetypes in which we can fish for insights both trivial and profound. These celebrations of the cycles of the year resonate deep within all of us, both from their intimate connection to the moods of the Mother, and from the echo of their symbols and ideas in modern celebrations. The weaving of the maypole and the death of John Barleycorn may no longer have the power to speak meaningfully to us, but the joys of spring and the bittersweet sorrow of sacrifice and transformation are always among us.

If you asked me how much of this book is really true, I would say all of it and none of it. It has wisdom that may speak to you if you will listen, and it has foolishness that you may safely ignore. Insofar as *Earthtime Moontime* touches you and brings you home to who you truly are, this book is true. Insofar as its metaphors and observations fail to connect you to the Mother, within whom we are all one, this book is untrue. I offer it to you for what you may make of it, and my blessings with it.

Appendix A:
Moon Summaries

Primary Energies of the Moons

Death Moon

Endings/New starts

Death/Rebirth

Transformation/Stability

Change/Stagnation

Recognition/Ignorance of the mysteries of transition

Birth Moon

Beginnings/Completions
Birth/Stasis
Hope/Despair
Creativity/ Destruction

Milk Moon

Recognition of Self/Others
Nurturing/Not nurturing
Generosity/Selfishness
Independence/Dependence

Fasting Moon

Forbearance/Indulgence
Wise/Unwise use of resources
Spiritual seeking/Contentment
Concern/Unconcern for community resources
and future
Recognition/Lack of recognition of the limits and
capacities of the physical self

Seed Moon

Beginning/Procrastinating
Commitment to action/Inaction
Faith/Fear
Renewal/Exhaustion

Courting Moon

Moderation/Excess
The ideal in reality/Fantasy
Freedom in/Slavery to time

Mating Moon

Joining/Separating
Relationship/Isolation
Fruitfulness/Sterility
Acceptance/Nonacceptance of self and others

Journey Moon

Love/Fear of the unknown
Risk/Safety
Innovative/Traditional
Unorthodox/Conforming
Progress/Stagnation
Time/Eternity

Mother's Moon

Motherlove/Fatherlove (unconditional/conditional)
Abundance/Scarcity
Relationship of material/spiritual value
Hope/Manifestation
Security/Insecurity
Independence/Dependence

Father's Moon

Sacrifice and transformation/Self-indulgence
and stagnation
Fatherlove/Motherlove
Knowledge of limits/Unlimited potential
Learning/Ignorance

Nesting Moon

Preparation/Unreadiness for trial
Wise/Unwise use of resources
Focus on now/The future
Protection/Vulnerability
Concern for others(Guardianship)/Self-centeredness

Harvest Moon

Gathering/Releasing
Endings/Beginnings
Responsibility/Irresponsibility for actions
Fulfillment/Incompletion

Sorting Moon

Discrimination/Acceptance
Choice/Failure to choose
Analysis/Synthesis
Specialization/Generalization
Free will/Fate
Order/Chaos

Date Ranges of the Moons

Death Moon	October 27 to December 25
Birth Moon	November 25 to January 24
Milk Moon	December 25 to February 22
Fasting Moon	January 24 to March 24
Seed Moon	February 23 to April 22
Courting Moon	March 23 to May 3
Mating Moon	April 4 to June 1
Journey Moon	May 3 to July 1
Mother's Moon	June 2 to July 30
Father's Moon	July 1 to August 29
Nesting Moon	July 31 to September 27
Harvest Moon	August 29 to October 27
Sorting Moon	September 27 to November 26

Moon Mirrors and Stages of Development (Waxing Year, Waning Year)

Beginning   Birth Moon, Mother's Moon
Commonality: Unconditional Acceptance

Growth   Milk Moon, Father's Moon
Commonality: Differentiation between Self and Others

Challenge   Fasting Moon, Nesting Moon
Commonality: Planning for Needs of Community and Self

Maturation   Seed Moon, Harvest Moon
Commonality: Providing for Needs of Community and Self

Initiation   Mating Moon, Sorting Moon
Commonality: Making Choices for Growth and Change

Cycle Change   Journey Moon, Death Moon
Commonality: The Results of Change

Moon Pair Focuses

Everyone's birthday falls in at least two moons. Birthdays from late March to early May may fall in three. Assuming that the energies of our birth moons make an important imprint on our personalities, I suspect that the secondary birth moon also has an influence, perhaps by setting the major focus of our interaction with our birth moon energies.

The following list is a preliminary speculation on how this might work. I offer a possible primary emphasis for each moon pair, with the understanding that it is an oversimplification of what is certainly a complex interaction of energies.

Death/Birth Moon	Beginnings and endings
Birth Moon/Milk Moon	Children
Milk Moon/Seed Moon	Education
Seed Moon/Mating Moon	Material creativity
Seed Moon/Courting Moon/ Mating Moon	Intellectual creativity
Mating Moon/Journey Moon	Seeking completion
Journey Moon/Mother's Moon	Seeking security
Mother's Moon/Father's Moon	Personal integration
Father's Moon/Nesting Moon	Taking care of others
Nesting Moon/Harvest Moon	Balancing need and desire
Harvest Moon/Sorting Moon	Making appropriate choices
Sorting Moon/Death Moon	Transformation by choice

Appendix B:
New Moon Dates

This table lists dates for new moons associated with the moon names from this calendar, from November, 1889 to October, 2019. The early dates allow readers to look up births and important life events for their parents and grandparents. The future dates are offered in the expectation that this table will be useful for many years into the future. All dates are based on times for Moon phase changes at the zero meridian, also known as Greenwich or Zulu Time. Local times, and sometimes dates, will differ by the same amount as local times differ from Greenwich Time.

Find the year you are interested in. Each "section" of tables covers one decade. Go down the year column until you find the two dates that bracket the date you are looking for. Follow the upper of the two dates to the left until you get to the "Moon" column. The name there is the moon you want. Please note that the Death Moon and the Birth Moon are always in the previous Gregorian calendar year. The phase tables in Appendix C give all four quarters of each moon and place the seasonal festivals in the moons.

Date Conversion Chart

Moon	1890	1891	1892	1893	1894	1895	1896	1897	1898	1899
Death	11/23	11/12	11/01	11/19	11/08	10/28	11/16	11/05	11/24	11/14
Birth	12/22	12/12	12/01	12/19	12/08	11/27	12/16	12/04	12/23	12/13
Milk	01/20	01/10	12/31	01/18	01/07	12/27	01/14	01/03	01/22	01/11
Fasting	02/19	02/09	01/29	02/16	02/05	01/25	02/13	02/01	02/20	02/10
Seed	03/20	03/10	02/28	03/18	03/07	02/24	03/14	03/03	03/22	03/11
Courting	none	none	03/28	none	none	03/26	none	04/02	none	none
Mating	04/19	04/08	04/26	04/16	04/06	04/25	04/13	05/01	04/20	04/10
Journey	05/18	05/08	05/26	05/15	05/05	05/24	05/12	05/31	05/20	05/09
Mother's	06/17	06/06	06/24	06/14	06/03	06/22	06/11	06/30	06/19	06/08
Father's	07/17	07/06	07/23	07/13	07/03	07/22	07/10	07/29	07/18	07/07
Nesting	08/15	08/04	08/22	08/11	08/01	08/20	08/09	08/28	08/17	08/06
Harvest	09/14	09/03	09/21	09/10	08/30	09/18	09/07	09/26	09/16	09/05
Sorting	10/13	10/03	10/20	10/19	09/29	10/18	10/06	10/25	10/15	10/04

Moon	1900	1901	1902	1903	1904	1905	1906	1907	1908	1909
Death	11/03	11/22	11/11	10/31	11/19	11/07	10/28	11/16	11/05	11/23
Birth	12/03	12/22	12/11	11/30	12/18	12/07	11/26	12/15	12/05	12/23
Milk	01/01	01/20	01/09	12/29	01/17	01/05	12/26	01/14	01/03	01/22
Fasting	01/31	02/19	02/08	01/28	02/16	02/04	01/24	02/12	02/02	02/20
Seed	03/01	03/20	03/10	02/27	03/17	03/06	02/23	03/14	03/02	03/21
Courting	03/30	none	none	03/29	none	none	03/24	none	04/01	none
Mating	04/29	04/18	04/08	04/27	04/15	04/04	04/23	04/12	04/30	04/20
Journey	05/28	05/18	05/07	05/26	05/15	05/04	05/23	05/12	05/30	05/19
Mother's	06/27	06/16	06/06	06/25	06/13	06/03	06/21	06/10	06/28	06/17
Father's	07/26	07/15	07/05	07/24	07/13	07/02	07/21	07/10	07/28	07/17
Nesting	08/25	08/14	08/03	08/22	08/11	08/01	08/20	08/09	08/26	08/15
Harvest	09/23	09/12	09/02	09/21	09/09	08/30	09/18	09/07	09/25	09/14
Sorting	10/23	10/12	10/01	10/20	10/09	09/28	10/17	10/07	10/25	10/14

Moon	1910	1911	1912	1913	1914	1915	1916	1917	1918	1919
Death	11/13	11/02	11/20	11/09	10/29	11/17	11/07	11/25	11/14	11/03
Birth	12/12	12/01	12/20	12/08	11/28	12/17	12/06	12/24	12/14	12/03
Milk	01/11	12/31	01/19	01/07	12/27	01/15	01/05	01/23	01/12	01/02
Fasting	02/10	01/30	02/18	02/06	01/26	02/14	02/03	02/21	02/11	01/31
Seed	03/11	03/01	03/18	03/08	02/25	03/15	03/04	03/23	03/12	03/02
Courting	none	03/30	none	none	03/26	none	04/02	none	none	03/31
Mating	04/09	04/28	04/17	04/06	04/25	04/14	05/02	04/21	04/11	04/30
Journey	05/09	05/28	05/16	05/06	05/25	05/14	05/31	05/21	05/10	05/29
Mother's	06/07	06/26	06/15	06/04	06/23	06/12	06/30	06/19	06/08	06/27
Father's	07/06	07/25	07/14	07/04	07/23	07/12	07/30	07/19	07/08	07/27
Nesting	08/05	08/24	08/12	08/02	08/21	08/10	08/28	08/17	08/06	08/25
Harvest	09/03	09/22	09/11	08/31	09/19	09/09	09/27	09/16	09/05	09/24
Sorting	10/03	10/22	10/10	09/30	10/19	10/08	10/26	10/16	10/05	10/23

Moon	1920	1921	1922	1923	1924	1925	1926	1927	1928	1929
Death	11/22	11/10	10/30	11/19	11/08	10/28	11/16	11/05	11/24	11/12
Birth	12/22	12/10	11/29	12/18	12/08	11/26	12/15	12/05	12/24	12/12
Milk	01/21	01/09	12/29	01/17	01/06	12/26	01/14	01/03	01/22	01/11
Fasting	02/19	02/08	01/27	02/15	02/05	01/24	02/12	02/02	02/21	02/09
Seed	03/20	03/09	02/26	03/17	03/05	02/23	03/14	03/03	03/21	03/11
Courting	none	none	03/28	none	none	03/24	none	04/02	none	none
Mating	04/18	04/08	04/27	04/16	04/04	04/23	04/12	05/01	04/20	04/09
Journey	05/18	05/07	05/26	05/15	05/03	05/22	05/11	05/30	05/19	05/09
Mother's	06/16	06/06	06/25	06/14	06/02	06/21	06/10	06/29	06/17	06/07
Father's	07/15	07/05	07/24	07/14	07/02	07/20	07/09	07/28	07/17	07/06
Nesting	08/14	08/03	08/22	08/12	07/31	08/19	08/08	08/27	08/15	08/05
Harvest	09/12	09/02	09/21	09/10	08/30	09/18	09/07	09/25	09/14	09/03
Sorting	10/12	10/01	10/20	10/10	09/28	10/17	10/06	10/25	10/13	10/02

Moon	1930	1931	1932	1933	1934	1935	1936	1937	1938	1939
Death	11/01	11/20	11/09	10/29	11/17	11/07	11/26	11/14	11/03	11/22
Birth	12/01	12/20	12/09	11/28	12/17	12/06	12/25	12/13	12/02	12/21
Milk	12/30	01/18	01/07	12/27	01/15	01/05	01/24	01/12	01/01	01/20
Fasting	01/29	02/17	02/06	01/25	02/14	02/03	02/22	02/11	01/31	02/19
Seed	02/28	03/19	03/07	02/24	03/15	03/05	03/23	03/12	03/02	03/21
Courting	03/30	none	none	03/26	none	04/03	none	none	03/31	none
Mating	04/28	04/18	04/06	04/24	04/13	05/02	04/21	04/11	04/30	04/19
Journey	05/28	05/17	05/05	05/24	05/13	06/01	05/20	05/10	05/29	05/19
Mother's	06/26	06/16	06/04	06/23	06/12	06/30	06/19	06/08	06/27	06/17
Father's	07/25	07/15	07/03	07/22	07/11	07/30	07/18	07/08	07/27	07/16
Nesting	08/24	08/13	08/02	08/21	08/10	08/29	08/17	08/06	08/25	08/15
Harvest	09/22	09/12	08/31	09/19	09/09	09/27	09/15	09/04	09/23	09/13
Sorting	10/21	10/11	09/30	10/19	10/08	10/27	10/15	10/04	10/23	10/12

Moon	1940	1941	1942	1943	1944	1945	1946	1947	1948	1949
Death	11/11	10/30	11/19	11/08	10/29	11/15	11/04	11/23	11/12	11/01
Birth	12/10	11/29	12/18	12/08	11/27	12/15	12/04	12/23	12/12	11/30
Milk	01/09	12/28	01/16	01/06	12/27	01/14	01/03	01/22	01/11	12/30
Fasting	02/08	01/27	02/15	02/04	01/25	02/12	02/02	02/21	02/10	01/29
Seed	03/09	02/26	03/16	03/06	02/24	03/14	03/03	03/22	03/10	02/27
Courting	none	03/27	none	none	03/24	none	04/02	none	none	03/29
Mating	04/07	04/26	04/15	04/04	04/22	04/12	05/01	04/21	04/09	04/28
Journey	05/07	05/26	05/15	05/04	05/22	05/11	05/30	05/20	05/09	05/27
Mother's	06/06	06/24	06/13	06/02	06/20	06/10	06/29	06/18	06/07	06/26
Father's	07/05	07/24	07/13	07/02	07/20	07/09	07/28	07/18	07/06	07/25
Nesting	08/03	08/22	08/12	08/01	08/18	08/08	08/26	08/16	08/05	08/24
Harvest	09/02	09/21	09/10	08/30	09/17	09/06	09/25	09/14	09/03	09/22
Sorting	10/01	10/20	10/10	09/29	10/17	10/06	10/24	10/14	10/02	10/21

Moon	1950	1951	1952	1953	1954	1955	1956	1957	1958	1959
Death	11/20	11/09	10/30	11/17	11/06	11/25	11/14	11/02	11/21	11/11
Birth	12/19	12/09	11/29	12/17	12/06	12/25	12/14	12/02	12/21	12/10
Milk	01/18	01/07	12/28	01/15	01/05	01/24	01/13	01/01	01/19	01/09
Fasting	02/16	02/06	01/26	02/14	02/03	02/22	02/11	01/30	02/18	02/07
Seed	03/18	03/07	02/25	03/15	03/05	03/24	03/12	03/01	03/20	03/09
Courting	none	none	03/25	none	04/03	none	none	03/31	none	none
Mating	04/17	04/06	04/24	04/13	05/02	04/22	04/11	04/29	04/19	04/08
Journey	05/17	05/06	05/23	05/13	06/01	05/21	05/10	05/29	05/18	05/07
Mother's	06/15	06/04	06/22	06/11	06/30	06/20	06/08	06/27	06/17	06/06
Father's	07/15	07/04	07/21	07/11	07/29	07/19	07/08	07/27	07/16	07/06
Nesting	08/13	08/02	08/20	08/09	08/28	08/17	08/06	08/25	08/15	08/04
Harvest	09/12	09/01	09/19	09/08	09/27	09/16	09/04	09/23	09/13	09/03
Sorting	10/11	10/01	10/18	10/08	10/26	10/15	10/04	10/23	10/12	10/02

Moon	1960	1961	1962	1963	1964	1965	1966	1967	1968	1969
Death	10/31	11/18	11/08	10/28	11/16	11/04	11/23	11/12	11/02	11/20
Birth	11/30	12/18	12/07	11/27	12/16	12/04	12/22	12/12	12/01	12/19
Milk	12/29	01/16	01/06	12/26	01/14	01/02	01/21	01/10	12/31	01/18
Fasting	01/28	02/15	02/05	01/25	02/13	02/01	02/20	02/09	01/29	02/16
Seed	02/26	03/16	03/06	02/24	03/14	03/03	03/22	03/11	02/28	03/18
Courting	03/27	none	none	03/25	none	04/02	none	none	03/28	none
Mating	04/25	04/15	04/04	04/23	04/12	05/01	04/20	04/09	04/27	04/16
Journey	05/25	05/14	05/04	05/23	05/11	05/30	05/20	05/09	05/27	05/16
Mother's	06/24	06/13	06/02	06/21	06/10	06/29	06/18	06/08	06/25	06/14
Father's	07/23	07/12	07/01	07/20	07/09	07/28	07/18	07/07	07/25	07/14
Nesting	08/22	08/11	07/31	08/19	08/07	08/26	08/16	08/06	08/23	08/13
Harvest	09/20	09/10	08/30	09/17	09/06	09/25	09/14	09/04	09/22	09/11
Sorting	10/20	10/09	09/28	10/17	10/05	10/24	10/14	10/03	10/21	10/11

Moon	1970	1971	1972	1973	1974	1975	1976	1977	1978	1979
Death	11/09	10/30	11/18	11/06	11/24	11/14	11/03	11/21	11/11	10/31
Birth	12/09	11/28	12/17	12/05	12/24	12/13	12/03	12/21	12/10	11/30
Milk	01/07	12/28	01/16	01/04	01/23	01/12	01/01	01/19	01/09	12/29
Fasting	02/06	01/26	02/15	02/03	02/22	02/11	01/31	02/18	02/07	01/28
Seed	03/07	02/25	03/15	03/05	03/23	03/12	02/29	03/19	03/09	02/26
Courting	none	03/26	none	04/03	none	none	03/30	none	none	03/28
Mating	04/06	04/25	04/13	05/02	04/22	04/11	04/29	04/18	04/07	04/26
Journey	05/05	05/24	05/13	06/01	05/21	05/11	05/29	05/18	05/07	05/26
Mother's	06/04	06/22	06/11	06/30	06/20	06/09	06/27	06/16	06/05	06/24
Father's	07/03	07/22	07/10	07/29	07/19	07/09	07/27	07/16	07/05	07/24
Nesting	08/02	08/20	08/09	08/28	08/17	08/07	08/25	08/14	08/04	08/22
Harvest	08/31	09/19	09/07	09/26	09/16	09/05	09/23	09/13	09/02	09/21
Sorting	09/30	10/19	10/07	10/26	10/15	10/05	10/23	10/12	10/02	10/21

Moon	1980	1981	1982	1983	1984	1985	1986	1987	1988	1989
Death	11/19	11/07	10/27	11/15	11/04	11/22	11/12	11/02	11/21	11/09
Birth	12/19	12/07	11/26	12/15	12/04	12/22	12/12	12/01	12/20	12/09
Milk	01/17	01/06	12/26	01/14	01/03	01/21	01/10	12/31	01/19	01/07
Fasting	02/16	02/04	01/25	02/13	02/01	02/19	02/09	01/29	02/17	02/06
Seed	03/16	03/06	02/23	03/14	03/02	03/21	03/10	02/28	03/18	03/07
Courting	none	none	03/25	none	04/01	none	none	03/29	none	none
Mating	04/15	04/04	04/23	04/13	05/01	04/20	04/09	04/28	04/16	04/06
Journey	05/14	05/04	05/23	05/12	05/30	05/19	05/08	05/27	05/15	05/05
Mother's	06/12	06/02	06/21	06/11	06/29	06/18	06/07	06/26	06/14	06/03
Father's	07/12	07/01	07/20	07/10	07/28	07/17	07/07	07/25	07/13	07/03
Nesting	08/10	07/31	08/19	08/08	08/26	08/16	08/05	08/24	08/12	08/01
Harvest	09/09	08/29	09/17	09/07	09/25	09/14	09/04	09/23	09/11	08/31
Sorting	10/09	09/28	10/17	10/06	10/24	10/14	10/03	10/22	10/10	09/29

Moon	1990	1991	1992	1993	1994	1995	1996	1997	1998	1999
Death	10/29	11/17	11/06	11/24	11/13	11/03	11/22	11/11	10/31	11/19
Birth	11/28	12/17	12/06	12/24	12/13	12/02	12/22	12/10	11/30	12/18
Milk	12/28	01/15	01/04	01/22	01/11	01/01	01/20	01/09	12/29	01/17
Fasting	01/26	02/14	02/03	02/21	02/10	01/30	02/18	02/07	01/28	02/16
Seed	02/25	03/16	03/04	03/23	03/12	03/01	03/19	03/09	02/26	03/17
Courting	03/26	none	04/03	none	none	03/31	none	none	03/28	none
Mating	04/25	04/14	05/02	04/21	04/11	04/29	04/17	04/07	04/26	04/16
Journey	05/24	05/14	06/01	05/21	05/10	05/29	05/17	05/06	05/25	05/15
Mother's	06/22	06/12	06/30	06/20	06/09	06/28	06/16	06/05	06/24	06/13
Father's	07/22	07/11	07/29	07/19	07/08	07/27	07/15	07/04	07/23	07/13
Nesting	08/20	08/10	08/28	08/17	08/07	08/26	08/14	08/03	08/22	08/11
Harvest	09/19	09/08	09/26	09/16	09/05	09/24	09/12	09/01	09/20	09/09
Sorting	10/18	10/07	10/25	10/15	10/05	10/24	10/12	10/01	10/20	10/09

Moon	2000	2001	2002	2003	2004	2005	2006	2007	2008	2009
Death	11/08	10/27	11/15	11/04	11/23	11/12	11/02	11/20	11/09	10/28
Birth	12/07	11/25	12/14	12/04	12/23	12/12	12/01	12/20	12/09	11/27
Milk	01/06	12/25	01/13	01/02	01/21	01/10	12/31	01/19	01/08	12/27
Fasting	02/05	01/24	02/12	02/01	02/20	02/08	01/29	02/17	02/07	01/26
Seed	03/06	02/23	03/14	03/03	03/20	03/10	02/28	03/19	03/07	02/25
Courting	none	03/25	none	04/01	none	none	03/29	none	none	03/26
Mating	04/04	04/23	04/12	05/01	04/19	04/08	04/27	04/17	04/06	04/25
Journey	05/04	05/23	05/12	05/31	05/19	05/08	05/27	05/16	05/05	05/24
Mother's	06/02	06/21	06/10	06/29	06/17	06/06	06/25	06/15	06/03	06/22
Father's	07/01	07/20	07/10	07/29	07/17	07/06	07/25	07/14	07/03	07/22
Nesting	07/31	08/19	08/08	08/27	08/16	08/05	08/23	08/12	08/01	08/20
Harvest	08/29	09/17	09/07	09/26	09/14	09/03	09/22	09/11	08/30	09/18
Sorting	09/27	10/16	10/06	10/25	10/14	10/03	10/22	10/11	09/29	10/18

Moon	2010	2011	2012	2013	2014	2015	2016	2017	2018	2019
Death	11/16	11/06	11/25	11/13	11/03	11/22	11/11	10/30	11/18	11/07
Birth	12/16	12/05	12/24	12/13	12/03	12/22	12/11	11/29	12/18	12/07
Milk	01/15	01/04	01/23	01/11	01/01	01/20	01/10	12/29	01/17	01/06
Fasting	02/14	02/03	02/21	02/10	01/30	02/18	02/08	01/28	02/15	02/04
Seed	03/23	03/04	03/22	03/11	03/01	03/20	03/09	02/26	03/17	03/06
Courting	none	04/03	none	none	03/30	none	none	03/28	none	none
Mating	04/14	05/03	04/21	04/10	04/29	04/18	04/07	04/26	04/16	04/05
Journey	05/14	06/01	05/20	05/10	05/28	05/18	05/06	05/25	05/15	05/04
Mother's	06/12	07/01	06/19	06/08	06/27	06/16	06/05	06/24	06/13	06/03
Father's	07/11	07/30	07/19	07/08	07/26	07/16	07/04	07/23	07/13	07/02
Nesting	08/10	08/29	08/17	08/06	08/25	08/14	08/02	08/21	08/11	08/01
Harvest	09/08	09/27	09/16	09/05	09/24	09/13	09/01	09/20	09/09	08/31
Sorting	10/07	10/26	10/15	10/05	10/23	10/13	10/01	10/19	10/09	09/28

Appendix C:
Seasonal Festival Dates

The following tables give the dates of the seasonal festivals according to this calendar, as well as the name of the moon in which they occur, for the years 1920 to 2019. Please note that Yule is always in the previous calendar year relative to the date at the top of the column. All dates are based on Greenwich Time for the solar or lunar events that they represent. Local times for these events will vary by the number of hours that local time varies from Greenwich Time.

The "normal" placement of the seasonal festivals is as follows: Yule is in the Birth Moon; Imbolc is in the Milk Moon;

Ostara is in the Seed Moon; Beltane is in the Mating Moon; Litha is in the Mother's Moon; Lammas is in the Father's Moon; Mabon is in the Harvest Moon; and Samhain is in the Sorting Moon. Any variation from this pattern signals either the intercalation of a Courting Moon in the past year or the need for one in the coming year. During the period for which I developed this calendar, only Beltane is always in its "proper" moon.

Samhain in the Death Moon and Imbolc in the Fasting Moon signal that a Courting Moon needs to be inserted after the Seed Moon in the spring following these events. Litha moves to the Journey Moon after a Courting Moon. In the one exception in this table (1982), Litha occurs less than six hours after the new Mother's Moon.

Twice in the nineteen-year cycle, the Yule following a Courting Moon is in the Death Moon, followed in turn by Ostara in the Fasting Moon. When that happens, you will notice that year's Courting Moon occurs after only one year with *no* Courting Moon. The usual pattern is two years without a courtship moon and then one year with a Courting Moon. (See Appendix B, 1927 or 1935, for example, for a quick understanding of this point.) I understand that Yule falling in the Death Moon was considered a portent of a bad year.

Mabon may fall in the Nesting Moon after a Courting Moon and Lammas may appear in the Nesting Moon the year before one, but these placements do occur each time. Otherwise, the festivals are remarkably stable in the moon which best expresses the energies of the festival. The years with Courting Moons are starred.

	1920	**1921**	**1922***	**1923**	**1924**
Yule Moon	12/22 Birth	12/22 Birth	12/22 Birth	12/22 Birth	12/22 Birth
Imbolc Moon	02/04 Milk	01/23 Milk	02/12 Fasting	02/01 Milk	01/22 Milk
Ostara Moon	03/20 Seed	03/21 Seed	03/21 Seed	03/21 Seed	03/20 Seed
Beltane Moon	05/03 Mating	04/22 Mating	05/11 Mating	04/30 Mating	04/19 Mating
Litha Moon	06/21 Mother's	06/21 Mother's	06/22 Journey	06/22 Mother's	06/21 Mother's
Lammas Moon	07/30 Father's	08/18 Nesting	08/07 Father's	07/27 Father's	08/14 Nesting
Mabon Moon	09/23 Harvest	09/23 Harvest	09/23 Harvest	09/24 Harvest	09/23 Harvest
Samhain Moon	10/27 Sorting	11/15 Death	11/04 Sorting	10/24 Sorting	11/11 Death

	1925*	**1926**	**1927***	**1928**	**1929**
Yule Moon	12/22 Birth	12/22 Birth	12/22 Birth	12/22 Death	12/22 Birth
Imbolc Moon	02/08 Fasting	01/28 Milk	02/16 Fasting	02/05 Milk	01/25 Milk
Ostara Moon	03/21 Seed	03/21 Seed	03/21 Seed	03/20 Fasting	03/21 Seed
Beltane Moon	05/08 Mating	04/28 Mating	05/16 Mating	05/04 Mating	04/23 Mating
Litha Moon	06/21 Mother's	06/22 Mother's	06/22 Journey	06/21 Mother's	06/21 Mother's
Lammas Moon	08/04 Father's	07/25 Father's	08/13 Father's	08/01 Father's	07/21 Father's
Mabon Moon	09/23 Harvest	09/23 Harvest	09/24 Nesting	09/23 Harvest	09/23 Harvest
Samhain Moon	10/31 Sorting	11/19 Death	11/09 Sorting	10/28 Sorting	11/17 Death

	1930*	**1931**	**1932**	**1933***	**1934**
Yule Moon	12/22 Birth	12/22 Birth	12/22 Birth	12/22 Birth	12/22 Birth
Imbolc Moon	02/13 Fasting	02/03 Milk	01/23 Milk	02/10 Fasting	01/30 Milk
Ostara Moon	03/21 Seed	03/21 Seed	03/20 Seed	03/21 Seed	03/21 Seed
Beltane Moon	05/12 Mating	05/02 Mating	04/20 Mating	05/09 Mating	04/29 Mating
Litha Moon	06/22 Journey	06/22 Mother's	06/21 Mother's	06/21 Journey	06/22 Mother
Lammas Moon	08/09 Father's	07/29 Father's	08/16 Nesting	08/05 Father's	07/26 Father's
Mabon Moon	09/23 Harvest	09/24 Harvest	09/23 Harvest	09/23 Harvest	09/23 Harvest
Samhain Moon	11/06 Sorting	10/26 Sorting	11/13 Death	11/02 Sorting	11/21 Death

	1935*	**1936**	**1937**	**1938***	**1939**
Yule Moon	12/22 Birth	12/22 Death	12/22 Birth	12/22 Birth	12/22 Birth
Imbolc Moon	12/28 Fasting	02/07 Milk	01/26 Milk	02/14 Fasting	02/04 Milk
Ostara Moon	03/21 Seed	03/20 Fasting	03/21 Seed	03/21 Seed	03/21 Seed
Beltane Moon	05/19 Mating	05/06 Mating	04/25 Mating	05/14 Mating	05/03 Mating
Litha Moon	06/22 Journey	06/21 Mother's	06/21 Mother's	06/22 Journey	06/22 Mother's
Lammas Moon	08/14 Father's	08/03 Father's	07/23 Father's	08/11 Father's	07/31 Father's
Mabon Moon	09/23 Nesting	09/23 Harvest	09/23 Harvest	09/23 Nesting	09/23 Harvest
Samhain Moon	11/10 Sorting	10/30 Sorting	11/18 Death	11/07 Sorting	10/28 Sorting

	1940	**1941***	**1942**	**1943**	**1944***
Yule Moon	12/22 Birth	12/21 Birth	12/22 Birth	12/22 Birth	12/22 Birth
Imbolc Moon	01/24 Milk	02/12 Fasting	02/01 Milk	01/21 Milk	02/09 Fasting
Ostara Moon	03/20 Seed	03/21 Seed	03/21 Seed	03/21 Seed	03/20 Seed
Beltane Moon	04/22 Mating	05/11 Mating	04/30 Mating	04/20 Mating	05/08 Mating
Litha Moon	06/21 Mother's	06/21 Journey	06/22 Mother's	06/22 Mother's	06/21 Mother's
Lammas Moon	08/17 Nesting	08/07 Father's	07/27 Father's	08/15 Nesting	08/04 Father's
Mabon Moon	09/23 Harvest	09/23 Harvest	09/23 Harvest	09/23 Harvest	09/23 Harvest
Samhain Moon	11/15 Death	11/04 Sorting	10/24 Sorting	11/12 Death	10/31 Sorting

	1945	**1946***	**1947**	**1948**	**1949***
Yule Moon	12/21 Birth	12/22 Birth	12/22 Death	12/22 Birth	12/21 Birth
Imbolc Moon	01/28 Milk	02/16 Fasting	02/05 Milk	01/26 Milk	02/13 Fasting
Ostara Moon	03/20 Seed	03/21 Seed	03/21 Fasting	03/20 Seed	03/20 Seed
Beltane Moon	04/27 Mating	05/16 Mating	05/05 Mating	04/23 Mating	05/12 Mating
Litha Moon	06/21 Mother's	06/22 Journey	06/22 Mother's	06/21 Mother's	06/21 Journey
Lammas Moon	07/25 Father's	08/12 Father's	08/02 Father's	07/21 Father's	08/08 Father's
Mabon Moon	09/23 Harvest	09/23 Nesting	09/23 Harvest	09/23 Harvest	09/23 Harvest
Samhain Moon	11/19 Death	11/09 Sorting	10/20 Sorting	11/16 Death	11/05 Sorting

	1950	**1951**	**1952***	**1953**	**1954***
Yule Moon	12/22 Birth	12/22 Birth	12/22 Birth	12/21 Birth	12/22 Birth
Imbolc Moon	02/02 Milk	02/23 Milk	02/11 Fasting	01/29 Milk	02/17 Fasting
Ostara Moon	03/21 Seed	03/21 Seed	03/21 Seed	03/20 Seed	03/21 Seed
Beltane Moon	05/02 Mating	04/21 Mating	05/09 Mating	04/29 Mating	05/17 Mating
Litha Moon	06/21 Mother's	06/22 Mother's	06/21 Journey	06/21 Mother's	06/21 Journey
Lammas Moon	07/29 Father's	08/17 Nesting	08/05 Father's	07/26 Father's	08/13 Father's
Mabon Moon	09/23 Harvest	09/23 Harvest	09/23 Harvest	09/23 Harvest	09/23 Nesting
Samhain Moon	10/25 Sorting	11/13 Death	11/01 Sorting	11/20 Death	11/10 Sorting

	1955	**1956**	**1957***	**1958**	**1959**
Yule Moon	12/22 Death	12/22 Birth	12/21 Birth	12/22 Birth	12/22 Birth
Imbolc Moon	02/07 Milk	01/27 Milk	02/14 Fasting	02/04 Milk	01/24 Milk
Ostara Moon	03/21 Fasting	03/20 Seed	03/23 Seed	03/21 Seed	03/21 Seed
Beltane Moon	05/06 Mating	04/25 Mating	05/13 Mating	05/03 Mating	04/23 Mating
Litha Moon	06/22 Mother's	06/21 Mother's	06/21 Journey	06/21 Mother's	06/22 Mother's
Lammas Moon	08/03 Father's	07/22 Father's	08/10 Father's	07/30 Father's	08/18 Nesting
Mabon Moon	09/23 Harvest	09/23 Harvest	09/23 Nesting	09/23 Harvest	09/23 Harvest
Samhain Moon	10/31 Sorting	11/18 Death	11/07 Sorting	10/27 Sorting	11/15 Death

	1960*	1961	1962	1963*	1964
Yule	12/22	12/21	12/22	12/22	12/22
Moon	Birth	Birth	Birth	Birth	Birth
Imbolc	02/12	01/31	01/20	02/08	01/28
Moon	Fasting	Milk	Milk	Fasting	Milk
Ostara	03/20	03/20	03/21	03/21	03/20
Moon	Seed	Seed	Seed	Seed	Seed
Beltane	05/11	04/30	04/20	05/08	04/26
Moon	Mating	Mating	Mating	Mating	Mating
Litha	06/21	06/21	06/21	06/22	06/21
Moon	Journey	Mother's	Mother's	Mother's	Mother's
Lammas	08/07	07/27	08/15	08/05	07/24
Moon	Father's	Father's	Nesting	Father's	Father's
Mabon	09/23	09/23	09/23	09/23	09/23
Moon	Harvest	Harvest	Harvest	Harvest	Harvest
Samhain	11/03	10/23	11/11	11/01	11/19
Moon	Sorting	Sorting	Death	Sorting	Death

	1965*	1966	1967	1968*	1969
Yule	12/21	12/22	12/22	12/22	12/21
Moon	Birth	Death	Birth	Birth	Birth
Imbolc	02/16	02/05	01/26	02/14	02/02
Moon	Fasting	Milk	Milk	Fasting	Milk
Ostara	03/20	03/21	03/21	03/20	03/20
Moon	Seed	Seed	Seed	Seed	Seed
Beltane	05/15	05/04	04/24	05/12	05/02
Moon	Mating	Mating	Mating	Mating	Mating
Litha	06/21	06/21	06/22	06/21	06/21
Moon	Journey	Mother's	Mother's	Journey	Mother's
Lammas	08/12	08/01	07/21	08/08	07/29
Moon	Father's	Father's	Father's	Father's	Father's
Mabon	09/23	09/23	09/23	09/22	09/23
Moon	Nesting	Harvest	Harvest	Harvest	Harvest
Samhain	11/09	10/29	11/17	11/05	10/25
Moon	Sorting	Sorting	Death	Sorting	Sorting

	1970	**1971***	**1972**	**1973***	**1974**
Yule Moon	12/22 Birth	12/22 Birth	12/22 Birth	12/21 Birth	12/22 Death
Imbolc Moon	01/22 Milk	02/10 Fasting	01/30 Milk	02/17 Fasting	02/06 Milk
Ostara Moon	03/21 Seed	03/21 Seed	03/20 Seed	03/20 Seed	03/21 Fasting
Beltane Moon	04/21 Mating	05/10 Mating	04/28 Mating	05/17 Mating	05/06 Mating
Litha Moon	06/21 Mother's	06/22 Journey	06/21 Mother's	06/21 Journey	06/21 Mother's
Lammas Moon	08/17 Nesting	08/06 Father's	07/26 Father's	08/14 Father's	08/03 Father's
Mabon Moon	09/23 Harvest	09/23 Harvest	09/22 Harvest	09/23 Nesting	09/23 Harvest
Samhain Moon	11/13 Death	11/02 Sorting	11/20 Death	11/10 Sorting	10/31 Sorting

	1975	**1976***	**1977**	**1978**	**1979***
Yule Moon	12/22 Birth	12/22 Birth	12/21 Birth	12/21 Birth	12/22 Birth
Imbolc Moon	01/27 Milk	02/15 Fasting	02/04 Milk	01/24 Milk	02/12 Fasting
Ostara Moon	03/21 Seed	03/20 Seed	03/20 Seed	03/20 Seed	03/21 Seed
Beltane Moon	04/25 Mating	05/13 Mating	05/03 Mating	04/23 Mating	05/12 Mating
Litha Moon	06/22 Mother's	06/21 Journey	06/21 Mother's	06/21 Mother's	06/21 Journey
Lammas Moon	07/23 Father's	08/09 Father's	07/30 Father's	08/18 Nesting	08/08 Father's
Mabon Moon	09/23 Harvest	09/22 Nesting	09/23 Harvest	09/23 Harvest	09/23 Harvest
Samhain Moon	11/18 Death	11/06 Sorting	10/26 Sorting	11/14 Death	11/04 Sorting

	1980	**1981**	**1982***	**1983**	**1984***
Yule	12/22	12/21	12/21	12/22	12/22
Moon	Birth	Birth	Birth	Birth	Birth
Imbolc	02/01	01/20	02/08	01/28	02/17
Moon	Milk	Milk	Fasting	Milk	Fasting
Ostara	03/20	03/20	03/20	03/21	03/24
Moon	Seed	Seed	Seed	Seed	Seed
Beltane	04/30	04/19	05/08	04/27	05/15
Moon	Mating	Mating	Mating	Mating	Mating
Litha	06/21	06/21	06/21	06/21	06/21
Moon	Mother's	Mother's	Mother's	Mother's	Journey
Lammas	07/27	08/15	08/04	07/24	08/11
Moon	Father's	Nesting	Father's	Father's	Father's
Mabon	09/22	09/23	09/23	09/23	09/22
Moon	Harvest	Harvest	Harvest	Harvest	Nesting
Samhain	10/23	11/11	11/01	11/20	11/08
Moon	Sorting	Death	Sorting	Death	Sorting

	1985	**1986**	**1987***	**1988**	**1989**
Yule	12/21	12/21	12/22	12/22	12/21
Moon	Death	Birth	Birth	Birth	Birth
Imbolc	02/05	01/26	02/13	02/02	01/21
Moon	Milk	Milk	Fasting	Milk	Milk
Ostara	03/20	03/20	03/21	03/20	03/20
Moon	Fasting	Seed	Seed	Seed	Seed
Beltane	05/04	04/24	05/13	05/01	04/21
Moon	Mating	Mating	Mating	Mating	Mating
Litha	06/21	06/21	06/21	06/21	06/21
Moon	Mother's	Mother's	Journey	Mother's	Mother's
Lammas	07/31	07/21	08/09	07/29	08/17
Moon	Father's	Father's	Father's	Father's	Nesting
Mabon	09/23	09/23	09/23	09/22	09/23
Moon	Harvest	Harvest	Harvest	Harvest	Harvest
Samhain	10/28	11/16	11/05	10/25	11/13
Moon	Sorting	Death	Sorting	Sorting	Death

	1990*	1991	1992*	1993	1994
Yule Moon	12/21 Birth	12/22 Birth	12/22 Birth	12/21 Death	12/21 Birth
Imbolc Moon	02/09 Fasting	01/30 Milk	02/18 Fasting	02/06 Milk	01/27 Milk
Ostara Moon	03/20 Seed	03/21 Seed	03/20 Seed	03/20 Fasting	03/20 Seed
Beltane Moon	05/09 Mating	04/28 Mating	05/16 Mating	05/06 Mating	04/25 Mating
Litha Moon	06/21 Journey	06/21 Mother's	06/21 Journey	06/21 Mother's	06/21 Mother's
Lammas Moon	08/06 Father's	07/26 Father's	08/13 Father's	08/02 Father's	07/22 Father's
Mabon Moon	09/23 Harvest	09/23 Harvest	09/22 Nesting	09/23 Harvest	09/23 Harvest
Samhain Moon	11/02 Sorting	11/21 Death	11/10 Sorting	10/30 Sorting	11/18 Death

	1995*	1996	1997	1998*	1999
Yule Moon	12/22 Birth	12/22 Birth	12/21 Birth	12/21 Birth	12/22 Birth
Imbolc Moon	02/15 Fasting	02/04 Milk	01/23 Milk	02/11 Fasting	01/31 Milk
Ostara Moon	03/21 Seed	03/20 Seed	03/20 Seed	03/20 Seed	03/21 Seed
Beltane Moon	05/14 Mating	05/03 Mating	04/22 Mating	05/11 Mating	04/30 Mating
Litha Moon	06/21 Journey	06/21 Mother's	06/21 Mother's	06/21 Journey	06/21 Mother's
Lammas Moon	08/10 Father's	07/30 Father's	08/18 Nesting	08/08 Father's	07/28 Father's
Mabon Moon	09/23 Nesting	09/22 Harvest	09/22 Harvest	09/23 Harvest	09/23 Harvest
Samhain Moon	11/07 Sorting	10/26 Sorting	11/14 Death	11/04 Sorting	10/24 Sorting

	2000	**2001***	**2002**	**2003***	**2004**
Yule Moon	12/22 Birth	12/21 Birth	12/21 Birth	12/22 Birth	12/22 Death
Imbolc Moon	01/21 Milk	02/08 Fasting	01/28 Milk	02/16 Fasting	02/06 Milk
Ostara Moon	03/20 Seed	03/20 Seed	03/20 Seed	03/21 Seed	03/20 Fasting
Beltane Moon	04/18 Mating	05/07 Mating	04/27 Mating	05/16 Mating	05/04 Mating
Litha Moon	06/21 Mother's	06/21 Journey	06/21 Mother's	06/21 Journey	06/21 Mother's
Lammas Moon	08/15 Nesting	08/04 Father's	07/24 Father's	08/12 Father's	07/31 Father's
Mabon Moon	09/22 Harvest	09/22 Harvest	09/23 Harvest	09/23 Nesting	09/22 Harvest
Samhain Moon	11/11 Death	11/01 Sorting	11/20 Death	11/09 Sorting	10/28 Sorting

	2005	**2006***	**2007**	**2008**	**2009***
Yule Moon	12/21 Birth	12/21 Birth	12/22 Birth	12/22 Birth	12/21 Birth
Imbolc Moon	01/25 Milk	02/13 Fasting	02/02 Milk	01/22 Milk	02/09 Fasting
Ostara Moon	03/20 Seed	03/20 Seed	03/21 Seed	03/20 Seed	03/20 Seed
Beltane Moon	04/24 Mating	05/13 Mating	05/02 Mating	04/20 Mating	05/09 Mating
Litha Moon	06/21 Mother's	06/21 Journey	06/21 Mother's	06/21 Mother's	06/21 Journey
Lammas Moon	07/21 Father's	08/09 Father's	07/30 Father's	08/16 Nesting	08/06 Father's
Mabon Moon	09/22 Harvest	09/23 Harvest	09/23 Harvest	09/22 Harvest	09/22 Harvest
Samhain Moon	11/16 Death	11/05 Sorting	10/26 Sorting	11/13 Death	11/02 Sorting

	2010	**2011***	**2012**	**2013**	**2014***
Yule Moon	12/21 Birth	12/21 Birth	12/22 Death	12/21 Birth	12/21 Birth
Imbolc Moon	01/30 Milk	02/18 Fasting	02/07 Milk	01/27 Milk	02/14 Fasting
Ostara Moon	03/20 Seed	03/20 Seed	03/20 Fasting	03/20 Seed	03/20 Seed
Beltane Moon	04/28 Mating	05/17 Mating	05/06 Mating	04/25 Mating	05/14 Mating
Litha Moon	06/21 Mother's	06/21 Journey	06/20 Mother's	06/21 Mother's	06/21 Journey
Lammas Moon	07/26 Father's	08/13 Father's	08/02 Father's	07/22 Father's	08/10 Father's
Mabon Moon	09/23 Harvest	09/23 Nesting	09/22 Harvest	09/22 Harvest	09/23 Harvest
Samhain Moon	11/21 Death	11/10 Sorting	10/29 Sorting	11/17 Death	11/06 Sorting

	2015	**2016**	**2017***	**2018**	**2019**
Yule Moon	12/21 Birth	12/22 Birth	12/21 Birth	12/21 Birth	12/21 Birth
Imbolc Moon	02/03 Milk	01/24 Milk	02/11 Fasting	01/31 Milk	01/21 Milk
Ostara Moon	03/20 Seed	03/20 Seed	03/20 Seed	03/20 Seed	03/20 Seed
Beltane Moon	05/04 Mating	04/22 Mating	05/10 Mating	04/30 Mating	04/19 Mating
Litha Moon	06/21 Mother's	06/20 Mother's	06/21 Journey	06/21 Mother's	06/21 Mother's
Lammas Moon	07/31 Father's	08/18 Nesting	08/07 Father's	07/27 Father's	08/15 Nesting
Mabon Moon	09/23 Harvest	09/22 Harvest	09/22 Harvest	09/23 Harvest	09/23 Harvest
Samhain Moon	10/27 Sorting	11/14 Death	11/04 Sorting	10/24 Sorting	11/12 Death

For Further Reading

Asimov, Isaac. *The Clock We Live On*. New York: Abelard-Schuman, 1959.
An excellent coverage of the history of marking time and solar and lunar calendar systems working together.

Blair, Lawrence. *Rhythms of Vision*. New York: Schocken, 1976.
A credible attempt to integrate scientific knowledge with traditional occult wisdom.

Bonheim, Jalaja. *The Serpent and the Wave: A Guide to Movement Meditation*. Berkeley: Celestial Arts, 1992.
A wise and wonderful book with some of the best exercises I've seen for knowing the spiritual through the material.

293

Busteed, Marilyn, Richard Tiffany, and Dorothy Wergin. *Phases of the Moon*. Boston: Shambhala, 1974
Personality effect of moon phase on natal astrology.

Campanelli, Pauline. *Wheel of the Year*. St. Paul: Llewellyn, 1989.
Folklore, folk practices, and practical occultism related to the months of the year. A point of interest is its inclusion of other systems of names for the moons of a year.

Eliade, Mircea. *The Myth of the Eternal Return*. Princeton: Princeton University Bollingen Series XLVI, 1954
Evidence in ancient literature and myth for the ideas of time that were held by early societies and the remnants of some of those ideas in our present culture.

Estes, Clarissa Pinkola. *Women Who Run With Wolves*. New York: Ballantine, 1992.
A good map of how the negative form of divine polarities can be constructive and the harm done when this side of polar energies is denied. A healing book directed at women, but one that many men can profit from as well.

Frazer, James. *Golden Bough, Condensed Version*. Various editions.
Frazer's classic study does not meet current scientific standards for anthropological study, but it is still a good source for folklore, particularly for northern European folk practices. Many of its examples show remnants of beliefs and practices that reflect the great story of the Goddess and her Lover/Son. Also a wealth of examples of local folklore related to the seasonal festivals.

Gallagher, Winifred. *The Power of Place*. New York: Poseidon Press, 1993.
This very readable book gathers scientific studies on the effect that weather, changing seasons, where we live, and other aspects of our external and internal environments affect the way we behave.

Glass-Koentop, Pattalee. *Year of Moons, Season of Trees*. St. Paul: Llewellyn, 1991.
Rituals for a year of moons that are named after trees. The book gives thirteen moons, but does not give a system for linking the moons with actual lunations.

Goodison, Lucy. *Moving Heaven and Earth: Sexuality, Spirituality and Social Change*. Cambridge, MA: Pandora Press, 1992.
A discussion of how symbols affect how people feel and a proposal for "immanent spirituality" in which spirit dwells within and not above matter. A thought-provoking and healing book.

Gould, Stephen Jay. *Wonderful Life*. New York: Norton, 1989.
A study of the Burgess Shale fauna and its implications for the diversity of life. Highly readable. The author does science as it ought to be, and history as it is. The book is a window into a non-teleological model of the history of life, where the purpose of the journey is the journeying.

Hall, Edward T. *Beyond Culture*. New York: Anchor Books, 1977.
The best book I've ever read on how human models of the world work. Specifically, an introduction of the effect of culture in how we perceive the world. Very readable.

Hall, Edward T. *The Dance of Life*. New York: Anchor Books, 1983.
A thoughtful and illuminating exposition on how ideas of time differ across cultures.

Hall, Edward T. *The Silent Language*. New York: Fawcett, 1959
One of the first popular books to address the different ways that cultures use time and space. Very readable.

Lovelock, J. E. *Gaia: A New Look at Life on Earth*. New York: Oxford, 1987.
An examination of the scientific evidence for the biosphere of the Earth being a single self-regulating organism which maintains itself through the activities of living organisms.

Parray, Danaan. *The Essene Book of Days*. Santa Fe: Sunstone Publications, Annual (same text, different astronomical data each year)
A daily meditation and focus for connecting to the earth as the seasons change. Very nice.

Pennick, Nigel. *Practical Magic in the Northern Tradition.* London: Aquarian, 1989.
Excellent chapter on different ways of dealing with time and laying out calendars. Interesting reflections that try to reconstruct some of the worldview of the place and time where the calendar in this book probably originated.

Priestly, J. B. *Man and Time.* New York: Dell, 1968.
A history of time measurement and cultural ideas of time, plus speculations on how time actually works.

Talbot, Michael. *The Holographic Universe.* New York: Harper-Collins, 1991.
A theory of reality that accounts for both scientific theories and paranormal phenomena. Some interesting implications on the "reality" of some of the ideas in this book.

Index

☾ REACH FOR THE MOON

Llewellyn publishes hundreds of books on your favorite subjects! To get these exciting books, including the ones on the following pages, check your local bookstore or order them directly from Llewellyn.

ORDER BY PHONE
- Call toll-free within the U.S. and Canada, 1–800–THE MOON
- In Minnesota, call (651) 291-1970
- We accept VISA, MasterCard, and American Express

ORDER BY MAIL
- Send the full price of your order (MN residents add 7% sales tax) in U.S. funds, plus postage & handling to:

  Llewellyn Worldwide
  P.O. Box 64383, Dept. K396–4
  St. Paul, MN 55164–0383, U.S.A.

POSTAGE & HANDLING
(For the U.S., Canada, and Mexico)
- $4.00 for orders $15.00 and under
- $5.00 for orders over $15.00
- No charge for orders over $100.00

We ship UPS in the continental United States. We ship standard mail to P.O. boxes. Orders shipped to Alaska, Hawaii, The Virgin Islands, and Puerto Rico are sent first-class mail. Orders shipped to Canada and Mexico are sent surface mail.

International orders: Airmail—add freight equal to price of each book to the total price of order, plus $5.00 for each non-book item (audio tapes, etc.).

Surface mail—Add $1.00 per item.

Allow 2 weeks for delivery on all orders.
Postage and handling rates subject to change.

DISCOUNTS
We offer a 20% discount to group leaders or agents. You must order a minimum of 5 copies of the same book to get our special quantity price.

FREE CATALOG
Get a free copy of our color catalog, *New Worlds of Mind and Spirit.* Subscribe for just $10.00 in the United States and Canada ($30.00 overseas, airmail). Many bookstores carry *New Worlds*— ask for it!

Visit our web site at www.llewellyn.com for more information.

Moon Magick

*Myth & Magic, Crafts & Recipes,
Rituals & Spells*

D. J. Conway

No creature on this planet is unaffected by the power of the Moon. Its effects range from making us feel energetic or adventurous to tense and despondent. By putting excess Moon energy to work for you, you can learn to plan projects, work and travel at the optimum times.

Moon Magick explains how each of the 13 lunar months is directly connected with a different type of seasonal energy flow and provides modern rituals and spells for tapping this energy and celebrating the Moon phases. Each chapter describes new Pagan rituals—79 in all—related to that particular Moon, plus related Moon lore, ancient holidays, spells, meditations and suggestions for foods, drinks and decorations to accompany your Moon rituals. This book includes two thorough dictionaries of Moon deities and symbols.

By moving through the year according to the 13 lunar months, you can become more attuned to the seasons, the Earth and your inner self. *Moon Magic* will show you how to let your life flow with the power and rhythms of the Moon to benefit your physical, emotional and spiritual well-being.

1-56718-167-8, 7 x 10, 320 pp., illus., softcover $14.95